DATE DUE

NOV 13 02			

Patent Law Essentials

A Concise Guide

Alan L. Durham

Q

QUORUM BOOKS
Westport, Connecticut • London

Library of Congress Cataloging-in-Publication Data

Durham, Alan L., 1963–
    Patent law essentials : a concise guide / Alan L. Durham.
      p. cm.
    Includes bibliographical references and index.
    ISBN 1–56720–242–X (alk. paper)
    1. Patent laws and legislation—United States. I. Title.
KF3114.3.D87   1999
346.7304'86—dc21   98–20133

British Library Cataloguing in Publication Data is available.

Library of Congress Catalog Card Number: 98–20133
ISBN: 1–56720–242–X

First published in 1999

Quorum Books, 88 Post Road West, Westport, CT 06881
An imprint of Greenwood Publishing Group, Inc.

Printed in the United States of America

The paper used in this book complies with the
Permanent Paper Standard issued by the National
Information Standards Organization (Z39.48–1984).

10 9 8 7 6

To my parents,
for putting me through
law school

Contents

Introduction

Patent Commissioner Charles H. Duell is said to have recommended in 1899 that the United States Patent Office be closed, because everything of importance that could be invented had been invented already. If the story is true, Mr. Duell's comments were premature to say the least. In the last five years alone, more than a half million new inventions have been patented, including everything from the most sophisticated electronic circuits and genetically engineered organisms to kitchen gadgets, toothbrushes and board games. Hopeful inventors of a "better mouse-trap" still beat a path to the Patent Office door.

In fact, patents are arguably a more powerful force in commerce than ever before. In technology-driven fields such as semiconductor manufacturing and biotechnology, a patent portfolio often numbers among a business's most valuable assets, either as a source of income in its own right or as a means of preserving competitive advantage. A business without a strong patent position may be left at the mercy of its more fortunate competitors. To appreciate the power of patents to make or break a business, one has only to consider the fate of Kodak, which was forced to terminate its multi-million dollar line of instant cameras as the result of patent litigation with Polaroid.

Patent law was once a relatively specialized field, but throughout the 1980s and 1990s it has experienced unprecedented growth. Law schools that in recent memory offered no courses in patent law now promote themselves as centers for the study of "intellectual property." Many a general litigation law firm now boasts a patent team. The increased number of patent-related lawsuits filed, and the enormous damages figures that sometimes result, undoubtedly account for this increased interest. In the litigation between Polaroid and Kodak, Polaroid received an award of more than $90 million. In a recent suit between Litton and Honeywell, Litton's allegations of patent infringement reaped it a jury award, successfully challenged, of more than $1.2 billion. In no other area of civil litigation are the potential rewards for the victor more abundant or the penalties for the loser more catastrophic.

Patent law is the subject of several multi-volume treatises, one of the best of which is the monumental work of Professor Donald Chisum. Readers interested in the historical development of the law, extensive case citations and a detailed analysis of theory should look there. The goal of this book is to present the essentials of patent law in the clearest and simplest terms possible, without oversimplifying the genuinely complex areas of the law. Every effort has been made to explain by example, often through reference to actual cases. If I have succeeded, the result is a book accessible to readers who do not have legal training, but still sufficiently complete and up-to-date to be of use to professionals. Of course, it must be emphasized that no book can be considered a substitute for consulting with an attorney, particularly in a field as complex and ever-evolving as patent law.

Although the goals of this book are largely practical, any skeptic who doubts that patent law can be entertaining in its own right is encouraged to track down an address by Judge Simon H. Rifkind, with the improbable title of "The Romance Discoverable in Patent Cases," reprinted in Volume 16 of the *Federal Rules Decisions*, at page 253. The judge reminds us that each patent case is a drama of a sort, touched by the mixture of cutting-edge science and legal metaphysics that gives patent law its unique richness and complexity and, occasionally, even a touch of "romance."

I would like to express my gratitude to the attorneys and staff of Morrison & Foerster LLP for their advice and support, and for allowing me the flexible schedule necessary to undertake this project. In particular, I would like to thank A. C. Johnston, Rachel Krevans and Mike Jacobs for smoothing the way. I would also like to thank friends and colleagues who at various times and in various ways have encouraged my interest in patent law and helped me to pursue a career in that field. In the jargon of claim drafting, that group "comprises" (but is not limited to) Jack Brown, Randy Bain, Lois Abraham, Phillip Berelson, Roger Borovoy, Martin Lagod, Karl Kramer, Don Kumamoto and Jeffrey Randall. Thanks also to Alissa Picker for general motivation, friendship and support. Finally, I would like to thank all of the colleagues with whom I have had thought-provoking discussions of patent law throughout the years, including, in addition to the persons I have already named, Sherman Kahn, Marc Pernick, Dahna Pasternak and many others. If you diasagree with anything I have said in this book, I know I will hear from you.

CHAPTER 1

Overview

1.1 ORIGINS

The historical antecedents of the United States patent system are often traced to seventeenth-century England. Until then, a "patent" often referred to nothing more than a legally sanctioned monopoly, granted to reward a loyal subject or sold to raise funds for the Exchequer. For example, a merchant guild might purchase a "patent" for the exclusive right to sell playing cards. The resulting freedom from competition allowed the patent owner to sell in larger volumes and at a higher price. While this system was undoubtedly popular with the government and with the patent owners, it was a source of resentment to consumers and potential competitors. In 1624, the Statute of Monopolies abolished the general power of the monarch to grant exclusive rights. However, the same statute that ended the general practice of monopolies specifically exempted patents granted to inventors.

The tradition of granting patents to inventors continued in colonial America and, in spite of some skepticism by influential thinkers such as Thomas Jefferson, it was incorporated in the laws of the United States. The framers of the Constitution provided to Congress, in Article I, Section 8, the power to "promote the progress of science and [the] useful arts, by securing for limited times to authors and inventors the exclusive right to their respective writings and discoveries." This brief language is the source of both patent law and copyright law in the United States.[1] The

---

[1] When the Constitution was drafted, the term "science" was used in a broader sense than it is today, and was generally synonymous with "knowledge." "Arts" also held a different meaning, and the term "useful arts" probably amounted to what we would refer to as

specifics were left to Congress, whose last wholesale revision of the Patent Act occurred in 1952, and to the Patent and Trademark Office (also known as the Patent Office or PTO), a division of the Department of Commerce created in 1836. The federal courts also have played a significant role in interpreting, supplementing, and some might say rewriting, the rules set down by Congress.

Although patent law has evolved in some ways with the passage of time, the theories behind it are the same today as they were 200 years ago. One theory, which still has an eighteenth-century flavor, is that inventors possess a "natural right" to their inventions that must be recognized by law. The creation is the property of the creator. The more common theory, and the one most clearly reflected in the Constitution, is that patents provide the encouragement necessary for industrial advancement. A budding Edison who feared that the rewards of his inventive efforts would be reaped by others, perhaps with greater power or resources, might abandon the laboratory for other pursuits. Society would then be denied the benefit of useful inventions. However, if that same inventor can obtain a patent ensuring that only he can enjoy the rewards of his invention, he is more likely to invest the time, effort and skill necessary to discover new technologies.

Patents also benefit society by making available precise descriptions of new inventions. A patent is a public document published by the United States government. One requirement of a patent is that it describe the invention, in both words and drawings, in such detail that other persons in the field can understand the invention and practice it themselves. During the term of the patent, this information may be of limited interest since only the patent owner and licensees have the legal right to practice the invention. Yet patents remain in force only for a time, and when the patent expires the invention enters the public domain. In theory at least, the more than 4 million patents that have expired to date are a resource that can be freely exploited by anyone. Even an unexpired patent can provide the inspiration for new and different approaches to technological problems.

The view that a patent is a kind of *bargain* between the inventor and the public, by which the inventor receives a limited monopoly in exchange for disclosing the invention to the public, is of more than theoretical interest. Together with the overall constitutional goal of promoting the "useful arts," the bargain model of patents helps to shape the specific rules that determine whether a patent is valid or invalid. In particular, this model will resurface as we examine the concepts of "enablement" and "best mode" in Sections 8.6–8.7.

"technology." Although somewhat counterintuitive, the prevailing view of legal historians is that patent law exists to advance the "arts," while copyright law exists to advance "science."

1.2 SUMMARY AND ROADMAP

A book about patent law is difficult to organize because an understanding of one principle is so often dependent on an understanding of other principles, ad infinitum. As a *New Yorker* article once observed, patent law is "apt to plunge all but the stoutest minds into dizzying swirls of logic."[2] What follows is a sort of roadmap to this book that may keep the reader better oriented as we wind our way through the maze.

Chapter 1 (this chapter) introduces the reader to some of the history and theory underpinning patent law, and concludes with a brief discussion of the laws, judicial opinions and other authorities that are cited throughout this book.

Chapter 2 distinguishes patents from other forms of intellectual property rights with which patents are often confused. Specifically, Chapter 2 briefly discusses copyrights, which protect works of authorship such as writings, musical compositions and illustrations; trademarks, which protect corporate names and logos; and trade secrets law, which protects confidential business information.

Chapter 3 leads the reader through a close examination of an actual United States patent found in Appendix A. This includes the patent drawings, the "specification," which is a detailed prose description of the inventor's work, and the "claims." The claims are the last portion of a patent, and they describe in careful terms exactly what the patented invention is.

Chapter 4 discusses the kinds of discoveries that can or cannot be patented, with sections devoted to abstract ideas, principles of nature, living organisms, artistic and literary creations, printed matter and methods of doing business. Whether computer software can be patented is a particularly thorny subject, and it is reserved for discussion with other specialized topics in Chapter 12.

Chapter 5 explains the process one goes through to obtain a patent from the United States Patent Office—a process known as "patent prosecution." Some of the complexities discussed include patent applications that spawn offspring, known as "continuations," "continuations-in-part" or "divisional" applications; "interferences," which are a procedure for determining which of two inventors having competing patents or patent applications actually invented first; and "reissue" and "reexamination," both procedures allowing the Patent Office a second look at applications that have already issued as patents.

Chapter 6 examines the issue of inventorship—that is, who should or should not be credited as an "inventor"—and how an inventor can convey rights to a patented invention, either by assignment or by license.

---

[2] John Seabrook, *The Flash of Genius*, **The New Yorker**, January 11, 1993, p. 40.

Chapter 6 also discusses how rights to a patented invention can be conveyed, intentionally or unintentionally, by an "implied license."

Chapter 7 deals with the issue of interpreting patent claims. This is a difficult but extremely important issue, because deciding what a patent claim *means* is the starting point for determining if the patent is valid or infringed. Chapter 7 reviews some of the tools used to interpret patent claims, including "plain meaning," the patent specification and the "prosecution history," which is a record of the applicant's dealings with the Patent Office. Chapter 7 also discusses special problems associated with claim "preambles" and certain specialized claim formats sometimes preferred by applicants. Among these are "product-by-process" claims, which describe the invention in terms of the way it is *made*, and "means-plus-function" claims, in which particular claim elements are described in terms of the function they perform.

Chapter 8 is one of the longer chapters in the book because it deals with the various conditions of patentability. If a patent application fails to meet any one of these conditions, it should be rejected by the Patent Office. If the application nevertheless slips through the Patent Office, the patent can be held invalid by a court. In fact, in nearly every case where a charge of infringement results in a lawsuit, the accused infringer argues that the patent is invalid.

Chapter 8 begins with a general discussion of the conditions of patentability, including the presumption that any patent is valid until proven otherwise. The specific topics covered in Chapter 8 include the "utility" requirement, which means that the patented invention must perform some useful function; the "definiteness" requirement, which means that the claims must be reasonably precise in identifying the patented invention; the "enablement" requirement, which means that the patent must include enough information so that others can practice the claimed invention without undue experimentation; the "best mode" requirement, which means that the inventor must have disclosed the best way he or she knew of practicing the invention at the time the application was filed; and the "written description" requirement, which means that the patent specification, as filed, must describe the invention ultimately claimed.

Chapter 8 then looks at the "novelty" requirement, which in many respects is the key to patentability. The "novelty" requirement means that the claimed invention must be *new* and *non-obvious*, in comparison to the "prior art." Chapter 8 discusses the various kinds of "prior art" that may be relevant, including prior inventions, prior patents, and prior publications. Chapter 8 also discusses how the "date of invention" is determined, which can be a critical issue when deciding if another invention, or a patent or publication, is actually *prior* art.

Chapter 8 discusses both "anticipation," which means that the claimed invention can be found in the prior art, and "obviousness" which means that even though nothing identical to the claimed invention is found in the prior art, the invention still would have been obvious to a person of ordinary skill. If an invention is obvious, perhaps as an elaboration or a combination of prior inventions, it is not considered an advance worthy of a patent. Obviousness is a difficult and subjective inquiry, invariably conducted in hindsight. Chapter 8 examines some of the "secondary considerations," such as commercial success, that are intended as more objective measures of whether an invention was obvious.

Chapter 8 continues with a discussion of the "statutory bar" provisions which can invalidate a patent if the applicant was too slow in filing an application after the occurrence of a critical event—such as offering for sale a product embodying the invention. Chapter 8 concludes with an examination of "double patenting." Double patenting is a ground for invalidating a patent if the same inventor had already patented the same invention. This prevents an inventor from obtaining multiple patents on the same thing, thereby extending the period of the patent monopoly beyond the intended span.

Chapter 9 examines two potential defenses to a charge of infringement which, if successful, result in a holding that a patent is "unenforceable." If a patent is unenforceable, a court will not use its powers to prevent that patent from being infringed. The first "unenforceability" defense discussed in Chapter 9 is "inequitable conduct." Because patent prosecution happens in secret, and only the applicant and the Patent Office participate, it is important to hold patent applicants to a high standard of candor and fair dealing during that process. Inequitable conduct occurs if an applicant intentionally deceives the Patent Office, or withholds critical information, during prosecution. The other unenforceability defense discussed in Chapter 9 is "misuse." "Misuse" refers to attempts to leverage the patent monopoly beyond its intended scope—for example, by requiring that anyone practicing the patented invention purchase an *unpatented* product from the patent owner. This kind of "tying" and other forms of misuse may violate the federal antitrust laws, in addition to rendering a patent unenforceable.

Chapter 10 is another lengthy chapter because it deals with the subject of infringement. After a preliminary discussion covering the temporal and geographical limitations of a patent, Chapter 10 discusses "direct" and "indirect" infringement. Direct infringement means making, using, selling, offering to sell or importing into the United States something that falls within the scope of a patent claim. Indirect infringement means inducing or contributing to infringement by someone else—for example, by supplying a part that can only be used in a patented combination. An indirect infringer is liable in the same way that a direct infringer is liable.

Chapter 10 then discusses "literal infringement," which occurs if the infringing product includes each and every element required by a patent claim, exactly as described. Next is a discussion of the "doctrine of equivalents," a doctrine holding that a product can still infringe a claim even though it is *different* from what the claim literally requires, as long as the differences are "insubstantial." This is a difficult concept, even for experts and judges, so it is covered in some detail. Chapter 10 discusses how the doctrine of equivalents has evolved, and it examines some of the tests used to determine if a product is or is not "equivalent" to a claimed invention. Chapter 10 also discusses limitations on the scope of "equivalency" imposed by the prosecution history, the patent disclosure and the prior art. Chapter 10 considers "equivalency" in the related context of "means-plus-function" claims, as well as the "reverse doctrine of equivalents," which holds that a product does not infringe, even though it is literally described by the patent claims, if it is sufficiently "changed in principle" from what the applicant actually invented.

Finally, Chapter 10 discusses a little-used "experimental use" exception to infringement.

Chapter 11 introduces the subject of patent litigation. Specific topics discussed include "jurisdiction" and "venue," which determine in what court a suit for infringement can be filed; actions for "declaratory judgment," which permit an accused infringer to sue a patent owner instead of waiting to be sued; burdens of proof, which determine who must prove what and how compelling the evidence must be; and the roles of judge and jury in deciding the various issues presented in a typical case. Chapter 11 also examines the kinds of relief that can be won in a suit for patent infringement. These include "preliminary injunctions," which bar the continuance of the allegedly infringing activity during the pendency of the lawsuit; permanent injunctions, which permanently bar infringing activity if the patent owner prevails; and money damages, which compensate the patent owner for past infringement. The last-named can be in the form of "lost profits" or a "reasonable royalty," and they can be increased as much as threefold if the infringement is found to have been "willful." Chapter 11 also discusses defenses that can limit the recovery of damages, including the six-year statute of limitations, the patent owner's failure to properly mark products that it has sold, "laches" and "equitable estoppel." "Laches" refers to unreasonable delay in filing suit which somehow prejudices the accused infringer. "Equitable estoppel" refers to conduct by the patent owner which leads the accused infringer to believe that the patent owner will not pursue a claim.

Chapter 11 ends with a brief discussion of the International Trade Commission, which is an alternative forum for raising a claim of patent infringement if the accused products are imported into the United States from abroad.

Chapter 12 concludes the work with a discussion of several specialized topics, including design patents, plant patents, foreign patents and patents claiming computer programs.

Appendices A and B provide, respectively, samples of actual utility and design patents issued by the United States Patent Office.

1.3 SOURCES OF LAW

Several important sources of patent law will be referred to throughout this book. One is the Patent Act, found at Title 35 of the United States Code. The Patent Act contains most of the legislation enacted by Congress that relates to patents. References to particular sections of the Act will generally be in the format "35 U.S.C. § _____." Other important authorities are the Code of Federal Regulations (37 C.F.R.) and the Manual of Patent Examining Procedure (MPEP), which set forth detailed rules and regulations for obtaining a patent.

In addition to the statutes, rules and regulations, one can find hundreds, perhaps thousands, of reported court decisions interpreting the patent laws. As in any other field of federal law, the controlling precedents are those of the U.S. Supreme Court. However, during the latter half of this century the Supreme Court has only rarely accepted appeals in patent cases, leaving most of the decision making to the lower courts. The most significant of these lower courts, at present, is the Federal Circuit Court of Appeals. Established in 1982, the Federal Circuit or CAFC, based in Washington, D.C., hears all appeals of patent-related cases, regardless of the place where the suit initially was filed. Except on those occasions when the Supreme Court intervenes, the Federal Circuit is the ultimate authority on what patent laws mean, and all inferior courts, as well as the Patent Office, are bound by its interpretations.

Cases referred to in this book are accompanied by citations, generally in the footnotes. The standard citation format includes the name of the case, followed by the volume of the official reporter in which it appears, the abbreviated name of the official reporter, the relevant page numbers, and in parentheses an identification of the court and the date of the decision. For example, *Vitronics Corp. v. Conceptronic, Inc.*, 90 F.3d 1576, 1582–83 (Fed. Cir. 1996), refers to a case of that name reported in Volume 90 of the *Federal Reporter* (Third Series) beginning at page 1576. The pages of particular interest are pages 1582–83, and the decision was rendered by the Federal Circuit Court of Appeals in 1996. These citations are provided in case the reader needs additional information or authority to support a particular proposition.

CHAPTER 2

Patents
Distinguished from
Other Rights

People sometimes confuse patents with copyrights or trademarks, saying, for example, that Lucasfilm has a "patent" on the name "Star Wars." Patents, copyrights, trademarks and trade secrets are all legal means of protecting "intellectual property"—a term referring to the intangible creations of the human mind. However, patents, copyrights, trademarks and trade secrets are each governed by a unique body of rules and requirements, and, in spite of some overlap, they are generally designed to protect different sorts of intellectual creations. Therefore, a good starting point for explaining what a patent *is* may be to emphasize what it is *not*.

2.1 COPYRIGHTS

Copyrights protect *works of authorship*, which is broadly defined by statute to include writings in the conventional sense, dramatic works, musical compositions, choreography, paintings, sculptures, photographs, motion pictures, audio recordings and architecture. To some degree, any "work of authorship" has an aspect of creative "expression." Copyright protects this "expression," not the underlying "ideas." Although idea and expression are not always easy to sort out, one could, for example, borrow the information published in this book without violating its copyright. The copyright would be violated only by duplicating the book's language or organization. Language is a matter of "expression" and an extension of the author's creative faculties. The information itself is on the side of "ideas," and, no matter what labor was expended to compile it, it can be freely used without violation of copyright.

A copyright cannot be used to protect a utilitarian invention or a useful feature of a product. For example, a new and more efficient spark plug design could not be "copyrighted." Some useful products do have an aesthetic aspect that can be copyrighted, but the artistic component of the design must be distinguishable from the utilitarian component, which can only be patented. For example, a belt buckle might be copyrighted as a sculpture,[1] but the copyright cannot prevent the copying of some mechanical aspect of the design, such as an improved latching mechanism or the like. In this respect a copyright is the antithesis of a patent, which is specifically intended to protect such technological advancements. If one had both a copyright and a patent on the same belt buckle, the copyright would protect *only* the aesthetic appearance of the belt buckle, and the patent would protect *only* the mechanism by which it worked.[2]

As we will see in Section 8.9, an invention is patentable only if it is sufficiently new and different when compared to prior inventions that persons skilled in the field would not have considered it obvious. In contrast, copyright law has no requirement of novelty per se. As long as the "work of authorship" is an original product of the author's imagination, a copyright cannot be denied simply because the work is similar to others that have gone before. This may be the case because of the difficulty of judging novelty or obviousness in relation to the kinds of creative works that are traditionally protected by copyright. Who can say whether the latest mystery novel is an obvious variation of the thousands that have gone before? By the same token, independent creation is a complete defense to infringement of copyright, regardless of the similarity of two works. If two songs are nearly identical to one another, but it can be shown that the second composer worked entirely on his own, without knowledge of the first composition, the second composer cannot be held to have infringed the copyright of the first.[3] Patent law is very different. One who innocently infringes a patent, perhaps not even knowing that the patent exists, can still be held accountable in the courts.

One area in which patent and copyright converge is in the protection of computer software. Software blurs the boundaries between a "work of authorship" and a machine. From the perspective of a programmer, a computer program is a kind of writing. It is expressed in a language, which resembles in some respects ordinary human languages, and the process of authorship involves some of the aesthetic choices and personal style associated with other forms of writing. Copyright, rather than patent, would seem the proper vehicle for protecting this "expression." On the

---

[1] *See Kieselstein-Cord v. Accessories By Pearl, Inc.*, 632 F.2d 989 (2d Cir. 1980).

[2] Unless the patent were a "design patent," a special category of patent discussed in Section 12.1.

[3] Of course, the similarity of the two works can be considered evidence that the second composer *was* influenced by the composition of the first.

other hand, a program is akin to a machine part as soon as it is executed by a computer. The program controls the operation of the computer much as cogs and wheels may have controlled a machine of an earlier era. From this perspective, a computer program seems outside of the subject matter protected by copyright and more suitable for protection by patent.

Courts and scholars have struggled for decades to determine the proper application of copyright and patent law to computer software. At present, both forms of protection appear to be available, though each has its limitations. A computer program can be copyrighted, but this may not prevent someone else from extracting the functional aspects of the program to incorporate in a new program. The functional aspects of computer software can be patented as long as they meet the various requirements of patentability (such as novelty and non-obviousness) and as long as the patent steers clear of monopolizing an abstract idea, mathematical algorithm or principle of nature. These special concerns are discussed in some detail in Section 12.4.

2.2 TRADEMARKS

Trademarks are governed both by federal statutes and by common law. A trademark generally is a phrase, or a symbol, that is used to represent the origin of a product. A consumer who finds the word "Nike" on a shoe box, or the familiar Nike "swoosh" symbol, is entitled to presume that the shoe sold in the box is the genuine article. The purpose of trademark law is the protection of consumers, and disputes in this area are usually resolved by determining whether consumers would be confused by the use of a mark that is similar to the mark of another business. If another shoe manufacturer adopted the name "Nikke" for its line of products, one could be sure that the original Nike would challenge such use as unfair and confusing. Patents are granted only on inventions—not on labels, logos or brand names. Trademarks, on the other hand, cannot be used to protect the utilitarian aspects of a product.

2.3 TRADE SECRETS

Patents are not the only way that inventors can prevent others from taking advantage of their labors. Another option is to keep the invention a secret. Generally speaking, an inventor cannot do both. As soon as a patent issues, the invention becomes public. This is a part of the bargain that the inventor strikes with the government in order to obtain a limited monopoly. However, the patent *application* process is secret. If an inventor applies for a patent, but the application is rejected, the inventor can abandon the attempt and still retain some protection by keeping the invention a secret.

Whether an inventor is better advised to patent an invention or simply keep it a secret may depend on the nature of the invention. If it is something that will be revealed as soon as a product incorporating the invention is placed on the market, the notion of keeping the invention secret may be self-defeating. On the other hand, certain inventions can be exploited without making them public. For example, an ordinary product, indistinguishable from any other, might be manufactured less expensively because of an innovative process. Such a process might be better protected through secrecy than it would be by patent, since a patent would only last for a limited term. Similarly, the legendary secret formula of Coca-Cola has never been patented, apparently because the original ingredients cannot be accurately determined by analyzing the finished product. Under these circumstances, secrecy provides Coca-Cola with better and longer-lasting protection of its formula than could patent law.

If secret information is of the kind that gives one an advantage in business, it may be protectable under "trade secret" law. Trade secrets are governed by state laws, rather than federal law, so there is some geographic variation. However, about 40 states have adopted, in some form, a model statute known as the Uniform Trade Secrets Act. The definition of "trade secret" under the Uniform Act extends to various forms of information, including "a formula, pattern, compilation, program, device, method, technique or process."[4] Such things as formulas, devices and processes are also within the area of potentially patentable inventions.[5] However, trade secret law imposes a different set of requirements. In order to qualify as a protectable "trade secret" under the Uniform Act, the information must "derive independent economic value, actual or potential, from not being generally known to, and not being readily ascertainable by proper means by, other persons who can obtain economic value from its disclosure or use."[6] In other words, not only must the information be secret, it must also be *valuable*. In addition, the information must be "the subject of efforts that are reasonable under the circumstances to maintain its secrecy."[7] A company that is lax about security may be unable to resort to trade secret law to protect its information from use or disclosure. Patent law, in contrast, requires neither that an invention be eco-

---

[4] Uniform Trade Secrets Act §1(4).

[5] Trade secret law can also be used to protect certain kinds of business information that would *not* be patentable—for example, customer lists and marketing plans. As long as information is secret and valuable to a business, it can be protected as a trade secret, even though it is not an "invention" in the usual sense.

[6] Uniform Trade Secrets Act §1(4)(i).

[7] Uniform Trade Secrets Act §1(4)(ii).

nomically valuable nor (under most circumstances) that it have been kept secret.[8]

While patent law speaks of "infringement," trade secret law forbids "misappropriation." Misappropriation includes unauthorized disclosure or use of the trade secret information by someone who has a duty to keep the information secret or limit its use.[9] Employees, for example, are generally duty-bound to refrain from using or disclosing the trade secret information of their employers. So is anyone who has signed a contract or confidentiality agreement promising to protect the information. An employee of a soda company who published his employer's secret formula on the Internet, or who used the formula to devise a rival soda, would likely be held guilty of trade secret misappropriation.

Misappropriation also includes the use of information known to be derived from someone under a duty to keep it confidential and acquisition of the secret information by "improper means."[10] A person who bribed a soda company employee in order to obtain its secret formula would likely be guilty of misappropriation. Finally, misappropriation can occur, under the Uniform Act, if trade secret information is used by persons who know that the information has come into their possession only because of a mistake. If a soda manufacturer received a fax from a competitor setting out a secret formula, and it was evident that the fax had actually been intended for someone else, the rival would probably not be permitted to keep the fax and use the formula.

Trade secret law differs from patent law in requiring either some connection with a "duty," contractual or otherwise, to protect the confidential information, the use of "improper means" to acquire the information, or an evident mistake. If the information was acquired under other circumstances, it can be freely used. For example, the Uniform Act allows the acquisition of information by "reverse engineering." "Reverse engineering" means beginning with the finished product and analyzing it to determine the process by which it was developed or the principle of its operation. As long as the finished product was acquired legitimately, by purchasing it on the open market, for example, it is not a violation of trade secret law to "reverse engineer" the product and use the resulting information in a competing product.

Hence, if a rival soda manufacturer could analyze a beverage and determine the formula by which it was manufactured, trade secret law (applying the Uniform Act) would not prevent the rival from discovering and using that information. Patent law, in contrast, does not distinguish be-

---

[8] An exception arises if the invention was disclosed more than one year before a patent application was filed. See Section 8.10.

[9] Uniform Trade Secrets Act §1(2)(ii).

[10] Uniform Trade Secrets Act §1(2)(ii).

tween information acquired legitimately or illegitimately. A product can still infringe a patent, even though it was the result of reverse engineering or even independent development.

Trade secret law might seem at odds with patent law, which requires the public disclosure of information in exchange for exclusive rights. However, the Supreme Court has ruled that the two bodies of law are not incompatible, and federal patent law does not preempt state trade secret laws.[11] One complements the other, and inventors are provided with a choice of means to protect their inventions, the most appropriate of which will be determined by the circumstances.

2.4 PATENTS

Patents cover practical inventions in the "useful arts." Any technological advance from a new microchip to an improved formula for bubble gum can be the subject of a patent. A special form of patent known as a "design patent" can protect some forms of artistic creation (see Section 12.1), but the usual kind of patent, the "utility patent," applies only to technological inventions. As a result, a patent cannot be granted for a painting, a novel, a song, a product name or a company logo.

In order to obtain a patent, an inventor must file an application with the United States Patent and Trademark Office, and the application must describe the invention in such a way that persons skilled in the field could practice the invention. The application must conclude with numbered "claims" that describe in precise terms exactly what the patent covers. A patent can be granted, or if granted can be held valid in the courts, only if the claims describe an invention that is both *new* and *non-obvious*. Patent law thus includes a requirement of "novelty" that is absent from copyright and trademark law.

A patent remains in force for 20 years from the date the application was filed. During that time, no one without the permission of the patent owner can (within the geographical limits of the United States) make, use, sell, offer to sell or import the invention described by the patent claims. To do so is an infringement of the patent, regardless of whether the infringer copied the inventor's ideas or discovered them independently. In contrast to trademark law, which requires that the protected mark be *used* in business, a patent owner can choose to practice the claimed invention, license it to others or prevent its practice altogether.

---

[11] *Kewanee Oil Co. v. Bicron Corp.*, 416 U.S. 470, 94 S. Ct. 1879 (1974).

CHAPTER 3

Reading a Patent

Anyone interested in patent law should take the time to study an actual patent. Copies of three United States patents can be found in Appendix A of this book. The examples have been chosen for the sake of simplicity and brevity, and to show that inventors are still searching for a better mousetrap.

The first patent claims a device for trapping a mouse with the help of a ping-pong ball. The mouse enters a tube, the tube tips forward as the mouse heads for the "smelly bait" and a ping-pong ball rolls down to block the mouse's escape. In the second patent, bait is used to lure the mouse onto a bridge. Although the bridge appears to be secure, the weight of the mouse causes the bridge to spin sideways, sending the mouse plunging headlong into a bucket. The trap claimed in the third patent is made from a soda can.

Although none of these inventions is complex, each patent includes the basic components found in patents awarded to the most sophisticated advancements. The first patent will be used as an example for most of the following discussion, but the reader should examine all three, in order to get a feel for the way patents are organized.

3.1 GENERAL INFORMATION

Patents are officially known by their serial numbers, printed at the top right-hand corner of the patent. However, for the sake of convenience patents are often referred to by the last name of the first listed inventor or by the last three digits of the patent's serial number. The first patent in Appendix A would be referred to as the Oviatt patent, or as the '918 patent. The date on which the patent issued appears directly below the serial number.[1]

The title of the patent appears at the top of the left-hand column: for example, "Mousetrap for Catching Mice Live." The title of a patent has little official significance and can sometimes be misleading. The "Mousetrap for Catching Mice Live" patent suggests that the trap can be immersed and the rodent drowned. The name of the inventor, or inventors, appears directly below the title, together with the inventor's address or home town. Beneath the inventor's name is the name of any person or company to whom the inventor assigned rights in the patent, prior to the date of issue.[2] Since the Oviatt patent shows no assignee, ownership of the patent evidently was retained by the inventor. Patent rights can be assigned after the patent issues. When this is the case, the transfer of ownership will not be evident from the patent itself, but it may be recorded in the Patent Office's prosecution history file.

Moving down the left-hand column, the next item to appear is the number of the application on which the patent was based. Each patent application submitted to the Patent Office is assigned a serial number. However, it is not the same serial number ultimately assigned to the patent itself. Although this can result in some confusion, it allows reference to applications that never issued as patents. The Oviatt patent is the result of a single application, numbered 347,890. Often the situation is more complicated. The applicant may have filed one application, which was objected to and abandoned in favor of a "continuation" or a "continuation-in-part" application. Sometimes this happens several times, resulting in a chain of applications preceding a particular patent. These complications are discussed in Sections 5.2–5.3. For now, it is enough to note that the "family history" of the patent, if any, can be found in the upper left-hand column of the patent, next to the bracketed number [63].

All patented inventions are assigned by the Patent Office to subject matter categories, which are sometimes narrowed to very particular fields. This is done so that the Patent Office (or anyone else for that matter) can conveniently search a given area and determine what has been patented so far. This classification information appears beneath the application "family history," next to the bracketed numbers [51] and [52], the first number relating to international classification and the second to

---

[1] The bracketed number "[11]" to the left of the patent serial number, like the other bracketed numbers found at various places on the patent, is a matter of Patent Office formatting. All patents of a certain era have the number [11] next to the serial number, [45] next to the date of issue, [54] next to the title, [75] next to the names of the inventors and so forth. The numbers have no significance, other than in identifying the location of certain information.

[2] See Section 6.2.

U.S. classification. In the case of the Oviatt patent, the mousetrap invention has been assigned to U.S. subject matter Class 43: "Fishing, Trapping and Vermin Destroying." It can be found specifically under subclasses 60 ("Traps:Imprisoning"), 61 ("Traps:Imprisoning:Swinging or Sliding Closure") and 66 ("Traps:Self and Ever Set:Nonreturn Entrance:Victim Opened").

As discussed in Section 5.1, part of the Patent Office's duty on receiving an application is to search its collection of prior patents to determine whether the application claims something new. The Field of Search area shows the categories that were reviewed by the Patent Office in its search for earlier patents. In the case of the Oviatt patent, the Patent Office searched the same subclasses noted above, with the addition of subclasses 58 ("Traps"), 67 ("Traps:Self and Ever Set:Nonreturn Entrance:Victim Opened") and 75 ("Traps:Self-Reset:Smiting"). The search categories established by the Patent Office provide a brief catalog of modern technology. Class 43, for example, is a testament to man's continuing war with the mouse, including subcategories for "impaling," "explosive," "choking or squeezing" and "electrocuting" traps, in addition to those that "smite."

Moving downwards, the next section of the patent is a list of prior art references cited by the Patent Office during prosecution of the application. Prior art, discussed in Section 8.9.1, includes earlier patents and publications disclosing inventions similar to the one claimed by the patent applicant. The cited references are those that the Patent Office considered closest to the patented invention, though not so close as to prevent the patent from issuing. Looking once again to the Oviatt patent, the Patent Office cited three patents as prior art, two of them more than 75 years old: the Turnbo patent, issued in 1909, the Cushing patent, issued in 1917, and the Sackett patent, issued in 1988. All disclose some form of rat or mouse trap with a tilting mechanism to prevent the victim's escape.

Next to appear are the name of the patent examiner, or examiners, who reviewed the application for the Patent Office, and the name of the counsel or patent agent who represented the inventor during this process.

The paragraph entitled "Abstract" provides a summary of the invention. This is the place to look for the gist of the invention, before tackling the detailed description of the invention that follows the drawings. The abstract typically includes a brief description of how the invention works and what it is good for.

3.2 DRAWINGS

After the abstract appear the patent drawings. These are often far more helpful in understanding the invention than a written description alone would be. Although drawings are not required for every patent, nearly all include some form of illustration. The Oviatt patent, like most patents, shows the invention from a variety of views so that all details are readily visible. Figures 3 and 8 show the invention before the mouse has sprung the trap. Figure 9 shows the movement of the ping-pong ball and the appearance of the trap after it has tipped forward on its pivot. Figure 2 is described as a "mouse eye view." Patents sometimes include exploded views, cross sections or views of individual components when those views are helpful to understand the invention. Some patents include graphs or flow charts.

Patent drawings are generally surrounded by numbers and arrows, as are the drawings in the Oviatt patent. These are reference numbers corresponding to the written description of the invention found in the body of the patent. For example, the Oviatt patent identifies sphere 9 as the ping-pong ball, lump 10 as the bait and rodent M as the mouse. Reading a patent sometimes requires a great deal of flipping back and forth to identify the components numbered in the drawings.[3]

Patent drawings sometimes depict different embodiments of the invention. Figure 1 of the Oviatt patent shows the trap set up on a stand made of wire, whereas Figure 5 shows the trap resting on the edge of a plastic ring. The inclusion of alternative embodiments shows that the inventor's ideas were not limited to a particular implementation of the invention.

3.3 SPECIFICATION

After the drawings comes the section of the patent referred to as the "specification." The specification describes the invention, or technology related to the invention, in words rather than pictures. Often the specification begins with a "background of the invention" section discussing the technology as it existed before the patented invention was made. This allows the inventor to point out the shortcomings of what has gone before and highlight the advantages of the patented invention. The Oviatt patent begins in typical fashion by describing the health menace posed by mice and the disadvantages of typical traps that kill the mouse, where it is left to decompose, smell and endanger children and pets. Oviatt then explains that his own invention avoids these problems by trapping the mouse live.

Many specifications include a "Summary of the Invention" section which is used to list the objectives of the patented invention. Oviatt states that the "main object" of his invention is to "trap a mouse alive." Other,

---

[3] Note that the numbers used in labeling a patent drawing need not be consecutive. The Oviatt patent uses numbers 90 and 100, but there is no 89 or 99.

subsidiary objectives are to provide an inexpensive trap, a trap that can be immersed in water to drown the mouse and a trap that is reusable.

The next section of the Oviatt patent is, again in typical fashion, a "Brief Description of the Drawings." This portion of the patent explains in the most general way what is depicted in the drawings—for example, Figure 1 is a top view, Figure 3 is a cross section and Figure 5 is an alternative embodiment.

The next section of the Oviatt patent is entitled "Description of the Preferred Embodiment." Almost any patent has a similar section where the inventor describes the "preferred embodiment" in great detail, identifying in the process all of the components visible in the drawings. The "preferred embodiment" means the inventor's favored implementation of the invention. Inventions are usually general concepts that, at a detailed level, could be implemented in any number of ways. For example, in the Oviatt patent, the tilting tube and the rolling ball are general concepts that characterize the invention. Oviatt might be entitled to claim any mousetrap that shares those features. But in the specification, we learn of the inventor's preference for a ping-pong ball, and we are given two possible designs for the fulcrum on which the trap teeters—one a stand preferably made of wire, and the other a plastic ring with one flat edge.

Disclosure at this level of detail satisfies two requirements of the patent laws: that inventors provide in the specification sufficient information to allow persons skilled in the field to practice the invention, and that inventors disclose the *best* way they know of to practice the invention. These requirements, known respectively as the "enablement" and "best mode" requirements, are discussed in Sections 8.6 and 8.7. However, it is important to realize that these details discussed in the specification do not, under most circumstances, limit what the patent covers. Even though the specification describes a ping-pong ball, the patent might still cover a similar mousetrap that used a rubber ball.

In fact, the Oviatt specification includes warnings to that effect. Just before the numbered claims, we find the following caveat:

Although the present invention has been described with reference to preferred embodiments, numerous modifications and variations can be made and still the result will come within the scope of the invention. No limitation with respect to the specific embodiments disclosed herein is intended or should be inferred.

Such warnings are common, though they are probably unnecessary.

3.4 CLAIMS

The last, and most important, section of a patent consists of the numbered "claims." The claims, not the drawings or the specification, define what the patent "covers" and what will infringe. In the Oviatt patent we find eight claims.

Claims generally come in two forms—independent and dependent. An independent claim stands by itself, whereas a dependent claim explicitly refers to another claim and incorporates its terms by reference. Claim 1 of the Oviatt patent is an independent claim. Claim 2 is a dependent claim because it refers to "The mousetrap of claim 1 wherein . . .". As a result, Claim 2 is read as though it incorporates all of the language of Claim 1, plus the additional language of Claim 2. Claim 3 is another dependent claim, which this time refers to Claim 2 ("The mousetrap of claim 2 wherein . . ."). Since Claim 2 depends from Claim 1, the effect of Claim 3 is to incorporate *all* of the language of Claims 1, 2 and 3.

Claims generally begin with a "preamble" that establishes the context of the invention. As discussed in Section 7.6, the preamble is sometimes treated as a limitation on the scope of the claim and sometimes as a mere introduction to the claim which has no legal effect. This can have important consequences. For example, Claim 1 of the Oviatt patent begins with the preamble "A mousetrap comprising . . .". If this were the last reference in the claim to a "mouse," the question could be raised as to whether the claim covered, for example, a squirrel trap that was otherwise identical to the device described in the claim.

The preamble usually ends with the term "consisting of" or "comprising."[4] The indented paragraphs following are the claim "elements" or claim "limitations." The vast majority of patent claims are designed to cover a *combination* of elements or limitations. Looking at Claim 1 of the Oviatt patent, we find the following combination set forth:

1. A mousetrap comprising:

   a main tube having a central fulcrum means, a bait end, and a ball end;

   a base stand having a means to support the main tube at the fulcrum;

   said bait end further comprising mouse bait and a main tube closure;

   said ball end further comprising a ball and a main tube closure;

   an entrance tube depending down from the main tube at the central fulcrum means, and angled toward the ball end;

   said entrance tube having a mouse entrance adjacent a supporting surface for the base stand; and

   said main tube having a horizontal load position where said ball rests at the ball end, wherein a mouse enters the mouse entrance, walks toward the base up the entrance tube, and passes the fulcrum means, thereby causing the main tube to teeter down at the bait end, and cause the ball to roll down the main tube and

---

[4] See Section 7.6.

then down the entrance tube, functioning to block an egress of the mouse out the mouse entrance.

Claim 1 of the Oviatt patent would cover any mousetrap that included each of the elements described. If a mousetrap did not incorporate one or more of the described elements, it would be outside the scope of the claim. For example, if a mousetrap did not tip like the Oviatt mousetrap, but instead relied on a spring-loaded mechanism to shoot a ping-pong ball down the tube to trap the mouse, that trap would lack the "fulcrum means" required by Claim 1, and it would fall outside the literal scope of the claim.[5]

The language used in patent claims is generally more formal and technical, and sometimes more obscure, than everyday language. Claim 1 of the Oviatt patent is not a particularly bad example, but it does include terms such as "fulcrum means," "supporting surface," "horizontal load position" and "egress" that might seem more grandiose than the invention requires. Claim drafters, whether inventors or attorneys, resort to such technical or pseudotechnical language because of the importance of the words to the legal effect of the patent. Insofar as possible, the claim language is required to describe exactly what the patent covers. Claim drafters therefore must be precise in their description of the invention but must not limit themselves by the choice of language to something narrower than the inventor intends to claim.

The Oviatt patent has three independent claims—Claims 1, 6 and 8— and five dependent claims. A patent can have as many claims as the inventor desires, although more claims can mean paying the Patent Office a higher fee. Each claim can be treated in some respects as if it were a separate patent. Although people often speak of a patent being infringed, it is really a claim, or a series of claims, that is infringed. A device may infringe one claim of a patent but not another, perhaps because of a small difference in language. An inventor who describes the invention through more than one claim decreases the chance that a potentially infringing product will escape because of some small difference. Using more than one claim is also a hedge against the possibility that a claim will be held invalid by the courts. One claim may be held invalid, while another, with slightly different language, survives.

Note how the Oviatt patent describes the same concept, in slightly different terms, in Claims 1, 6 and 8. Claim 1 speaks of a pair of tubes—a "main tube" and an "entrance tube." Claim 8, on the other hand, speaks of a " 'Y' shaped tube." The Oviatt patent also illustrates how dependent claims are often used to include details described in the specification but omitted from the broader claims. For example, Claim 4 specifically limits

---

[5] See Section 10.5.

the "ball" of Claim 1 to a "ping-pong ball." If it proved to be the case that a moustrap had been invented prior to Oviatt's that used a rubber ball, the broader claim might be held invalid while the narrow claim might not.

CHAPTER 4

Patentable Subject Matter

The Supreme Court has suggested that the realm of patents embraces "anything under the sun that is made by man."[1] This is not literally true. First, the Constitution limits the power of Congress to the promotion of the "useful arts." These are generally understood to include technological endeavors, rather than, for example, artistic or social endeavors. The types of creations that can be patented are further limited by the language of the Patent Act. Section 101 of the Patent Act (35 U.S.C. § 101) provides as follows:

Whoever invents or discovers any new and useful process, machine, manufacture, or composition of matter, or any new and useful improvement thereof, may obtain a patent therefor, subject to the conditions and requirements of this title.[2]

In order to be patented, an invention must fall within one of the statutory categories of "process, machine, manufacture, or composition of matter." Since these terms are deliberately broad, this is seldom an obstacle. However, certain categories of invention or discovery have been held to exceed the statutory boundaries of patentable subject matter, or are sufficiently close to those boundaries as to generate controversy. The most important of these fall under the rubric of abstract ideas, principles

---

[1] *Diamond v. Chakrabarty*, 447 U.S. 303, 309, 100 S. Ct. 2204, 2207–08 (1980).

[2] "Manufacture" is an abbreviated term for a product produced by a manufacturing process. "Composition of matter" is a broad term that is most often applied to chemical compounds and the like, but that could literally refer to any agglomeration of physical substances.

of nature, living organisms, literary or artistic creations, printed matter, methods of doing business and computer programs.

4.1 ABSTRACT IDEAS

The most general category of unpatentable subject matter, and perhaps the hardest to define, is the category of "abstract ideas." Obviously, one can patent an "idea" if it is in the form of a new process, machine, manufacture or composition of matter. On the other hand, one cannot patent an "idea" that is without a material form or a practical application. For example, one probably could not patent the idea of "renewable energy resources." The idea is a useful one, but to be patentable it should take the form of a particular kind of renewable energy resource. Patents are intended to reward and encourage those who make tangible contributions to the useful arts. If patents were awarded to abstract ideas, rather than to practical applications of those ideas, the effect might be to discourage, rather than promote, advancements in those arts.

4.2 PRINCIPLES OF NATURE

Although the Patent Act defines "invention" as meaning "invention *or discovery*,"[3] the courts have long held that the truths of nature per se cannot be patented, even by the people who discover those truths. The clearest examples can be found in the formulas of mathematics or the physical sciences. While Pythagoras may have been the first to appreciate that the sums of the squares of the two sides of a right triangle are equal to the square of the hypotenuse, this discovery does not qualify as a patentable invention. Similarly, Einstein could not have patented the relationship of mass to energy: $E = mc^2$. What *can* be patented is an apparatus, method or composition of matter that puts a principle of nature to practical application. The Pythagorean theorem is not patentable subject matter as such, but its use in an apparatus for surveying might be. Einstein might have patented a nuclear reactor that put his formula to use. Because the formulas of science and mathematics are generalized descriptions of the universe, any invention, at some level, can be described by those formulas. As long as the invention is not the formula itself but a useful application or embodiment of the formula, it is potentially patentable.

The rule against patenting a principle of nature has been applied to materials discovered in nature, as well as abstract relationships and physical laws. It has been said, for example, that the discoverer of a new mineral could not patent that mineral as such. However, the discoverer of a natural material is permitted to patent the *use* of that material in a par-

[3] 35 U.S.C. § 100.

ticular application—for example, the use of the mineral to treat a disease. If the mineral were later discovered to be useful in some other application, that too could be patented. Some problems can be avoided through careful claim drafting. For example, one inventor was denied a patent on a shrimp that was beheaded and cleaned, but still protected by its shell.[4] Although the shrimp was no longer whole, that which remained was still a "product of nature" and in its original state. Had the inventor instead claimed a *method* of preparing a shrimp, that method would more likely be held patentable subject matter, at least in today's judicial climate.

It might be argued that investigation into the principles of nature is a pursuit just as valuable as the development of technology, and that awarding patents to significant discoveries would encourage such investigation. Why then are patents unobtainable on newly discovered natural laws? At least two theories have been advanced. One holds that a patent on a principle of nature would simply be too broad. A principle may lead to a vast spectrum of practical applications, many of which could not have been foreseen by the discoverer of the principle. This may well be true. However, as we will see in Section 10.6.5, even inventions of the ordinary kind (e.g., machines, processes and compositions of matter) may be applied after their invention in ways that the inventor could not have predicted. This is particularly true of "pioneering" inventions, which establish an entirely new field of industry. These inventions, however, are often regarded as those *most* worthy of a patent. Another, perhaps sounder argument is that patent law should not take from the public that which it has formerly possessed. New inventions take nothing from the public because, by definition, the inventions did not exist before. On the other hand, principles of nature exist even before they are discovered, and the public may, in some sense, have "used" these principles before they were appreciated. The nuclear reactions that cause the sun to shine are described, in part, by Einstein's formula, but no one would suggest that the discovery of that formula should have entitled Einstein to a monopoly on sunshine.

4.3 LIVING ORGANISMS

Advances in technology sometimes compel a reassessment of the scope of protection available through the patent laws. Genetic engineering provides an example. Until recently, the idea of patenting a living animal hardly arose. Even when an explorer discovered a species that was previously unknown, the explorer could not claim to have "invented" the species; the explorer merely "discovered" what was already there. The situation has changed with the development of techniques allowing sci-

[4] *Ex Parte Grayson*, 51 U.S.P.Q. 413 (Pat. Off. Bd. App. 1941).

entists to rearrange the genetic codes of existing species. Now biologists can truly claim to have "invented" a form of life that did not exist before. Still, the notion that a person or a company can claim a property interest in a life form is one that is unsettling to many people.

In one of its rare forays into patent law, the Supreme Court, in *Diamond v. Chakrabarty*, 447 U.S. 303, 100 S. Ct. 2204 (1980), addressed the question of whether a genetically engineered bacteria, so devised that it could break down crude oil, could be patented. The bacteria was undeniably useful, since it could be used to treat oil spills. It was also new. No naturally occurring bacteria possessed the same ability to break down all of the components found in crude oil. However, the Patent Office rejected Chakrabarty's patent application on the grounds that a living organism cannot be patented. The majority of the court disagreed, holding that Congress had established a broad scope of patentability, and that if Congress wished to exclude genetically engineered life forms it would have to do so explicitly. The court also observed that the most important inventions may be those least foreseeable to the legislature. Literally speaking, new bacteria are "manufactures" and "compositions of matter," and are patentable as such.

The principles of *Chakrabarty*[5] have since been extended to multicellular organisms. In 1988, Harvard University obtained a celebrated patent on a genetically engineered mouse. The mouse is useful in laboratory studies because it is particularly susceptible to cancer. The PTO Board of Appeals and Interferences[6] has also held patentable a genetically altered oyster that can be enjoyed year-round, in contrast to naturally occurring oysters which must be avoided during the summer months.[7] Nevertheless, the Patent Office has announced that it will not permit a patent on a human being.

A special kind of patent, discussed in Section 12.2, is available for plant life. However, plant life has also been found to be appropriate subject matter for a utility patent.[8] This is a natural extension of *Chakrabarty*, although if Congress saw fit to create a specific set of rules governing plants, one might infer that plants were outside the scope of the pre-existing statute.

---

[5] Cases are typically referred to by the name of the *first* litigant—for example, *Smith v. Jones* would be referred to as the *Smith* case. *Diamond v. Chakrabarty*, however, is generally referred to as the *Chakrabarty* case rather than the *Diamond* case. Diamond was the name of the acting Commissioner of Patents at the time the suit was filed. Since a number of cases can include the name of the Patent Commissioner (i.e., *Diamond v. Chakrabarty* and *Diamond v. Diehr*), using the name of the patent applicant (Chakrabarty) to refer to the cases reduces ambiguity.

[6] See Section 5.1.

[7] *Ex Parte Allen*, 2 U.S.P.Q.2d 1425 (PTO Bd. App. & Int. 1987).

[8] *See Ex Parte Hibbard*, 227 U.S.P.Q.2d 443 (PTO Bd. App. & Int. 1985).

4.4 ARTISTIC AND LITERARY CREATIONS

Generally speaking, the proper vehicle for protecting artistic and literary creations is copyright.[9] Utility patents are intended to protect, as the name implies, *useful* inventions. In this context, "useful" is meant in the narrow sense of a practical advancement in a technological art. Patents *are* available for ornamental design as applied to utilitarian objects, but design patents are a different kind of patent subject to a different set of rules.[10] If an inventor attempts to obtain a utility patent on what is essentially an ornamental feature, that patent may be held outside of the subject matter permitted under § 101. For example, a court in New York recently addressed the matter of whether garments that had been treated to produce a characteristic "stone-washed" jeans pattern could be patented.[11] The court determined that because the patterns did not affect the usefulness of the garments, the garments could only be protected by a design patent, not a utility patent.

4.5 PRINTED MATTER

Another generally recognized exception to patentability is the "printed matter" exception. This rule holds that a manufactured article or composition of matter is not patentable if the only thing that distinguishes it from prior inventions is the presence of pictures or writing. For example, one could not obtain a utility patent for a baseball cap merely because it bears a new team logo, even though the cap is "new" and "useful," and caps, as such, are articles of manufacture.

On the other hand, an invention that involves printed matter may be patentable, as long as the invention as a whole calls for a new structure, or the printed matter bears a novel functional relationship to the "substrate"—that is, the physical object on which the matter is printed. In one instance, an inventor applied for a patent on a scheme for deliberately mislabeling a measuring cup to solve the problem of measuring when making less than a full recipe. A cook who wishes to prepare, for example, one-third of the amount specified in a recipe may be left with the difficult task of measuring quantities such as 1/3 of 2/3 of a cup. The inventor conceived of a measuring cup for fractional portions. The cook who wishes to make a 1/3 recipe simply selects the 1/3 recipe cup, and when he fills the cup to the 2/3 cup mark, he actually has the desired 2/9 cup. The Patent Office rejected the claims as drawn to unpatentable "printed matter," because the only difference between the inventor's measuring

---

[9] See Section 2.1.
[10] See Section 12.1.
[11] *Levi Strauss & Co. v. Golden Trade S.r.L.*, 1995 U.S. Dist. LEXIS 4899 (S.D.N.Y. 1995).

cup and other measuring cups was the markings. The appellate court reversed, however, finding a useful functional relationship between the markings and the cup.[12]

A similar problem can arise in the case of computer storage media, which function to store information, though not in "printed" form. Is a computer disk patentable merely because it contains new information? The answer may depend on the nature of the information. Under its current guidelines, the Patent Office will presume that a computer-readable storage medium that can be used to direct a computer to operate in a particular manner is an "article of manufacture" and falls within the scope of patentable subject matter. A CD-ROM, for example, that contains a new computer program will presumptively qualify as patentable subject matter. However, a known storage medium encoding data representing "creative or artistic expression" such as a work of art, literature or music, would be considered non-statutory.[13]

4.6 METHODS OF DOING BUSINESS

Perhaps because the constitutional phrase "useful arts" is generally regarded as equivalent to technological arts, methods of doing business have traditionally been held beyond the purview of the patent laws. For example, an accounting method allowing users to enter, categorize and total expenditures, and display the results in an expense analysis report, has been held unpatentable subject matter.[14] Arguably, such techniques are simply too remote from the disciplines of science and engineering to be thought suitable for the patent system. On the other hand, an *apparatus* used in business (i.e., a cash register) would usually be considered patentable, as a technological means to an end.

In recent years, computers have emerged as the universal tool for the

---

[12] *Application of Miller*, 418 F.2d 1392 (C.C.P.A. 1969).

[13] MPEP § 2106. The Federal Circuit has opined that the "printed matter" cases have no relevance where the "matter" is to be processed not by a human mind, but by a computer. *In re Lowry*, 32 F.3d 1579, 1583 (Fed. Cir. 1994). However, if the distinguishing feature of the invention is in the form of stored information rather than revised structure, whether in the form of printing or information stored on a computer disk, the same concerns can be raised about the suitability of the invention for patent protection. The information, for example, might represent an advance in a literary or an artistic field rather than an advance in technology. Although it could be argued that a computer disk storing new data differs *structurally* from other disks, at a microscopic level, the same could be said of the printed page. The Patent Office seems to have embarked on a reasonable course by attempting to distinguish between a computer program that causes a computer to function in a particular way, and stored data that merely represents a musical, literary or artistic creation. Still, future court decisions will likely be necessary to sort out just when a computer disk with stored data is patentable and when it is not.

[14] *Ex Parte Murray*, 9 U.S.P.Q.2d 1819 (PTO Bd. Pat. App. & Int. 1988).

conduct of a broad range of human activities, including the conduct of business. Any "method of doing business" in use today probably involves a computer in some way. A clever draftsman, instead of claiming the method per se, will now claim the programmed computer as a "system" or "apparatus," thereby giving the invention a flavor of the technological arts. Should a method of doing business that would once have been considered unpatentable be patentable today, merely because the instrumentality has changed from pen and paper to a high-tech computer?

This question still has not been answered definitively. However, one federal district court has concluded that a computer can make an otherwise unpatentable business method an invention suitable for patenting.[15] In this case, Merrill Lynch had the idea of combining in one financial service a brokerage account, a money market account and a checking/credit card account. The combination of the three kinds of accounts supposedly produced "synergistic" benefits for the customer. The claims described a computerized "system," including means for entering, storing, manipulating and communicating the information necessary to manage such a combined account. Although the court recognized that the account scheme itself would be "unpatentable if done by hand," the court held that drafting the claims in terms of a computerized system brought the invention within the realm of the "technological arts."[16]

In the similar case of *State Street Bank & Trust Co. v. Signature Financial Gp.*,[17] the Federal Circuit recently went so far as to reject the method of doing business exception to patentability altogether. The patented invention in *State Street* involved a system for organizing a group of mutual funds under the common ownership of a partnership, an arrangement that produced economies of scale and tax advantages. The claims described a system and method for performing the necessary accounting, though in such broad terms that anyone creating such a fund and using a computer would necessarily infringe. The court found that the claims did not describe an unpatentably abstract algorithm[18] because the manipulation of data representing money is a "useful, concrete and tangible result." Examining the authority for a "business methods" exception to patentable subject matter, the court found such authority so unpersuasive that it took the opportunity to "lay this ill-conceived exception to rest." The court did not, however, address the interesting question of whether the patented invention in *State Street* represented any advancement in the "useful" or "technological" arts.

---

[15] *Paine, Webber, Jackson & Curtis, Inc. v. Merrill Lynch, Pierce, Fenner & Smith, Inc.*, 564 F. Supp. 1358 (D. Del. 1983).

[16] *Paine, Webber*, 564 F. Supp. at 1369.

[17] 149 F.3d 1368 (Fed. Cir. 1998).

[18] See Section 12.4.

As methods of doing business become increasingly dependent on computers, questions regarding the patentability of business methods will often be subsumed within the larger question of when computer programs can be patented. This complex question is discussed in Section 12.4.

CHAPTER 5

Patent Prosecution

5.1 EXAMINATION

The process of applying for a patent, also known as patent "prosecution," begins when the inventor, on his own or through his agent or attorney, files an application with the Patent Office for "examination." The application includes essentially the same things that a patent would include—a specification describing the invention in detail, drawings and claims. The Patent Office assigns the application to a "patent examiner" who has expert knowledge in the field of the invention. Since the Patent Office requires a filing fee, an issue fee and various other fees, obtaining a patent can easily cost several thousand dollars, exclusive of any fees paid to a patent attorney or agent.[1]

The patent examiner searches for "prior art" patents already granted on similar inventions in order to determine if the invention claimed in the application is new and non-obvious.[2] The examiner also reviews the application to determine if it meets the other requirements of a valid patent, such as having claims that are sufficiently definite.[3] After reviewing the application and searching for prior art, the examiner prepares a written "Office Action" to tell the applicant which claims are "allowed" or rejected and to explain any problems with the application. In many cases

---

[1] Reduced fees are available to individuals and "small entities" (see MPEP § 509.02), but the costs are still considerable. A current fee schedule can be obtained by calling the Public Service Center at 703) 308–4357.

[2] See Section 8.9.

[3] See Section 8.5.

the examiner will reject the claims as originally filed on grounds that the invention is already disclosed in prior patents or that it is obvious in light of those prior patents.

Following such a rejection, the applicant is permitted to file a written response. Sometimes the response is to argue the point with the examiner and attempt to explain, on legal or technical grounds, why the claims should be allowed after all. Often, however, the response is to *amend* the claims in an effort to distinguish the invention from what has gone before. It is also possible to cancel claims or add new claims. When claims are amended, or new claims added, the applicant should explain why the changes overcome the problems found by the examiner.[4]

After a response from the applicant, the examiner prepares another Office Action which may allow the claims or reject them once again. This back-and-forth process continues until the claims are allowed or until the examiner announces that the rejection is "final." A final rejection can be appealed to the Patent Office Board of Appeals and Interferences, and from there to the Federal Circuit Court of Appeals. If the situation appears hopeless, the application can be abandoned.

Although patent prosecution resembles a court proceeding in some respects—applicants are typically represented by attorneys who present legal arguments to the examiner "judge"—the situation differs in a very significant respect. In a typical court proceeding, the judge hears argument and evidence presented by adversaries having opposite points of view. Patent prosecution, on the other hand, is "ex parte," meaning that there is no one to represent an opposing viewpoint. For example, a company that might infringe the patent has no opportunity to argue to the examiner that the patent should not issue. In fact, since patent prosecution is secret, a potential infringer would have no way even of knowing that the application was under consideration. It is the job of the examiner to represent the interests of the public and to ensure that a patent is not issued unless it meets all of the legal requirements. However, the opportunity to present unrebutted arguments provides applicants with a great advantage, and that advantage is magnified in litigation by the presumption that all issued patents are valid.[5]

Because patent prosecution is ex parte, the individuals involved are held to a higher standard of candor and fair dealing than is typical of court proceedings. For example, if the applicant is aware of information that might call into question whether the patent should issue (for example, a close prior art reference), the applicant is required to bring that to the

---

[4] Although the claims can be amended, the specification cannot be changed to add "new matter." 37 C.F.R. § 1.118. "New matter" can be added only by filing a continuation-in-part. See Section 5.2.

[5] See Section 8.2.

attention of the examiner. If the applicant, or the applicant's attorney, fails in that duty of candor, the patent may later be held "unenforceable" by a court.[6]

Prosecution is a slow process that may take months or even years. All of the documents filed by the applicant or by the examiner become part of the "prosecution history" of the patent. The prosecution history (also known as the "file wrapper") is made available to the public if the patent issues, and it is an important resource for interpreting what the claims mean. For example, if in response to a rejection the applicant argues in favor of a narrow claim interpretation, that same interpretation is likely to be adopted by a court in any subsequent litigation.[7]

5.2 CONTINUATIONS AND CONTINUATIONS-IN-PART

In some instances, an applicant may choose to start over, in a sense, by filing a "continuation." A continuation is an application that has the same disclosure as the prior application (i.e., the same specification) but new claims.[8] As long as the continuation is filed before the original application is abandoned, and as long as the continuation includes an explicit reference to the original application, the continuation, and any patent claims that issue from it, will be treated as though it were filed on the date that the original application was filed.[9] This earlier filing date may be important in determining the priority of the invention as compared to other inventions or references.[10] The original application may be abandoned after the continuation is filed, or prosecution of the two applications may continue in parallel.

The second application may lead in turn to another, and a "chain" of applications can be created in this way. The application that comes last on the chain will receive the benefit of the first application's filing date, as long as each link in the chain meets the requirements of continuity— that is, each application included the same disclosure as the one preceding it, and it was filed before the preceding application was abandoned. Related applications are often referred to using a "family tree" analogy,

---

[6] See Section 9.1.

[7] See Section 7.3.

[8] *See Transco Prods. Inc. v. Performance Contracting, Inc.*, 38 F.3d 551, 555 (Fed. Cir. 1994); M.P.E.P. § 201.07. There can be any number of reasons for filing a continuation. One is to permit the amendment of claims that have already been subject to a "final" rejection. *See Transco*, 38 F.3d at 559.

[9] *See Mendenhall v. Cedarapids, Inc.*, 5 F.3d 1557, 1565 (Fed. Cir. 1993); 35 U.S.C. § 120; M.P.E.P. § 201.11. If the original application names more than one joint inventor, the continuation must name the same inventors, or a subset of them. 35 U.S.C. § 120; *In re Chu*, 66 F.3d 292, 297 (Fed. Cir. 1995).

[10] See Section 8.9.2.

in which case an earlier application may be referred to as the "parent" or "grandparent" of a later application.

On other occasions, an applicant may choose to file a "continuation-in-part" (or "C-I-P"). A continuation-in-part is like a continuation, but it includes *additional* disclosure in the "specification."[11] A continuation-in-part might be filed if the applicant discovers an improvement on the basic invention disclosed in the original application and desires a patent claim to match. The important difference between a continuation and a continuation-in-part is that the latter is entitled to the filing date of the original application *only* as to claims supported by the disclosure of the original application.[12] Any claim supported by newly added material (referred to as "new matter") is entitled only to the filing date of the continuation-in-part application.[13]

Suppose, for example, that an inventor files an application for a basic mousetrap on January 1, 2001. The application discloses and claims the combination of a spring, a latch and a trigger to release the spring when disturbed by the mouse. Later that month, the inventor discovers a new kind of trigger that is less likely to release the spring prematurely. Since the original application is still in prosecution, the inventor files a continuation-in-part which discloses both the basic mousetrap design of the first application and the improved trigger. That application is filed on February 1, 2001. If the second application includes a claim having nothing to do with the new trigger, and the claim is fully supported by the disclosure of the original application, that claim will receive the benefit of the January 1 filing date. However, a claim that did refer to the new trigger would be entitled only to the February 1 filing date. If another inventor happened to have filed an application on a mousetrap trigger on January 15, the difference could be significant in determining priority.[14]

An exception to the rules just described arises if the matter newly added to the continuation-in-part application is *inherent* in the original application, even though not explicitly disclosed. Suppose, for example, that the inventor of the mousetrap realized that the design disclosed in the original application was more compact than most, so that the trap could be slipped into a smaller space. The inventor might decide to file a second application, styled as a continuation-in-part, explicitly pointing out this newly discovered advantage, and a claim might be drafted that referred explicitly to the trap's dimensions. As long as this characteristic had been

[11] *See Transco,* 38 F.3d at 555; M.P.E.P. § 201.08.
[12] The support must be adequate to satisfy the written description requirement of 35 U.S.C. § 112. See Section 8.8.
[13] *See Waldemar Link GmbH v. Osteonics Corp.,* 32 F.3d 556, 558 (Fed. Cir. 1994).
[14] See Section 8.9.2.

inherent in the design originally disclosed, though not discussed, the claim would be entitled to the filing date of the original application.[15]

5.3 DIVISIONAL APPLICATIONS

Another complication in a patent "family tree" arises when, in the view of the examiner, the application claims more than one distinct invention. For example, the same application might claim both a new mousetrap design and a new "artificial cheese" to be used as bait, either of which could be used without the other. The examiner might determine that each was a separate invention, which should be claimed in its own application subject to its own fees and prior art search. When this occurs, the examiner issues a "restriction requirement" compelling the applicant to choose which of the two inventions to pursue. The other invention can be made the subject of a "divisional" application. The divisional application includes the pertinent part of the original disclosure, and it is entitled to the same filing date.[16]

5.4 INTERFERENCES

One responsibility of a patent examiner is to search for other patent applications that claim the same invention as the application under consideration. Since it is not uncommon for an invention to occur to two inventors at nearly the same time, it is also not uncommon for two patent applications to claim essentially the same thing. If such an application is discovered, the Patent Office will conduct an "interference" proceeding to determine which of the applications deserves priority.[17] Interference proceedings are conducted by the Board of Patent Appeals and Interferences, and examination of the interfering applications is generally halted until the interference is decided. In contrast to the usual course of patent prosecution, an interference is a trial-like adversarial proceeding in which each applicant has an opportunity to present evidence and argument in favor of its position.[18] An interference is time consuming and can delay issue of a patent for years.

---

[15] See *Therma-Tru Corp. v. Peachtree Doors Inc.*, 44 F.3d 988, 992–93 (Fed. Cir. 1995); *Kennecott Corp. v. Kyocera Int'l, Inc.*, 835 F.2d 1419, 1421–23 (Fed. Cir. 1987).

[16] See 35 U.S.C. § 121; M.P.E.P. § 201.06; *Transco Prods. Inc. v. Performance Contracting, Inc.*, 38 F.3d 551, 555 (Fed. Cir. 1994).

[17] See 35 U.S.C. § 135; *Case v. CPC Int'l, Inc.*, 730 F.2d 745, 748 (Fed. Cir. 1984). Two applications claim the "same invention" if the invention of one is the same as, or obvious in light of, the invention of the other. 37 C.F.R. § 1.601 (i), (n).

[18] Note that similar contests over priority can arise in the course of infringement litigation. See Section 8.9.1.3.

Although interferences are generally a contest between two or more pending applications, occasionally an interference occurs between an application and a patent that has already issued. In this case, the interference may occur at the instigation of the applicant, but the applicant must claim entitlement to an interference no more than one year after the patent has issued.[19]

Even if two applicants describe essentially the same invention, they are likely to use different language in their claims. In order to clarify what the disputed invention is, the Patent Office devises its own claims, known as "counts," to describe the subject matter of the interference. A "count" may be identical to a claim submitted by one of the applicants, or it may be a new description of the invention. The purpose of the interference is to decide if both applications support a claim to the invention described by the count, and, if so, which applicant invented first. Although an applicant may be able to avoid an interference by denying any intention to claim the subject matter described by the count, the denial will prevent the applicant from afterwards obtaining a patent on that invention.[20]

In an interference, the applicant who was first to file is known as the "senior party" and other applicants are known as "junior parties." The senior party is presumed to have invented first, but that presumption can be overcome by evidence presented by a junior party.[21] Ultimately, the issue of which applicant was first to invent turns on questions of conception, reduction to practice and diligence, all of which are discussed in Section 8.9.2. The victor in an interference can proceed with patent prosecution. The loser, barring an appeal,[22] must abandon his application or pursue claims to a different invention.

5.5 REISSUE

Apart from an interference, there are two instances in which an already issued patent may return to the Patent Office to undergo further prosecution. They are known as "reissue" and "reexamination." Reissue is a means for applicants to correct errors in a patent. The error may be a defect in the specification or drawings, or the applicant's claims may have been too broad or too narrow in comparison to what the applicant could rightfully claim.[23] If the claims are too narrow, they may fail to protect

---

[19] 35 U.S.C. § 135(b). An interference can occur between *two* issued patents, but in this case the Patent Office has no jurisdiction. An interference between two issued patents must be conducted by a federal court. *See* 35 U.S.C. § 291.

[20] *See* 37 C.F.R. § 1.605(a).

[21] *See Bosies v. Benedict*, 27 F.3d 539, 541 (Fed. Cir. 1994).

[22] An appeal can be taken either to the Federal Circuit Court of Appeals or to a federal district court. *See* 35 U.S.C. § 146.

[23] *See* 35 U.S.C. § 251. Minor errors of a clerical or typographical nature can be rectified without further examination by a "certificate of correction." *See* 35 U.S.C. §§ 254–255.

the full measure of the invention; if too broad, they may run afoul of the prior art.[24]

The reissue application cannot add "new matter" to the original application,[25] and any claims sought through reissue that would broaden the scope of the original claims must be applied for within two years of issue.[26] If a reissued patent is allowed, the original patent is "surrendered" in favor of the revised version.[27] The latter is enforceable from its own date of issue, and it expires when the original patent would have expired.[28] If any claims from the original patent are carried forward in substantially identical form in the reissued patent, those claims are enforceable as though they had been in effect from the issue date of the original patent. (In other words, damages can be assessed for infringement after and *before* the reissue, even though the original claims were "surrendered.")[29] Patents that are the result of reissue proceedings can be identified by their serial numbers, which begin with the initials "Re."[30]

When applying for a reissue, the applicant must file a declaration identifying the error to be corrected, explaining how it occurred and affirming that the error occurred without any deceptive intent.[31] What constitutes "error" can be a difficult issue. For example, the applicant's deliberate choice to cancel a broad claim in favor of a narrow one in order to avoid prior art is not an "error" that can be corrected by reissue, even if the applicant has second thoughts.[32] On the other hand, a patent attorney's

---

[24] See Section 8.9.

[25] See Section 5.2.

[26] 35 U.S.C. § 251. This rule is strictly interpreted. If there is any conceivable device or method that would infringe the new claims but would not have infringed the original claims, the new claims are "broader" and cannot be obtained more than two years after the patent issued. *See Tillotson, Ltd. v. Walbro Corp.*, 831 F.2d 1033, 1037 n.2 (Fed. Cir. 1987). On the other hand, an original claim and a reissue claim may be identical in scope, even if they do not use precisely the same words (e.g., one could refer to "12 inches" where the other refers to "one foot").

[27] 35 U.S.C. §§ 251–52.

[28] 35 U.S.C. § 251.

[29] *See* 35 U.S.C. § 252; *Laitram Corp. v. NEC Corp.*, 952 F.2d 1357, 1360–61 (Fed. Cir. 1991).

[30] Note that *all* claims of a patent are examined during a reissue proceeding, including those that are unchanged from the original patent. A patentee who initiates a reissue proceeding therefore runs some risk that a claim already issued will be held invalid when looked at again. *See Hewlett-Packard Co. v. Bausch & Lomb Inc.*, 882 F.2d 1556, 1563 (Fed. Cir. 1989).

[31] *See* 37 C.F.R. § 1.175.

[32] "Error under the reissue statute does not include a deliberate decision to surrender specific subject matter in order to overcome prior art, a decision which in light of subsequent developments in the marketplace might be regretted. It is precisely because the patentee amended his claims to overcome prior art that a member of the public is entitled to occupy the space abandoned by the patent applicant." *Mentor Corp. v. Coloplast, Inc.*, 998 F.2d 992, 994–95 (Fed. Cir. 1993); *see also Hewlett-Packard*, 882 F.2d at 1565 ("error" must involve "inadvertence, accident, or mistake"). The rationale for the "recapture rule" is also relevant to prosecution history estoppel, discussed in Section 10.6.8.

"failure to appreciate the full scope of the invention" generally is recognized as an "error" justifying reissue with broadened claims.[33]

Although patent claims can be broadened by reissue, the legislature foresaw the potential unfairness to anyone who steered clear of the original narrow claims, but not the new broader ones. To protect such persons, the law recognizes "intervening rights."[34] If, prior to the reissue, a person or corporation had made, used, or purchased a product that did not infringe the original narrow claims, that person or corporation may continue to use that product, or may sell it to someone else, even if doing so would infringe the broadened claims.[35] Thus, for example, if a business had in its inventory items manufactured before the reissue that would infringe only the modified claims, that business would have the absolute right to sell those products after the reissue without incurring liability. Moreover, a court may allow additional items of this nature to be made, used, or sold after the date of the reissue if "substantial preparation" to do so occurred before the reissue, and the court deems such measures equitable in light of the investments made and businesses commenced before the reissue.[36] Thus, for example, a business that had invested in a factory to manufacture the newly infringing item would likely be allowed to produce and sell the item even after the reissue. Naturally, these rights do not extend to anyone who made no investments in an infringing activity until after the date of reissue.

5.6 REEXAMINATION

"Reexamination" allows the Patent Office to reconsider the validity of already issued claims in light of newly discovered prior art patents or printed publications. The purpose of reexamination is to provide a quicker and less expensive alternative to litigation when, for one reason or another, the Patent Office failed to consider important prior art during the initial prosecution, and as a result the validity of the patent is in doubt. Reexamination differs from most Patent Office proceedings in one important respect. Whereas the public is generally denied any participation in patent prosecution, reexamination can be requested by *anyone*, including a licensee, an accused infringer, a government agency or someone who simply likes to meddle.[37] All that is necessary to begin (besides the money to pay the reexamination fee) is knowledge of a prior patent or

[33] *See Mentor*, 998 F.2d at 995.
[34] *See* 35 U.S.C. § 252.
[35] *See* 35 U.S.C. § 252; *BIC Leisure Prods., Inc. v. Windsurfing Int'l, Inc.*, 1 F.3d 1214, 1220–21 (Fed. Cir. 1993).
[36] *See* 35 U.S.C. § 252; *BIC*, 1 F.3d at 1220–21.
[37] *See* 35 U.S.C. § 302; *In re Freeman*, 30 F.3d 1459, 1468 (Fed. Cir. 1994); *Syntex (U.S.A.) Inc. v. U.S. PTO*, 882 F.2d 1570, 1573 (Fed. Cir. 1989).

printed publication that casts doubt on the validity of some or all of the patent claims.[38]

The party requesting the reexamination must submit to the Patent Office a list of prior art and a statement explaining why it is pertinent.[39] A copy of the request is sent to the patent owner. Within three months, the Patent Office must decide whether the request raises "a substantial new question of patentability."[40] If the answer is no, the decision is final and unappealable. If the answer is yes, the Patent Office orders a reexamination. At that point the patent owner may file a statement, including any proposed changes to the claims, and the party requesting the reexamination may file a reply.[41] From that point onward, reexamination proceeds by the rules devised for ordinary patent prosecution, and the party requesting reexamination has no further involvement.[42]

If necessary, claims can be narrowed during reexamination so that they avoid the newly discovered prior art. However, the patentee is not allowed to enlarge the scope of the claims.[43] When the reexamination is concluded, the examiner issues a certificate canceling any claims held invalid, confirming any claims held patentable and incorporating into the patent any new or revised claims.[44]

Although one would expect reexamination to be requested by someone wishing to attack the patent, sometimes it is requested by the patentee, as a way of *strengthening* a patent that might be held invalid in litigation. If the Patent Office finds that the claims are valid in spite of the additional prior art, a court is unlikely to hold otherwise. On the other hand, if the prior art is so close that the claims must be modified, reexamination provides an opportunity to do so. Thus, while a request for reexamination may signal doubts as to the validity of the patent, if the patent survives the process it is likely to be stronger than ever.

---

[38] Reexamination can be based only on prior patents or printed publications, not, for example, a claim of invalidity based on sales of the patented product prior to the application's "critical date." See Section 8.10.1. This limitation helps to keep reexamination proceedings comparatively simple and expedient.

[39] *See* 35 U.S.C. § 302.

[40] 35 U.S.C. § 303; *Freeman*, 30 F.3d at 1468.

[41] 35 U.S.C. § 304. If the request for reexamination is made by someone other than the patentee, the patentee has no opportunity to make its views known until *after* the Patent Office has decided whether there is a "substantial new question of patentability." *See* 37 C.F.R. § 1.530(a); *Platlex Corp. v. Mossinghoff*, 771 F.2d 480, 483–84 (Fed. Cir. 1985).

[42] *See In re Opprecht*, 868 F.2d 1264, 1265 (Fed. Cir. 1989).

[43] 35 U.S.C. § 305; *Freeman*, 30 F.3d at 1468.

[44] 35 U.S.C. § 307.

CHAPTER 6

Ownership and Other Rights

6.1 INVENTORSHIP

The right to obtain a patent initially belongs to the inventor.[1] So when a patent application is filed, it is important to designate the proper inventor of the subject matter claimed. A patent can name a single inventor, or it can name two or more joint inventors. It is typically in the latter case that questions arise regarding who should or should not receive credit.

An inventor is anyone who participated in the mental act of *conceiving* the invention.[2] If two people work together on a project and both contribute to a patentable idea, both can be named on the application as joint inventors. This is true whether the specific contribution of each is difficult to identify, as may be the case when an idea arises from collaborative "brainstorming," or whether the contribution of each inventor is a discrete component of the whole.

Not all contributions rise to the level of invention. Someone who had supervisory responsibility for a project but added nothing to the conception of the invention would not properly be considered an inventor. Similarly, someone who built or tested the completed invention, but did not contribute to its conception, could not be considered an inventor, no matter how important that person's contribution to the project as a

---

[1] *See* 35 U.S.C. §§ 111, 115–16; *Beech Aircraft Corp. v. EDO Corp.*, 990 F.2d 1237, 1248 (Fed. Cir. 1993).

[2] *See Burroughs Wellcome Co. v. Barr Labs., Inc.*, 40 F.3d 1223, 1227–28 (Fed. Cir. 1994) ("Conception is the touchstone of inventorship, the completion of the mental part of invention."); *Sewell v. Walters*, 21 F.3d 411, 415 (Fed. Cir. 1994).

whole.[3] Even someone who identifies a problem is not considered a co-inventor of the solution, in spite of the fact that identifying the problem is often a significant step. As one court observed, "[i]t is one thing to suggest that a better mousetrap ought to be built; it is another thing to build it."[4]

Deciding who should be credited as an inventor can be a difficult task, as illustrated by the recent case of *Hess v. Advanced Cardiovascular Sys., Inc.*[5] The invention was a balloon angioplasty catheter—a device that can be threaded through a narrowed artery and then inflated in order to reduce the blockage. The doctors responsible for the invention had tried various materials without success, when they were referred to Mr. Hess, an engineer with Raychem who was familiar with their line of heat-shrinkable plastics. Hess identified specific materials and fabrication techniques that would provide the doctors with what they needed. The materials worked, the doctors obtained a patent and the invention was a commercial success.

Eventually, Hess claimed that he should have been named on the patent as a co-inventor, because the invention would not have worked without his contribution. The Federal Circuit disagreed, noting that the inventors named on an issued patent are presumed to be the correct ones.[6] Hess's contribution was compared to that of a scientific treatise or a product catalog—he merely provided information regarding existing technology. "The principles [Hess] explained to [the doctors] were well known and found in textbooks. Mr. Hess did no more than a skilled salesman would do in explaining how his employer's product could be used to meet a customer's requirements."[7] Nevertheless, one can understand why Hess felt that identifying the right materials for the new application added more to the inventive idea than the passive contributions of a textbook author.

For two or more persons to be named as joint inventors, they must have *collaborated* in some way.[8] Two inventors who were unaware of each other's work could not be considered joint inventors, even if their efforts overlapped and even if the two inventors were employed by the same company.[9] Similarly, if inventor B simply builds on the published work of

---

[3] *See Sewell*, 21 F.3d at 416–17; *Application of Herschler*, 591 F.2d 693, 699 (C.C.P.A. 1979); *Mattor v. Coolegem*, 530 F.2d 1391, 1395 (Ct. Cl. 1976).

[4] *See Buildex Inc. v. Kason Indus. Inc.*, 4 U.S.P.Q.2d 1803, 1805–6 (E.D.N.Y. 1987).

[5] 106 F.3d 976 (Fed. Cir. 1997).

[6] *Hess*, 106 F.3d at 980. The presumption can only be overcome by clear and convincing evidence. *Id.*

[7] *Hess*, 106 F.2d at 981.

[8] *Burroughs*, 40 F.3d at 1227 ("A joint invention is the product of a collaboration between two or more persons working together to solve the problem addressed."); *Credle v. Bond*, 25 F.3d 1566, 1574 (Fed. Cir. 1994).

[9] *Kimberly-Clark Corp. v. Procter & Gamble Dist. Co.*, 973 F.2d 911, 916 (Fed. Cir. 1992).

inventor A, the result is the sole invention of inventor B, not the joint invention of A and B.

On the other hand, joint inventors need not have physically worked together at the same time, nor is it necessary that the contribution of each be equivalent in type or amount.[10] If inventor A partially completed an invention, then passed it along to inventor B with the intention that inventor B complete it, A and B could be considered joint inventors of the finished invention. There are no distinctions drawn between co-inventors based on the significance, ingenuity or timing of their contributions.

Each joint inventor named on an application need not have contributed to every claim.[11] For example, if an application names A, B and C as joint inventors, some claims may represent the work of A and B alone, or B and C alone, or A alone, or B alone and so forth. Under one possible interpretation of the statute,[12] at least one claim of the joint application must embody the collective work of all the named inventors. However, the Patent Office has adopted the more liberal view that the application is proper as long as each inventor, jointly or *individually*, has contributed to at least one claim.[13] Although this could lead to joint applications including claims to unrelated inventions, the Patent Office has the power to issue a restriction requirement when this is the case.[14]

If an application names the wrong inventors (as can easily happen given the ambiguities in defining the role of "inventor"), the application, or issued patent, can be corrected to name the proper inventors without affecting the validity of the patent.[15] The incorrect naming of the inventors must, however, have occurred through error and without deceptive intent.[16] It cannot, for example, have been the product of a scheme to obtain an earlier priority date.

6.2 ASSIGNMENTS

Although the right to apply for a patent belongs to the inventor, and an application must at least be filed on the inventor's behalf,[17] a patent is commonly *owned* by someone other than the inventor. The transfer of

---

[10] 35 U.S.C. § 116; *Burroughs*, 40 F.3d at 1227.

[11] 35 U.S.C. § 116.

[12] 35 U.S.C. § 116.

[13] *See* 37 C.F.R. § 1.45 ("each named inventor must have made a contribution, individually or jointly, to the subject matter of at least one claim of the application").

[14] See Section 5.3.

[15] *See* 35 U.S.C. §§ 116 (correction of inventorship in a pending application), 256 (correction of inventorship of issued patent); *Stark v. Advanced Magnetics, Inc.*, 29 F.3d 1570, 1573 (Fed. Cir. 1994).

[16] 35 U.S.C. §§ 116, 256.

[17] *See* 35 U.S.C. §§ 115–16.

ownership rights from the inventor to someone else is known as "assignment." A common element of an employment contract, particularly in the case of engineers and scientists, is that any patentable inventions made by the employee in the course of employment must be assigned to the employer. Even if such a provision is not explicit in the employment contract, it is very likely to be implied if invention falls within the natural scope of the employee's duties.[18] Thus, while patents bear the name of individual inventors (hence the "Smith patent" or the "Jones patent"), actual rights to the patent often belong to a corporate assignee from the day the application is filed. In fact, a corporate assignee can prosecute a patent in the name of the inventor and ultimately obtain rights to the invention, even if the inventor refuses to cooperate.[19]

Patent rights are freely assignable like other forms of property.[20] A patent can be assigned not only from an employee to a corporation, but also from one corporation (or individual) to another. In a typical assignment, all rights, including the right to sue for infringement, pass to the new owner.[21]

6.3 LICENSES

A patent license is a more limited transfer of rights than an assignment. A licensor retains ownership of the patent but grants the licensee the right to practice the claimed invention, usually in exchange for some sort of royalty. A license can be exclusive or non-exclusive. If it is exclusive, there is only one licensee, and only that licensee has the right to practice the claimed invention. An exclusive licensee has the right to file suit against an infringer in order to preserve that exclusivity, though it may be necessary to sue in the patent owner's name or to join the patent owner as a co-plaintiff.[22] A non-exclusive licensee must rely on the patent owner to

---

[18] *See Teets v. Chromalloy Gas Turbine Corp.*, 83 F.3d 403, 407 (Fed. Cir. 1996). Even if no agreement to assign is express or implied, if the invention was made by the employee on company time and using company materials, or if the employee introduced the practice of the invention into the employer's business, a court is likely to recognize a "shop right" benefiting the employer. A shop right is a non-exclusive, non-transferable right allowing the employer to practice the invention, royalty-free, even if the employee is allowed to patent the invention as an individual. *See McElmurry v. Arkansas Power & Light Co.*, 995 F.2d 1576, 1580–82 (Fed. Cir. 1993).

[19] *See* 37 C.F.R. § 1.47.

[20] *See* 35 U.S.C. § 261.

[21] *See Rite-Hite Corp. v. Kelley Co.*, 56 F.3d 1538, 1551 (Fed. Cir. 1995); *Ortho Pharmaceuticals Corp. v. General Institute, Inc.*, 52 F.3d 1026, 1030 (Fed. Cir. 1995). More limited assignments are also possible—for example, assignment of the rights to a patent as they pertain to a particular geographical area of the United States. *See* 35 U.S.C. § 261.

[22] *See Rite-Hite Corp. v. Kelley Co.*, 56 F.3d 1538, 1552 (Fed. Cir. 1995); *Ortho Pharmaceuticals Corp. v. General Institute, Inc.*, 52 F.3d 1026, 1030–31 (Fed. Cir. 1995); *Abbott Labs. v. Diamedix Corp.*, 47 F.3d 1128, 1131 (Fed. Cir. 1995).

file suit.[23] Sometimes, but not always, a licensee obtains the right to "sub-license" others.

Some patent owners license their patents in order to obtain the royalty income. However, there is no requirement that a patent owner license anyone.[24] In some cases, the patent owner prefers the monopolistic, but perfectly legal, advantages of being the only producer of the patented product. On occasion patent owners "cross-license" their patents, each patent owner granting to the other the right to practice some or all of the inventions in its patent portfolio. Where two or more companies hold basic patents in the same field of technology, this can be an expedient way to ensure that mutually destructive litigation does not take the place of competition in the marketplace.

6.3.1 Implied Licenses

Sometimes patent licenses are not express but implied.[25] An implied license is a reflection of the shared expectations of parties who have had dealings with one another, even if those expectations were not made explicit.[26] An implied license, like an express license, is a defense to a claim of infringement.[27]

6.3.1.1 *"First Sale"*

Because a patent owner has, among other rights, the exclusive right to "use" the patented invention, a patent owner might sell a patented article, only to forbid its use by the purchaser. Needless to say, most purchasers expect to use the things they buy. In order to fulfill this expectation and similar ones, whenever a patented article is purchased from the patent owner, without any express restrictions or reservation of rights, the law recognizes an implied license allowing the purchaser to use the article, repair it[28] or sell it to someone else. As stated in one Federal Circuit opinion, "an authorized sale of a patented product places that product beyond the reach of the patent. . . . The patent owner's rights with respect to the product end with its sale, . . . and a purchaser of such

---

[23] *See Rite-Hite,* 56 F.3d at 1552; *Ortho,* 52 F.3d at 1031; *Abbott,* 47 F.3d at 1131.

[24] *See* 35 U.S.C. § 271(d)(4).

[25] *Carborundum Co. v. Molten Metal Equipment Innovations, Inc.,* 72 F.3d 872, 878 (Fed. Cir. 1995).

[26] *See Carborundum,* 72 F.3d at 878; *McCoy v. Mitsuboshi Cutlery, Inc.,* 67 F.3d 917, 920 (Fed. Cir. 1995) (implied license arises from "entire course of conduct" between the parties).

[27] *Carborundum,* 72 F.3d at 878.

[28] Unless the repairs are so extensive that they are really a "reconstruction" of the patented invention. See Section 10.4.

a product may use or resell the product free of the patent."[29] A patent owner who intends otherwise must make those intentions explicit.[30]

The "first sale" of a patented article, without restrictions, is said to "exhaust" the rights of the patent owner.[31] In other words, whatever compensation the patent owner receives from the "first sale" is all the patent owner can expect, even if the article is sold and re-sold, used and re-used, many times.[32] A similar result follows a "first sale" by a licensee of the patent owner. The licensee may owe royalties to the patent owner, but the article sold is afterwards "free of the patent."[33]

The "first sale" rule can also apply where a patent claims a *method* and the patent owner sells an *apparatus* used in that method. For example, a patent might claim a "method of catching mice," and the apparatus sold might be a kind of mousetrap. Anyone who purchases a mousetrap expects to use it for catching mice, and if the only method of using the mousetrap is the same one claimed in the patent, the purchaser reasonably expects to use that method. Such expectations lead to the following rule: an unrestricted sale of an apparatus by the patent owner confers an implied license to practice a patented method if (1) the apparatus sold has no noninfringing uses, and (2) the circumstances of the sale otherwise plainly indicate that a license should be inferred.[34] On the other hand, if the apparatus has other uses, one cannot imply a license to the patented method.[35]

---

[29] *Intel Corp. v. ULSI Sys. Technology, Inc.*, 995 F.2d 1566, 1568 (Fed. Cir. 1993).

[30] Explicit restrictions *are* possible. For example, a patentee could sell an item with the requirement that it be used only once. Re-use of that item by the purchaser might then be considered an infringement. See *Mallinckrodt, Inc. v. Medipart, Inc.*, 976 F.2d 700 (Fed. Cir. 1992). However, some restrictions may constitute misuse or an antitrust violation. See Section 9.2.

[31] See *United States v. Univis Lens Co.*, 316 U.S. 241, 250, 62 S. Ct. 1088, 1093 (1942); *Bandag, Inc. v. Al Bolser's Tire Stores, Inc.*, 750 F.2d 903, 924 (Fed. Cir. 1984).

[32] The "first sale" must be an authorized sale by the patent owner or a licensee of the patent owner. If the product originated with an infringer, downstream purchasers can be held to infringe by using or re-selling the product. See *Intel*, 995 F.2d at 1572–73 (Plager, J., dissenting). However, if the infringer was sued and compelled to pay money damages to the patentee, that payment amounts to a "first sale" and the infringing goods are subsequently beyond the reach of the patent. See *King Instrument Corp. v. Otari Corp.*, 814 F.2d 1560, 1564 (Fed. Cir. 1987).

[33] See *Unidisco, Inc. v. Schattner*, 824 F.2d 965, 968 (Fed Cir. 1987).

[34] *Met-Coil Sys. Corp. v. Korners Unlimited, Inc.*, 803 F.2d 684, 686 (Fed. Cir. 1986). The scope of the implied license may still depend on "what the parties reasonably intended . . . based on the circumstances of the sale." See *Carborundum*, 72 F.3d at 878. In *Carborundum*, for example, the parties disputed whether the implied license to practice a patented method lasted for the life of the patent, or expired when the purchased apparatus wore out. The court found that the parties could not have intended the license to outlast the apparatus. *Id.* at 878–79.

[35] See *Bandag*, 750 F.2d at 924.

6.3.1.2 Legal Estoppel

Another situation in which a patent license can be implied falls under the heading of "legal estoppel." Simply put, "legal estoppel" is a doctrine that prevents a patent owner from licensing one patent, only to make that license worthless by enforcing another.[36] Suppose that an inventor obtained two patents—one a broad patent covering a new mousetrap design, and the other a narrow patent covering a particular variation of that design. A mousetrap within the scope of the narrower patent would necessarily fall within the scope of the broader patent as well. Anyone who received an express license to the second patent would likely receive an implied license to the first under the principle of "legal estoppel." Otherwise the patent owner could prevent the licensee from taking any benefit from the license it obtained.

6.3.1.3 Industry Standards

The preceding examples are merely specific instances in which a patent license is commonly implied. Any conduct by a patentee which could lead one to infer a waiver or an abandonment of the patentee's rights may result in an implied license.[37] An increasingly common example involves the adoption of a patented technology as an "industry standard." Many industries, such as the computer and telecommunications industries, depend on such standards to ensure that equipment from different manufacturers can work together. Once such a standard is adopted, companies in the industry are virtually compelled to conform. If the industry standard is covered by a patent, should all companies in the industry be forced to pay a royalty? In some cases the answer is yes, but if the patent owner promoted the adoption of the technology as a standard and gave the impression that the standard could be practiced free of obligations, the circumstances could establish an implied license.[38] Otherwise an industry could be lured into adopting a standard, only later to be faced with claims of infringement.

---

[36] *See Spindelfabrik Suessen-Schurr Stahlecker & Grill GmbH v. Schubert & Salzer Maschinenfabrik Atiengesellschaft*, 829 F.2d 1075, 1080 (Fed. Cir. 1987). "The rationale . . . is to estop the grantor from taking back that for which he received consideration." *Id.*

[37] *See Wang Labs., Inc. v. Mitsubishi Electronics America, Inc.*, 103 F.3d 1571, 1580 (Fed. Cir. 1997).

[38] *See Wang*, 103 F.2d at 1575, 1581–82.

CHAPTER 7

Interpreting Patent Claims

The claims are the most important part of any patent. They define what the patented "invention" is. Hence, the first step in determining whether a patent is valid or infringed is to analyze the claims and determine precisely what they mean. This analysis is known as "claim construction" or "claim interpretation."

Claims are written in the English language, but they often employ a technical vocabulary the meaning of which is not immediately apparent. The following is an example of patent claim language, chosen more or less at random:

1. An aqueous cosmetic emulsion comprising:
   i) an isoparaffin;
   ii) a C_8-C_{22} alkyl phosphate salt;
   wherein the isoparaffin and alkyl phosphate salt are present in a respective weight ratio of from about 40:1 to about 1:1, and said emulsion having a viscosity ranging from about 35 to about 90 Brookfield units as measured with a Brookfield Viscometer Model LTV using a #4 spindle rotating at 60 rpm at 25° C.[1]

The claim is to a hand lotion.

The obscurity of claim language can be traced to two sources. First, because patents are awarded to technological advancements, a technical vocabulary is often best suited to describe what the invention is. The language of the preceding example is probably meaningful to the chemist who invented the lotion and to other chemists who are likely to be reading

---

[1] *Conopco, Inc. v. May Dept. Stores Co.*, 46 F.3d 1556, 1560 (Fed. Cir. 1994).

the patent. Second, because of its legal significance, claim language must describe the invention precisely. If a narrow term is used instead of a more accurate broader term, the claims may fail to cover a product that was legitimately within the scope of the applicant's invention. For example, if the preceding example had used the term "hand lotion" instead of "cosmetic emulsion," the claim might have been too narrow to cover a face cream that consisted of the same combination of materials. On the other hand, if a claim term is too broad, the patent may be anticipated by a prior art reference and made invalid.[2] The specific measure of viscosity in the preceding example may have been all that distinguished the invention from other lotions. Thus, everyday language that would serve as a casual description of an invention will not do for a patent claim. Finding the right words to describe an invention, from both a technical and legal viewpoint, is one of the most important tasks faced by a patent attorney.

When deciding what a patent claim means, guidance can be found from the following sources:

• The "ordinary meaning" or "plain meaning" of a word.
• The specification.
• The prosecution history.
• Other claims.

Although patentees sometimes testify as to what they *intended* a claim to mean, such subjective, post-hoc testimony carries little weight.[3]

7.1 "PLAIN MEANING"

The starting point for interpreting any term used in a patent claim is its "ordinary meaning" or "plain meaning" in the field of the invention.[4] Sometimes a general dictionary of the "Webster's" variety is used as an aid to deciphering a patent claim.[5] However, the best guide to the "plain meaning" of a technical term is often the technical literature, including specialized dictionaries, textbooks, research papers and even other patents.[6] "Experts" may also be permitted to offer their opinion on how a

---

[2] See Section 8.9.5.
[3] *See Senmed, Inc. v. Richard-Allan Medical Indus., Inc.,* 888 F.2d 815, 819 (Fed. Cir. 1989).
[4] *Hoechst Celanese Corp. v. BP Chemicals Ltd.,* 78 F.3d 1575, 1578 (Fed. Cir. 1996).
[5] *See, e.g., Greenberg v. Ethicon Endo-Surgery, Inc.,* 91 F.3d 1580, 1583 (Fed. Cir. 1996); *Athletic Alternatives, Inc. v. Prince Mfg. Co.,* 73 F.3d 1573, 1579 (Fed. Cir. 1996).
[6] "[A] general dictionary definition is secondary to the specific meaning of a technical term as it is used and understood in a particular technical field." *See Hoechst Celanese,* 78 F.3d at 1580.

term is understood in the field, but this kind of testimony is increasingly frowned upon, perhaps because it so often seems a matter of litigation-induced hindsight.[7] If the meaning of a claim is not apparent from the patent itself, the claims are not serving their intended function.

7.2 SPECIFICATION

If a word has an "ordinary" or "plain meaning," one might suppose that its interpretation would be uncontroversial, yet words as simple as "on" and "a" have been the subject of intense debate in the context of infringement litigation.[8] One reason is that a patent applicant can be "his own lexicographer"—which is to say, an applicant can devise his own vocabulary to describe the invention.[9] Words can be used in ways that differ from their ordinary sense, or new words can be invented. Nevertheless, since patents are meant to be read and understood by persons "skilled in the art" of the invention, the applicant must make his meaning clear. If he chooses to be "his own lexicographer" by using words in a specialized or unusual sense, that sense must be explained in the patent specification.[10] Words used in a patent claim cannot have a secret meaning.[11]

The patent specification is a place for the applicant to elaborate on the invention, and it serves as a "dictionary" to define, expressly or by implication, any specialized meaning to be given terms used in the claims.[12] Accordingly, the specification is "the single best guide to the meaning of a disputed term."[13] In all cases it is relevant, and in many it is dispositive.[14] If the specification shows that the applicant did not use a term in its ordinary sense, the specification takes precedence. If the specification states that "black" means white and "white" means black, that is how those terms will be interpreted in the context of the claims.

Although the specification is an indispensable tool for claim interpretation, there is always a danger that it will be used not to *define* a term

---

[7] *See Vitronics Corp. v. Conceptronic, Inc.,* 90 F.3d 1576, 1582–83 (Fed. Cir. 1996) ("extrinsic evidence," such as expert testimony, cannot be allowed to alter the public record regarding the meaning of the claims, as apparent from the language of the claims, the specification and the prosecution history); *Southwall Technologies, Inc. v. Cardinal IG Co.,* 54 F.3d 1570, 1578 (Fed. Cir. 1995).

[8] *Senmed, Inc. v. Richard-Allan Medical Indus., Inc.,* 888 F.2d 815, 819 (Fed. Cir. 1989); *North American Vaccine, Inc. v. American Cyanamid Co.,* 7 F.3d 1571, 1575–76 (Fed. Cir. 1993).

[9] *Vitronics Corp. v. Conceptronic, Inc.,* 90 F.3d 1576, 1582 (Fed. Cir. 1996); *Novo Nordisk of North America, Inc. v. Genentech, Inc.,* 77 F.3d 1364, 1368 (Fed. Cir. 1996).

[10] *See Vitronics,* 90 F.3d at 1582; *Novo Nordisk,* 77 F.3d at 1368.

[11] *Intellicall, Inc. v. Phonometrics, Inc.,* 952 F.2d 1384, 1387–88 (Fed. Cir. 1992).

[12] *See Vitronics,* 90 F.3d at 1582.

[13] *Vitronics,* 90 F.3d at 1582.

[14] *Vitronics,* 90 F.3d at 1582.

used in a claim, but to *add limitations* that do not appear in the claim at all. A specification is required to describe specific examples, or "preferred embodiments," that fall within the scope of the patent claims, but are not co-extensive with them.[15] The details of these preferred embodiments do not limit the scope of the claims, unless the claims say so.[16]

Consider, for example, the claims in *In re Paulsen*,[17] which described a "portable computer" with a hinged case allowing the display screen to be latched in an upright position during use. The patentee argued that the term "portable computer" did not include a calculator. If the claims did cover a calculator, they would be found invalid because of a pre-existing Japanese patent. The patentee pointed out that the specific "portable computer" disclosed in the specification incorporated a sophisticated display, advanced data processing capability, communications ports and other attributes that are characteristic of a laptop personal computer rather than a calculator. Nevertheless, the court found that none of these things were required by the claims. Since the claims merely said "portable computer," and the court found that a calculator was a kind of "portable computer" as that term is generally understood, the claims were broad enough to include a calculator.[18]

Sometimes, as in *Paulsen*, the patentee is motivated to "read in" to the claims limitations found in the specification, in order to narrow the claims sufficiently to avoid the prior art. In other cases, it is the accused infringer who seeks to read in those limitations in order to narrow the claim and avoid infringement. In neither case is the practice allowed. Note that there is sometimes a fine line between "reading in" a limitation absent from the claims and using the specification to *interpret* the claims in a particular fashion. The patentee in *Paulsen*, for example, might have argued that "computer" is a term with various meanings and that reading the claim language *in light of* the specification would suggest the narrower meaning.[19]

There is one important exception to the rule that limitations found only in the specification cannot be read into the claims. This exception applies to claims drafted in the "means-plus-function" format provided

---

[15] See Section 3.3.
[16] *Electro Medical Sys. S.A. v. Cooper Life Sciences, Inc.*, 34 F.3d 1048, 1054 (Fed. Cir. 1994) ("[A]lthough the specifications may well indicate that certain embodiments are preferred, particular embodiments appearing in a specification will not be read into the claims when the claim language is broader than such embodiments."); *Intervet America, Inc. v. Kee-Vet Labs., Inc.*, 887 F.2d 1050, 1053 (Fed. Cir. 1989) (interpreting what is *meant* by a word in a claim is proper; reading into the claims limitations found only in the specification is not).
[17] 30 F.3d 1475 (Fed. Cir. 1994).
[18] *Paulsen*, 30 F.3d at 1479–80.
[19] *See, e.g., Ethicon Endo-Surgery, Inc. v. U.S. Surgical Corp.*, 93 F.3d 1572, 1578 (Fed. Cir. 1996).

for in Paragraph 6 of 35 U.S.C. § 112. Claims of this type are discussed in Section 7.7.4.

7.3 PROSECUTION HISTORY

Another resource for interpreting claim language is the prosecution history.[20] This is (ideally) a complete record of the proceedings before the Patent Office at the time the patent was applied for, and it includes any remarks or representations that may have been made by the applicant concerning the proper interpretation of the claims.[21] Claims must be interpreted in the same way in litigation as they were in the Patent Office.[22] Otherwise applicants could treat their claims as the proverbial "nose of wax" to be twisted one direction in prosecution (perhaps to avoid a close prior art reference), then another direction in litigation (perhaps to encompass an accused product similar to that reference).[23] Such inconsistency in interpretation would pervert the prosecution process, and it would hinder potential competitors who should be entitled to rely on the public record in judging the scope of the patentee's claims.[24]

7.4 OTHER CLAIMS

Sometimes the meaning of language in one claim is clarified by comparison to the language of another claim. This particularly arises in the context of the so-called doctrine of claim differentiation, which holds that each claim should be presumed to differ in scope from every other claim. The assumption is that an applicant would not intentionally draft two claims that covered, in different words, precisely the same subject matter.[25] The doctrine of claim differentiation is not absolute, however. On occa-

---

[20] See Section 5.1.

[22] *Vitronics Corp. v. Conceptronic, Inc.*, 90 F.3d 1576, 1583 (Fed. Cir. 1996); *Southwall Technologies, Inc. v. Cardnal IG Co.*, 54 F.3d 1570, 1576 (Fed. Cir. 1995).

[23] *See Vitronics*, 90 F.3d at 1583; *Southwall*, 54 F.3d at 1578.

[24] *See Vitronics*, 90 F.3d at 1583. It should not be necessary for competitors to look beyond the patent itself to understand what the claims mean. The specification ought to provide all of the information required. If the claim interpretation suggested by the patent itself is one that favors a competitor, it could be argued that the patentee should not be entitled to rely on the prosecution history for a different interpretation.

[25] *See Beachcombers v. Wildwood Creative Prods., Inc.*, 31 F.3d 1154, 1162 (Fed. Cir. 1994) (interpretation that would render a claim superfluous is "presumptively unreasonable"); *Tandon Corp. v. U.S. Int'l Trade Comm'n*, 831 F.2d 1017, 1023 (Fed. Cir. 1987).

sion the only reasonable interpretation of a claim is one that makes it redundant.[26]

7.5 VALIDITY

Another basic principle of claim interpretation is that claims should, if possible, be read in a manner that preserves their validity.[27] The source of this rule is obscure, but probably the underlying assumption is that a claim approved by the Patent Office should be presumed valid,[28] and the interpretation that supports validity must be the one that the Patent Office had in mind. Like the doctrine of claim differentiation, this principle does not justify a claim interpretation that is unreasonable or simply contrary to the evidence.[29]

One rule of claim interpretation that *is* absolute is that a claim must be interpreted in the same way when the issue is infringement as it is when the issue is validity.[30] If, for example, a claim is interpreted in a narrow fashion to avoid a potentially invalidating prior art reference, that same narrow interpretation must be applied when comparing the claim to the accused product. The meaning of a claim cannot change to suit the convenience of the patent owner.[31]

7.6 PREAMBLES

One peculiar rule of claim interpretation involves the "preamble"— the first paragraph of a patent claim that typically ends with the word "comprising." In the claim set out at the beginning of this section, the preamble language is "An aqueous cosmetic emulsion comprising." The preamble generally characterizes the category of invention involved, or its intended use (i.e., a mousetrap or a "cosmetic emulsion"), but it does

---

[26] *See Hormone Research Found., Inc v. Genentech, Inc.*, 904 F.2d 1558, 1567 n.15 (Fed. Cir. 1990); *Tandon*, 831 F.2d at 1023–24.

[27] *Whittaker Corp. v. UNR Indus., Inc.*, 911 F.2d 709, 712 (Fed. Cir. 1990); *Texas Instruments Inc. v. U.S. Int'l Trade Comm'n*, 871 F.2d 1054, 1065 (Fed. Cir. 1989).

[28] See Section 8.2.

[29] "Although [courts] construe claims, if possible, so as to sustain their validity . . . it is well settled that no matter how great the temptations of fairness or policy making, courts do not redraft claims." *Quantum Corp. v. Rodime, PLC*, 65 F.3d 1577, 1584 (Fed. Cir. 1995); *see also Texas Instruments*, 871 F.2d at 1065.

[30] *Atlantic Thermoplastics Co. v. Faytex Corp.*, 970 F.2d 834, 846 (Fed. Cir. 1992); *Lemelson v. General Mills, Inc.*, 968 F.2d 1202, 1206 n.4 (Fed. Cir. 1992); *Smithkline Diagnostics, Inc. v. Helena Labs. Corp.*, 859 F.2d 878, 882 (Fed. Cir. 1988).

[31] A disadvantage borne by patent owners in litigation is that they must find a single claim interpretation that supports a finding of *both* validity and infringement. An accused infringer, on the other hand, can be satisfied with an interpretation that renders the claim invalid *or* a different interpretation that renders the claim not infringed. Which interpretation the court chooses may be a matter of indifference to the accused infringer.

not in itself recite the checklist of claim elements that defines the patented invention. In some cases, the preamble is not considered a claim limitation, and this can have important consequences. Imagine, for example, a product identical to the "cosmetic emulsion" described in the example but used as an industrial lubricant. *If* the preamble were disregarded, the lubricant would infringe the claim.

Whether or not a preamble is ignored or treated as a claim limitation depends on whether it is necessary to "give life and meaning to the claim and properly define the invention."[32] This is a nebulous distinction. On occasion the preamble is clearly a substantive part of the claim because the "body" of the claim that follows includes references to the preamble. For instance, the body of the claim used as an example refers to "said emulsion." It is therefore likely that a court would consider the "aqueous cosmetic emulsion" language to be a claim limitation.[33]

Often the line is harder to draw, but if the claim read without the preamble would leave one guessing as to what the invention really was, the preamble would probably be considered a claim limitation. In *Diversitech Corp. v. Century Steps, Inc.*,[34] for example, the claim referred to an equipment-supporting base comprising a foam core and a cementitious coating. Without the preamble, the claim would have referred to the core and the coating, but one would have no idea what the invention really was. In *Diversitech* the court found that the preamble was necessary to define the invention. On the other hand, if the preamble states an intended use or environment for the invention, but the remainder of the claim is sufficient by itself to describe what the invention *is*, then the preamble may not be considered a part of the claim.[35]

Recently, the Federal Circuit has stated that interpretation of a claim preamble is subject to the same rules as interpretation of any other portion of a claim.[36] Possibly this signals a move away from the special rules developed for interpreting, and in some cases ignoring, claim preambles. If so, it is a reasonable and perhaps overdue development.

On the subject of preambles, it is important to note the difference

---

[32] *See In re Paulsen*, 30 F.3d 1475, 1479 (Fed. Cir. 1994). However, the courts have denied that there is any "litmus test" for deciding if a preamble should be considered a claim limitation. *See Corning Glass Works v. Sumitomo Electric U.S.A., Inc.*, 868 F.2d 1251, 1257 (Fed. Cir. 1989). "To say that a preamble is a limitation if it gives 'meaning to the claim' may merely state the problem rather than lead one to the answer." *Id.*

[33] *See Gerber Garment Technology, Inc. v. Lectra Sys., Inc.*, 916 F.2d 683, 689 (Fed. Cir. 1990).

[34] 850 F.2d 675, 677–78 (Fed. Cir. 1988).

[35] *See Paulsen*, 30 F.3d at 1479.

[36] *Bell Communications Research, Inc. v. Vitalink Communications Corp.*, 55 F.3d 615 (Fed. Cir. 1995) ("We construe claim preambles, like all other claim language, consistently with these principles. . . . [W]hen the claim drafter chooses to use *both* the preamble and the body to define the subject matter of the claimed invention, the invention so defined, and not some other, is the one the patent protects. . . . Preamble construction . . . presents no deeper mystery than the broader task of claim construction, of which it is but a part.").

between "comprising" and "consisting of," the two phrases that typically conclude a claim preamble. "Comprising" is a term of art, understood to mean that the invention consists of the following combination of claim elements, by themselves or in combination with additional elements.[37] "Consisting of," on the other hand, is understood to mean "the following elements *and no others.*" "Comprising" is the broader and generally more useful term. If the preamble ends with "consisting essentially of," the claim allows additional unrecited ingredients, but only if they do not change the basic characteristics of the combination.[38]

7.7 SPECIAL CLAIM FORMATS

Several specialized claim formats are available to inventors who wish to use them.

7.7.1 Jepson Claims

One specialized claim format is known as a "Jepson claim."[39] A Jepson claim is a claim to an improvement on a product that already exists. The Jepson format includes a recitation of the pre-existing components in the preamble and the improvement in the body of the claim.[40] For example:

In an instrument marker pen body including an ink reservoir and means for receiving a writing tip, *the improvement comprising* a pen arm holding means consisting of an integrally molded hinged member adapted to fold against a surface of the pen body and to be locked against said surface by engageable locking means and to receive and secure in place against said surface a pen arm when said hinged member is in its folded and locked position.[41]

The words "In a [pre-existing device], the improvement comprising" are typical of a Jepson claim. The significance of a Jepson claim is that the elements recited in the preamble are claim limitations, and the patent applicant, by implication, admits that those elements exist in the prior art.[42]

---

[37] *See Carl Zeiss Stiftung v. Renishaw* PLC, 945 F.2d 1173, 1178 (Fed. Cir. 1991); *Water Technologies Corp. v. Calco, Ltd.*, 850 F.2d 660, 666 (Fed. Cir. 1988).

[38] *See Water Technologies*, 850 F.2d at 666.

[39] Named after *Ex parte Jepson*, 243 O.G. 525 (Ass't Comm'r Pat. 1917), the case that first approved the format.

[40] *See Ethicon Endo-Surgery, Inc. v. U.S. Surgical Corp.*, 93 F.3d 1572, 1577 (Fed. Cir. 1996).

[41] *Pentec, Inc. v. Graphic Controls Corp.*, 776 F.2d 309, 312 (Fed. Cir. 1985) (emphasis supplied).

[42] *Pentec*, 776 F.2d at 315.

7.7.2 Markush Claims

Another specialized claim format is the "Markush claim," generally used to describe chemical and biological inventions. A Markush claim includes a claim element selected from a group of possibilities—for example, "a sugar selected from the group consisting of sucrose, fructose, and lactose."[43] "Markush groups" are used when there is no generic term that conveniently describes the desired claim element.[44]

7.7.3 Product-by-Process Claims

While most patent claims can be characterized as process, apparatus or composition of matter claims, a so-called product-by-process claim straddles the usual categories. A product-by-process claim, as the name suggests, describes a product made by a specific process. Traditionally, product-by-process claims have been used when the invention is one best described in terms of how it is made rather than what it is.[45] By way of analogy, consider how an omelet could be described to someone who had never seen one. One might attempt to describe an omelet in physical or chemical terms, but a better approach would be to provide the recipe. At one time product-by-process claims were allowed only when the invention could not be described except by way of the "recipe"—for example, when the precise physical characteristics of the product could not be determined. Now they are allowed even if they are not "necessary."

There has been much debate about the role to be given the process in interpreting a product-by-process claim. In *Scripps Clinic & Research Foundation v. Genentech, Inc.*,[46] the Federal Circuit held that the process described in a product-by-process claim could be ignored when determining the scope of the claim. In other words, if the claim recited the product of process X, an *identical product* made by a *different process* would still infringe.[47] According to this way of thinking, the process recited in a product-by-process claim is provided only as a way to define the product. The subject matter of the claim is still the omelet, not the recipe. This interpretation of the law follows the practice of the Patent Office in determining if a product-by-process claim should issue. The Patent Office will not

---

[43] For an actual example of a Markush claim, see *North American Vaccine, Inc. v. American Cyanamid Co.*, 7 F.3d 1571, 1573 (Fed. Cir. 1993).

[44] *See Application of Weber*, 580 F.2d 455, 457 n.4 (C.C.P.A. 1978).

[45] *See In re Thorpe*, 777 F.2d 695, 697 (Fed. Cir. 1985).

[46] 927 F.2d 1565 (Fed. Cir. 1991).

[47] "[T]he correct reading of product-by-process claims is that they are not limited to product prepared by the process set forth in the claims." *Scripps Clinic & Research Foundation v. Genentech, Inc.*, 927 F.2d 1565, 1583 (Fed. Cir. 1991).

issue a product-by-process claim unless it finds that the product, not just the process, is something new.[48]

However, in *Atlantic Thermoplastics Co. v. Faytex Corp.*,[49] a different panel of Federal Circuit judges rejected the earlier interpretation and held that the process set forth in a product-by-process claim does limit the claim, at least in litigation, so an identical product made by a different process does not infringe.[50] According to this court, the *Scripps Clinic* rule was contrary to Supreme Court authority and the hornbook principle of patent law that all elements of a claim are essential in determining infringement. Although it acknowledged that different standards are applied in patent prosecution, the court noted that this discrepancy is not unique. For example, the Patent Office will give claims their "broadest reasonable interpretation," whereas no such rule applies in litigation.[51]

Conflict in the Federal Circuit can be resolved through a procedure allowing an expanded, or "en banc," panel of all the judges on the Federal Circuit to review the case and decide collectively how the conflict will be settled. Unfortunately, the procedure was not followed in this instance, and the conflict between *Scripps Clinic* and *Atlantic Thermoplastics* remains. As a rule, if two decisions of the Federal Circuit conflict, the earlier one (i.e., *Scripps Clinic*) takes precedence.[52] However, if *Scripps Clinic* really was contrary to Supreme Court precedent (a matter on which the Federal Circuit judges disagree), then the Supreme Court authority would control. Accordingly, it is impossible for anyone to say at this juncture precisely what the law is.

7.7.4 "Means-Plus-Function" Claims

One form of specialized claim format that has become extremely common is the "means-plus-function" format authorized by 35 U.S.C. § 112, Paragraph 6. At one time, courts held that a claim to an apparatus must describe the features of the apparatus in precise physical terms rather than in terms of the functions they perform. So, for example, a claim to a mousetrap could properly refer to a "steel spring" but could not refer simply to a "means for snapping the trap shut." The latter claim would literally cover a mousetrap with a steel spring, a plastic spring, a rubber

---

[48] *See Thorpe,* 777 F.2d at 697.

[49] 970 F.2d 834 (Fed. Cir. 1992).

[50] *Atlantic Thermoplastics,* 970 F.2d at 847.

[51] *Atlantic Thermoplastics,* 970 F.2d at 846. The court suggested, but did not clearly state, that a product-by-process claim involving a new process but an old product would be held valid in litigation, even though it would be (or should be) rejected by the Patent Office. If this were not true, it would violate the principle that claims must be given the same interpretation for infringement as for validity. *See Id.*

[52] *Newell Co. v. Kenney Mfg. Co.,* 846 F.2d 787, 765 (Fed. Cir. 1988).

band or any other mechanism that might be conceived of for closing the trap. Such a claim would not adequately define the invention, since it could cover many things that the patentee had not invented or disclosed.

Permitting a patentee to describe a feature of the invention in terms of its function does have certain advantages, however. In the prior example, for instance, the inventor might have in mind the steel spring, the plastic spring, the rubber band and dozens of other means for snapping the trap shut, and the choice of which to use might have little to do with the essence of the invention. A person skilled in designing mousetraps who read the patent might also realize that various forms of springs and elastic bands could be used. In this situation, it would seem pointless to require the inventor to provide a long list of every variety of spring, rubber band or similar device that the inventor could think of. Moreover, it might be too easy for a competitor to avoid the patent simply by coming up with a closing mechanism that the patentee had neglected to list.

The result of this tension between convenience and the need for specificity in claim drafting was legislative compromise, embodied in § 112(6):

An element in a claim for a combination may be expressed as a means or step for performing a specified function without the recital of structure, material or acts in support thereof, and such claim shall be construed to cover the corresponding structure, material or acts described in the specification and equivalents thereof.

Thus, an inventor can choose to describe an element of the invention as a physical structure (i.e., "steel spring") or as a "means" for performing a specified function (i.e., "means for snapping the trap shut"), leaving it to the specification to describe the physical structure that performs the function. If the inventor chooses the latter option, the claim will cover the specific structure disclosed in the specification and "equivalents" of that structure (i.e., a mousetrap with a steel spring or the "equivalent" of a steel spring). Deciding just what is "equivalent" is a matter discussed in Section 10.7.

Note that § 112(6) applies only to a "claim for a combination." A "single means claim" is still considered invalid.[53] For example, one could not claim just "a means for catching a mouse" and leave it at that. The "means-plus-function" format can be used only when the claim breaks down the invention into specific components.

7.7.5 "Step-Plus-Function" Claims

The language of § 112(6) also seems to provide for a "step-plus-function" claim—in other words, a process claim in which a step of the

---

[53] *See In re Hyatt*, 708 F.2d 712, 714 (Fed. Cir. 1983).

process is described solely in terms of the "function" performed by that step, without the recital of a specific "act." Such a claim would cover the "act" described in the specification and its equivalents. However, while it is comparatively easy to distinguish between a *function* and a *structure*, it is next to impossible to distinguish between a *function* and an *act*. Returning to the mousetrap example, a claim element that referred to a "means for snapping the trap shut" would clearly be a means-plus-function claim element, because other than the generic term "means," the physical structure is described solely in terms of the function it performs. Imagine, however, a mouse-trapping process claim, one element of which is "closing the trap to imprison the mouse." Is "closing the trap" (or for that matter "imprisoning the mouse") a "function" or an "act"? Does it describe the step itself or only the result of the step?

The Federal Circuit faced some of these issues in *O.I. Corp. v. Tekmar Co.*,[54] where the invention concerned a way of removing water vapor from material to be analyzed in a gas chromatograph. One element of the method claim referred to "the step[] of . . . passing the [material] through a passage." The court held that a "step" in a process claim might be described only in terms of accomplishing a "function," and that § 112(6) would limit the claim to the "act" described in the specification for accomplishing that function and equivalents of that "act." However, the court did not consider this such a claim. The court observed that "[i]f we were to construe every process claim containing steps described by an 'ing' verb, such as passing, heating, reacting, transferring, etc. into a step-plus-function limitation, we would be limiting process claims in a manner never intended by Congress."[55] Unfortunately, the court did not explain how it determined that "passing" is an "act" rather than a "function," nor did it give an example of a claim limitation that it *would* construe as a step-plus-function limitation.

O.I. Corp. is one of very few cases discussing step-plus-function claims and the only one in which the Federal Circuit has offered any views. While it seems apparent that the Federal Circuit will not interpret most process claims as step-plus-function claims, this is still an area of the law badly in need of clarification.

---

[54] 115 F.3d 1576 (Fed. Cir. 1997).
[55] *O.I. Corp.*, 115 F.3d at 1583.

CHAPTER 8

Conditions of Patentability

8.1 EXAMINATION VERSUS LITIGATION

Before a patent is issued, the application must go through a process of "examination" by the Patent Office.[1] The purpose of the examination is to ensure that the application meets the various requirements of "patentability." These requirements, which are explained in some detail in the pages that follow, include the following:

- The invention must have *utility*.
- The claims must be *definite*.
- The specification must *enable* the practice of the invention and must disclose the inventor's *best mode* of practicing the invention.
- The claimed invention must be *novel*—that is, it must be new and *non-obvious* in comparison to the prior art.

In spite of the examination process, patents are sometimes issued that fail to meet these fundamental requirements. This is not always the fault of the Patent Office. For example, the Patent Office cannot judge whether a claim is novel in comparison to an earlier product if, as not infrequently occurs, the Patent Office is not even aware of the earlier product. Moreover, patent examination is not a practical forum for inquiring into certain questions—such as whether the information disclosed in a specification really reflects the applicant's "best mode." Questions like these can be effectively explored only in an adversarial proceeding. For

[1] See Section 5.1.

all of these reasons, courts have the power to find an issued patent "invalid,"[2] and a finding of invalidity is a complete defense to any charge of infringement.[3]

The patentability requirements discussed in this chapter are relevant in the examination process, where they can be grounds for rejecting an application, and in the litigation context, where they can be grounds for holding an already issued patent invalid. There are some procedural differences in the way these requirements are enforced in the Patent Office as compared to a court. For example, when judging whether a claim is novel, the Patent Office will give the claim its "broadest reasonable construction." A court will not.[4] Nevertheless, the rules and precedent that apply in one context generally apply in the other context as well.

8.2 PRESUMPTION OF VALIDITY

Although courts have the power to hold an issued patent invalid, they do not discount the work of the Patent Office entirely. All patents are presumed to be valid, and the burden of overcoming that presumption rests with the accused infringer.[5] The presumption can only be overcome by "clear and convincing" evidence of invalidity.[6] This standard of proof is something less than the "beyond a reasonable doubt" standard of criminal law,[7] but it requires more than just a preponderance of the evidence. Consequently, a challenge to the validity of a patent is always an uphill battle. Note that the presumption of validity applies only after a patent has issued; there is no presumption in the Patent Office that an application meets the requirements of patentability.

Some older cases suggest that the presumption of validity is weakened or nullified when validity is challenged on grounds that were not considered by the Patent Office, such as a prior art reference of which the Patent Office was unaware. The Federal Circuit has adamantly maintained that the presumption of validity is ever-present and unchanging, no matter what grounds of invalidity may be asserted, but has admitted that the

---

[2] *See Quad Environmental Technologies Corp. v. Union Sanitary Dist.*, 946 F.2d 870, 876 (Fed. Cir. 1991) ("The courts are the final arbiter of patent validity and, although courts may take cognizance of, and benefit from, the proceedings before the patent examiner, the question is ultimately for the courts to decide, without deference to the rulings of the patent examiner.").

[3] *Lough v. Brunswick Corp.*, 86 F.3d 1113, 1123 (Fed. Cir. 1996).

[4] *See Atlantic Thermoplastics Co. v. Faytex Corp.*, 970 F.2d 834, 846 (Fed. Cir. 1992).

[5] 35 U.S.C. § 282; *Therma-Tru Corp. v. Peachtree Doors Inc.*, 44 F.3d 988, 992 (Fed. Cir. 1995); *Hybritech Inc. v. Monoclonal Antibodies, Inc.*, 802 F.2d 1367, 1375 (Fed. Cir. 1986).

[6] *Therma-Tru*, 44 F.3d at 992; *Richardson v. Suzuki Motor Co.*, 868 F.2d 1226, 1235 (Fed. Cir. 1989); *Hybritech*, 802 F.2d at 1375.

[7] *Trans-World Mfg. Corp. v. Al Nyman & Sons, Inc.*, 750 F.2d 1552, 1559 (Fed. Cir. 1984).

presumption is easier to overcome when the grounds are new.[8] Perhaps the difference is only one of semantics. In any event, deference to the Patent Office is more understandable when the Patent Office has already considered the issue than when it has not.

8.3 ASSIGNOR ESTOPPEL

Consider the following scenario. An inventor obtains a patent on a new apparatus and then assigns all rights to his employer.[9] The inventor receives valuable consideration for the assignment—perhaps a bonus. Afterward the inventor leaves his employer to form his own company and produces a product that is covered by the patent. If the former employer accuses the inventor of infringing the patent, can the inventor claim that the patent is invalid?

The answer is no. Anyone who assigns patent rights to another in exchange for valuable consideration[10] implicitly acknowledges the validity of the patent and gives up the right to challenge that validity at a later time. This principle, known as "assignor estoppel," is a matter of fairness; "an assignor should not be permitted to sell something and later assert that what was sold is worthless, all to the detriment of the assignee."[11] The rule applies to the individual who assigned the patent, and it may apply to others with whom that individual is involved. For example, if the company accused of infringing the patent is not owned by the inventor/ assignor, but it employs him in a position of responsibility, that company may still be barred from contesting the validity of the patent.[12]

8.4 UTILITY

Section 101 of the Patent Act states that a patent may be granted to the discoverer of a "new and useful" invention. Article 1, Section 8 of the Constitution also speaks of promoting the "useful arts." From these sources, the courts have derived the rule that an invention must be

---

[8] *Hybritech*, 802 F.2d at 1375 ("the presumption remains intact and on the challenger throughout the litigation, and the clear and convincing evidence standard does not change;" however, "the introduction of prior art not before the examiner may facilitate the challenger's meeting the burden of proof"); *Kalman v. Kimberly-Clark Corp.*, 713 F.2d 760, 773 n.3 (Fed. Cir. 1983).

[9] See Section 6.2.

[10] The "valuable consideration" need not be a separate payment or bonus. Where the inventor/assignor is an employee of a corporation, that employee's regular salary is likely to be considered adequate consideration, at least if the invention was within the scope of the inventor/assignor's employment. *See Diamond Scientific Co. v. Ambico, Inc.*, 848 F.2d 1220, 1225 (Fed. Cir. 1988).

[11] *Diamond Scientific*, 848 F.2d at 1224.

[12] *See Shamrock Technologies, Inc. v. Medical Sterilization, Inc.*, 903 F.2d 789, 793 (Fed. Cir. 1990).

"useful" before it can be patented.[13] This is known as the utility requirement.[14]

A broad range of inventions are considered "useful" in terms of patentability, even if they serve a relatively trivial purpose. Side by side with patents on such clearly useful inventions as microchips and pharmaceuticals, one can find many patents to toys, novelties and the like. If they serve their purpose, they are sufficiently "useful" to receive a patent.[15] The only kinds of invention categorically excluded from patentability on grounds of non-utility are those whose purpose is deemed illegal or "immoral." Until 1977, gambling machines were held to lack utility.[16] The exclusion still applies to any invention useful only in committing a crime or fraud—for example, a method of counterfeiting currency.[17]

Although it might be argued that an invention is "useful" only if it is an improvement over the prior art, this is not required. An invention can still be patented even if it is inferior to, or no better than, existing devices or methods.[18] As the Federal Circuit has observed, "[a]n invention need not be the best or the only way to accomplish a certain result, and it need only be useful to some extent and in certain applications."[19]

It would be difficult, and perhaps pointless, for the Patent Office to attempt to assess in every case whether the claimed invention is really an improvement. Although an invention is inferior to its predecessors in some respects, it may be superior in others. In many cases, the advantages of a particular invention cannot be fully appreciated until long after it is patented. In the end, the Patent Office is simply not in the business of judging whether one invention is better than another. This is one reason why the popular conception of a patent as an award for technological

---

[13] *See Stiftung v. Renishaw PLC,* 945 F.2d 1173, 1180 (Fed. Cir. 1991).

[14] The concept of utility does not apply to design patents, discussed in Section 12.1.

[15] One patent demonstrating the potential breadth of the concept of utility is U.S. patent No. 5,457,821, entitled "Hat Simulating a Fried Egg." According to the specification, "The hat finds utility, for example, as an attention-getting item in connection with promotional activities at trade shows, conventions, and the like. Further the hat is useful in connection with egg sale promotions in the egg industry." Perhaps a design patent would have been more appropriate. See Section 12.1.

[16] *See Tol-O-Matic, Inc. v. Proma Produkt-Und Marketing Gesellschaft M.b.H,* 945 F.2d 1546, 1552 (Fed. Cir. 1991).

[17] "All that the law requires is that the invention should not be frivolous, or injurious to the well-being, good policy, or good morals of society. The word useful therefore is incorporated into the act in contradistinction to mischievous or immoral." *Tol-O-Matic,* 945 F.2d at 1553 (emphasis in original, citation omitted).

[18] *Demaco Corp. v. F. Von Langsdorff Licensing Ltd.,* 851 F.2d 1387, 1390 ("The patent statute does not require that a patentable invention be superior to all prior devices.").

[19] *Stiftung,* 945 F.2d at 1180; *see also Envirotech Corp. v. Al George, Inc.,* 730 F.2d 753, 762 (Fed. Cir. 1984) ("the fact that an invention has only limited utility and is only operable in certain applications is not grounds for finding lack of utility").

achievement is off-base. In spite of the frequent attempts of advertising to imply that a product is "so good it's patented," patents are a reflection of novelty, not of merit.

Inventions are required to achieve a minimum level of operability, since an invention that fails to work at all cannot be said to have utility.[20] In most cases, the operability of the invention is taken for granted by the Patent Office, which is not equipped to perform experiments to test whether an invention works as advertised. Occasionally, however, the nature of the invention will be enough to raise suspicions. The Patent Office has received applications for perpetual motion machines, which are impossible according to the most fundamental principles of physics. When the Patent Office receives an application for an invention that so defies conventional wisdom, the applicant may be required to come forward with experimental evidence demonstrating that the invention actually does work.[21] In one case where the claimed device purported to produce more energy than it consumed, the Patent Office arranged for tests to be conducted by the Bureau of Standards. Unfortunately for the sake of our future energy needs, the tests were not a success.[22]

New pharmaceuticals present a special problem because years of testing may be required to demonstrate that they are safe and effective. In *In re Brana*,[23] the Federal Circuit held that animal studies could provide sufficient evidence of utility, even though FDA approval would require further testing.[24] The court explained that if full FDA approval were required before a patent could be granted, the costs would discourage some companies from patenting, and perhaps from developing, potentially important discoveries.

A patent specification must disclose the utility of the claimed invention, so difficulties can arise if it is unclear from the specification what the

---

[20] *Tol-O-Matic*, 945 F.2d at 1553 (referring to the "total incapacity" that could lead to a finding of non-utility). On the other hand, if a claimed invention achieves some of its objectives, but not others, it will still be deemed to have utility. *Stiftung*, 945 F.2d at 1180 ("When a properly claimed invention meets at least one stated objective, utility under § 101 is clearly shown." (citation omitted)). Note that if a claimed invention is an impossibility, the patent fails on grounds of enablement as well as utility. See Section 8.6.

[21] One example of an invention met with skepticism is discussed in *Fregau v. Mossinghoff*, 776 F.2d 1034 (Fed. Cir. 1985). The claimed method was supposed to enhance the density and flavor of beverages by passing them through a magnetic field. The Patent Office did not consider the experimental evidence offered by the applicant convincing. Curiously, the Patent Office also found several examples of close, and equally unbelievable, prior art.

[22] *See Newman v. Quigg*, 877 F.2d 1575 (Fed. Cir. 1989).

[23] 51 F.3d 1560 (Fed. Cir. 1995).

[24] "Usefulness in patent law, and in particular in the context of pharmaceutical inventions, necessarily includes the expectation of further research and development. The stage at which an invention in this field becomes useful is well before it is ready to be administered to humans." *Brana*, 51 F.3d at 1568.

invention is *supposed* to do. This is rarely, if ever, the case with apparatus claims, but it can occur when the invention is a chemical compound and the application fails to specify how the compound should be used. To state, for example, that a compound can be used to form a "film" may be an inadequate statement of utility, if the usefulness of such a film is not clear.[25] These problems are most likely to arise when the applicant attempts to rely on a foreign patent application in order to establish priority.[26] This is because other countries have different requirements regarding the disclosure of utility in a patent application.[27]

Although the Patent Office has limited means to challenge claims on grounds of inoperability or impossibility, this is not necessarily the case in litigation. A party charged with patent infringement may offer evidence demonstrating that whatever is required by the claim is either physically impossible or useless.[28] On the other hand, if a claim actually has been infringed, a court will be reluctant to find that the invention lacks utility. As one court has observed, "People rarely, if ever, appropriate useless inventions."[29]

8.5 DEFINITENESS

The function of patent claims is to identify what is covered by the patent. If patent infringement can be compared to trespassing, the claims serve as the boundary markers that define what is, or is not, an encroachment on the inventor's exclusive territory. The law therefore requires that the claims have a definite meaning understandable to those skilled in the art. This requirement is embodied in the second paragraph of 35 U.S.C. § 112, which provides that the "specification shall conclude with one or more claims particularly pointing out and distinctly claiming the subject matter which the applicant regards as his invention."

The test for compliance is "whether those skilled in the art would understand what is claimed when the claim is read in light of the specification."[30] If the claims are so vague or unclear that those in the industry

---

[25] *See In re Ziegler*, 992 F.2d 1197, 1201–1203 (Fed. Cir. 1993).

[26] See Section 12.3.

[27] *See Cross v. Iizuka*, 753 F.2d 1040 (Fed. Cir. 1985).

[28] *See Raytheon Co. v. Roper Corp.*, 724 F.2d 951, 956–57 (Fed. Cir. 1983).

[29] *Raytheon*, 724 F.2d at 959.

[30] *Beachcombers v. Wildwood Creative Products, Inc.*, 31 F.3d 1154, 1158 (Fed. Cir. 1994); *Morton Int'l, Inc. v. Cardinal Chemical Co.*, 5 F.3d 1464, 1470 (Fed. Cir. 1993); *Shatterproof Glass Corp. v. Libbey-Owens Ford Co.*, 758 F.2d 613, 624 (Fed. Cir. 1985) (" '[i]f the claims, read in light of the specification, reasonably apprise those skilled in the art both of the utilization and scope of the invention, and if the language is as precise as the subject matter permits, the courts can demand no more.' " (citation omitted)). Like enablement, discussed in Section 8.6, definiteness is determined from the perspective of one skilled in the art *at the time the patent application was filed.* W.L. Gore & Assoc, Inc. v. Garlock, Inc., 721 F.2d 1540, 1557 (Fed. Cir. 1983).

cannot reasonably determine what does or does not infringe the patent, the claims may be held unpatentable or invalid.[31] On the other hand, because language is inherently imprecise, the law requires only such precision in claim drafting as the subject matter permits.[32] In *Orthokinetics, Inc. v. Safety Travel Chairs, Inc.*,[33] for example, the patent claimed a wheel chair with a part "so dimensioned" that it could be inserted in the space between the seats and door frame of an automobile. The claim did not state exactly what those dimensions should be, nor could it have stated them precisely since they would vary depending on the model of the automobile. The dimensions for any particular automobile could easily be obtained by one skilled in the art. The court held that the claim language was not indefinite, since it was as precise as the subject matter permitted: "The patent law does not require that all possible lengths corresponding to the spaces in hundreds of different automobiles be listed in the patent, let alone that they be listed in the claims."[34]

The test for indefiniteness is whether the claim language is understandable when "read in light of the specification." One function of the specification is to serve as a dictionary or glossary for any claim terms that might have a specialized meaning.[35] The specification may provide a specific definition for otherwise vague claim language, or it may provide a test for measuring whether a product falls within the intended meaning of the claim.[36] Even if some experimentation is required to determine the boundaries of the claim, the claim will not be held indefinite if the language is as precise as the subject matter permits.[37] The prosecution history also may provide information to clarify the meaning of a disputed term.[38]

In spite of the requirement that claims use definite language, such "words of degree" as "generally," "approximately" and "substantially equal to" are commonly used.[39] While these terms are inherently inexact,

---

[31] *Morton*, 5 F.3d at 1470.
[32] *Hybritech Inc. v. Monoclonal Antibodies, Inc.*, 802 F.2d 1367, 1385 (Fed. Cir. 1986). It has been observed that a patent claim is "one of the most difficult legal instruments to draw with accuracy." *Slimfold Mfg. Co. v. Kinkead Indus., Inc.*, 810 F.2d 1113, 1117 (Fed. Cir. 1987) (citation omitted).
[33] 806 F.2d 1565 (Fed. Cir. 1986).
[34] *Orthokinetics*, 806 F.2d at 1576.
[35] *See Beachcombers*, 31 F.3d at 1158 ("As we have repeatedly said, a patentee can be his own lexicographer provided the patentee's definition, to the extent it differs from the conventional definition, is clearly set forth in the specification.").
[36] *See Seattle Box Co. v. Industrial Crating & Packing, Inc.*, 731 F.2d 818, 826 (Fed. Cir. 1984); *Shatterproof Glass*, 758 F.2d at 624; *W.L. Gore*, 721 F.2d at 1557–58.
[37] *Seattle Box*, 731 F.2d at 826.
[38] *See Texas Instruments Inc. v. U.S. Int'l Trade Comm'n*, 871 F.2d 1054, 1063 (Fed. Cir. 1989) ("The public is entitled to know the scope of the claims but must look to both the patent specification and the prosecution history, especially where there is doubt concerning the scope of the claims.").
[39] *See Andrew Corp. v. Gabriel Elec., Inc.*, 847 F.2d 819, 821 (Fed. Cir. 1988).

they are often tolerated because they are "as precise as the subject matter permits." For example, in *Rosemount, Inc. v. Beckman Instruments, Inc.*,[40] the patent claims described a device for measuring pH, having one component "in close proximity" to another. The court found that "close proximity" was a term used and understood in the industry. Had the inventor been forced to specify a precise dimension (e.g., "within .5 centimeters"), the claim would likely have been narrower than the true scope of the invention. Moreover, requiring a precise definition of "close proximity" in the patent specification would "turn the construction of a patent into a mere semantic quibble that serves no useful purpose."[41]

On the other hand, a court will treat "words of degree" with suspicion if, in litigation, the patentee argues that the term is broad enough to encompass the accused product but narrow enough to avoid the prior art, with no suggestion as to where the line in-between should be drawn. In *Amgen, Inc. v. Chugai Pharmaceuticals Co.*,[42] the patentee claimed a protein having a "specific activity" of "at least about 160,000 IU/AU." A prior art product exhibited a "specific activity" of 128,620 IU/AU. Since nothing in the claims, the specification, the prosecution history or the prior art provided any hint as to whether, for example, a protein having a "specific activity" of 145,000 IU/AU would come within the scope of the claims, the court held that the term "about" was insufficiently definite in the context of that particular patent.

When a claim is drafted in reasonably definite terms, it provides competitors of the patent owner with fair warning of what will or will not infringe the patent. If claim language is vague, competitors must proceed at their peril, and the uncertainty provides the patent owner with what is, in effect, a broader claim. However, the laudable effects of the definiteness requirement are undermined to some extent by the "doctrine of equivalents."[43] According to that doctrine, even a product that is not literally described by the claim language may infringe, if the differences are "insubstantial." The effect is to add an extra dimension of uncertainty to every patent claim. The tension between the definiteness requirement and the doctrine of equivalents is one of the reasons that the latter doctrine, though long established, has been criticized in recent years.[44]

---

[40] 727 F.2d 1540 (Fed. Cir. 1984).

[41] *Rosemount*, 727 F.2d at 1547. The Patent Office guidelines also require only a "reasonable degree of particularity and distinctness." M.P.E.P. § 2173.02. "Some latitude in the manner of expression and the aptness of terms should be permitted even though the claim language is not as precise as the examiner might desire." *Id. See also U.S. v. Telectronics, Inc.*, 857 F.2d 778, 786 (Fed. Cir. 1988) ("Section 112, para. 2, requires only reasonable precision in delineating the bounds of the claimed invention.").

[42] 927 F.2d 1200 (Fed. Cir. 1991).

[43] See Section 10.6.

[44] See Section 10.6.3.

8.6 ENABLEMENT

As discussed in Section 1.1, a patent can be regarded as a bargain between the inventor and the public. In exchange for a monopoly on the invention for a period of years, the inventor must disclose the invention in such clear terms that, when the patent has expired, the public at large can take advantage of the invention. This concept is behind the so-called "enablement" and "best mode" requirements.[45] The enablement requirement is derived from the following language of 35 U.S.C. § 112:

The specification shall contain a written description of the invention, and of the manner and process of making and using it, in such full, clear, concise, and exact terms as to *enable* any person skilled in the art to which it pertains, or with which it is most nearly connected, to make and use the same.

To satisfy the enablement requirement, the patent must describe the invention in such clear and exact terms that persons "skilled in the art"[46] can make and use the invention without "undue experimentation." Because patents are intended to be read and used by those "skilled in the art," the specification need not include information that such persons would already be aware of.[47] A patent on an improved radio antenna, for example, need not disclose the entire theory and practice of how to build a radio, beginning with Marconi. Persons skilled in the radio art would know the basics already and would only have to be informed of the inventor's improvement in order to take advantage of the invention.

It is also not required that a patent disclosure be so detailed that the invention can be practiced without experimentation. The only requirement is that such experimentation not be "undue." The definition of "undue" varies depending on the nature of the invention and expectations in the industry. Experimentation that takes a great deal of time may not be considered "undue" if the experiments are routine, and the specification provides clear guidance as to what must be done. In the biotechnology industry, for example, isolating cells that will produce a desired antibody may require testing many cells and discarding all but a few. However, if such screening is routine and the patent specification tells the experimenter how to proceed, the patent will not be considered non-

---

[45] The enablement requirement also helps to fix the date of invention for purposes of determining priority. See Section 8.9.2. The inclusion of an enabling disclosure in a patent application demonstrates that the applicant had a completed invention no later than the filing date.

[46] See Section 8.9.6.

[47] "[A] patent need not teach, and preferably omits, what is well known in the art." *Hybritech Inc. v. Monoclonal Antibodies, Inc.*, 802 F.2d 1367, 1384 (Fed. Cir. 1986).

enabling.[48] The test is whether, under the circumstances, the amount of experimentation required would be unreasonable.

Sometimes patentees risk violating the enablement requirement when they attempt to reserve as a trade secret some piece of information necessary to practice the claimed invention.[49] In one case a patentee obtained claims to a machine tool control system but did not disclose the proprietary software that made the system work.[50] Without better evidence that commercially available software could be substituted, the court found the patent non-enabling. To have constructed the necessary software from scratch would have required 1-1/2 to 2 years of "undue" experimentation. On the other hand, another patent that failed to disclose software necessary to practice the invention was held to be valid, where writing the necessary software would have been a comparatively quick and straightforward task for an experienced programmer.[51]

Under some circumstances, information can be "incorporated by reference" in a patent specification. This simply means that the patent refers the reader to information contained in another document. If the information is necessary to satisfy the enablement or best mode requirements, it can be incorporated by reference only if found in another U.S. patent or allowed patent application.[52] Foreign patents and non-patent publications can be incorporated by reference to provide background or context for the invention. In any case, a document incorporated by reference must be publicly available.

In the case of inventions that depend on the use of living materials, such as microorganisms or cultured cells, words alone may be insufficient to enable one skilled in the art to make and use the invention. A sample of the necessary biological materials may be necessary to begin. In such cases, inventors can satisfy the enablement requirement by depositing samples of the material in a certified depository where they are available to researchers in the field.[53] In other cases, it may be sufficient to direct researchers to commercial sources of supply or provide them with the directions necessary to produce the materials for themselves.

As far as the *enablement* requirement is concerned, the specification need disclose only some manner is which the invention can be practiced.

---

[48] *See In re Wands*, 858 F.2d 731 (Fed. Cir. 1988).

[49] See Section 2.3.

[50] *White Consolidated Indus. v. Vega Servo-Control, Inc.*, 713 F.2d 788 (Fed. Cir. 1983).

[51] *Northern Telecom, Inc. v. Datapoint Corp.*, 908 F.2d 931 (Fed. Cir. 1990). The absence of a specific disclosure of software is also a potential "best mode" violation. See Section 8.7. However, "it is generally sufficient if the functions of the software are disclosed, it usually being the case that creation of the specific source code is within the skill of the art." *Robotic Vision Sys., Inc. v. View Eng'g Inc.*, 112 F.3d 1163, 1166 (Fed. Cir. 1997).

[52] M.P.E.P. § 608.01(p).

[53] See 37 C.F.R. § 1.802; M.P.E.P. § 2401 *et seq.*

It need not disclose every manner of practicing the invention, or even the best manner.[54] It is also not required that the inventor understand or disclose the principles that make the invention work, as long as it does work. If the specification provides the information needed to make and use the invention, the patentee's theory as to why it works can be completely misguided.[55]

Whether a specification is enabling is measured at the time the patent application was filed. Later developments in the art are irrelevant.[56] If the invention requires a skill that was developed only after the filing date of the patent application, the patent cannot be considered enabling. By the same token, if a patent was enabling as of its filing date, no later developments in the art can undo that fact. For example, a patent on a bullet-proof vest could be enabling as of its filing date and remain a valid patent, even though later advancements in weaponry rendered the disclosed embodiments ineffective.

8.6.1 Scope of Enablement

Some of the most troubling enablement questions arise when the patent claims are substantially broader than the specific embodiments disclosed in the specification. Patent claims can be, and often are, generic. For example, a claim might (hypothetically) cover *every* mousetrap that included the combination of (1) a spring, (2) a latch and (3) a trigger to unhook the latch and release the spring when disturbed by a mouse. The specification might disclose in detail only *one* example of such a trap— with a particular kind of spring, latch and trigger. If the claim covers other versions of the trap that are not discussed at all, is the specification adequate to enable one skilled in the art to practice the claimed invention?

It is often said that the enabling disclosure in the specification must be "commensurate in scope" with the breadth of the claims.[57] However, the rules to be applied generally depend on the kind of invention that is claimed. If the invention is a mechanical one or an electrical circuit, the art is regarded as "predictable," meaning that if one embodiment of the invention is disclosed, persons skilled in the art will understand how to make and use other variations.[58] If, for example, the specification discloses

---

[54] *Engel Indus., Inc. v. Lockformer Co.*, 946 F.2d 1528, 1533 (Fed. Cir. 1991). However, failure to disclose the best manner known to the inventor may violate the "best mode" requirement. See Section 8.7.

[55] *See Newman v. Quigg,* 877 F.2d 1575, 1581 (Fed. Cir. 1989).

[56] *See In re Wright,* 999 F.2d at 1557, 1562–63 (Fed. Cir. 1993).

[57] *See, e.g., Amgen, Inc. v. Chugai Pharmaceutical Co.,* 927 F.2d 1200, 1213 (Fed. Cir. 1991).

[58] "If an invention pertains to an art where the results are predictable, e.g., the mechanical as opposed to the chemical arts, a broad claim can be enabled by disclosure of a single embodiment. . . ." *Spectra-Physics, Inc. v. Coherent, Inc.,* 827 F.2d 1524, 1533 (Fed. Cir. 1987).

a plastic spring for the mousetrap, persons skilled in the art will know how to substitute a steel spring.

However, other arts, such as chemistry and biotechnology, are considered "unpredictable." Even a tiny change in the structure of a molecule may have large and unanticipated effects. Here, the patentee may be forced to draft claims that are more limited in scope and closer to the specific embodiments disclosed in the specification. For example, one patentee claimed all possible sequences of DNA that would produce the protein EPO, which stimulates the production of red blood cells, or any "analog" of EPO that would have a similar effect.[59] The specification disclosed the information needed to prepare EPO and just a few of its analogs. The court found that the number of possible DNA sequences within the scope of the claim vastly outstripped the enabling disclosure: "There may be many other genetic sequences that code for EPO-type products. [The patentee] has told us how to make and use only a few of them and is therefore not entitled to claim all of them."[60]

This distinction between the "predictable" and "unpredictable" arts strikes some as unsatisfactory. If a claim in the mechanical arts can be considered enabled even though it encompasses embodiments that are "inadequately disclosed" in the specification,[61] of what use is the "predictability" of the art? Is it true that mechanical contrivances are invariably more "predictable" than chemistry? Where do new arts, such as that of computer programming, fall? However, at least until the Federal Circuit or the Supreme Court decides to reexamine this issue, broad claims will be more readily tolerated in the mechanical and electrical arts than in the arts of chemistry and biotechnology.

8.7 "BEST MODE"

Like the enablement requirement, the "best mode" requirement arises from the language of 35 U.S.C. § 112, which provides that a specification "shall set forth the best mode contemplated by the inventor for carrying out his invention." The "best mode" means the best manner of practicing the invention, or the best operative example, known to the inventor. If, for example, the inventor of the hypothetical mousetrap envisioned two variants of the claimed invention, one using an inferior plastic spring and the other a superior steel spring, the best mode requirement would require that the better embodiment be disclosed in the patent, even though both came within the scope of the generic claim.

Like the enablement requirement, the best mode requirement reflects

---

[59] *Amgen,* 927 F.2d at 1212–14.
[60] *Amgen,* 927 F.2d at 1213–14.
[61] *Spectra-Physics,* 827 F.2d at 1533.

the bargain model of patent law. If a patentee is to be awarded a monopoly on an invention for a period of years, the public is entitled to disclosure of the best that the patentee has to offer. If there were no best mode requirement, patentees might be tempted to disclose the least effective or most impractical embodiments of their inventions, perhaps reserving the better embodiments as trade secrets. The result would do little to advance the "useful arts."[62]

Where the enablement requirement can be satisfied by the disclosure of *any* mode of practicing the invention, the best mode requirement compels disclosure of the one mode believed by the inventor to be the best. The relevant time period is the time at which the patent application was filed, and the relevant perspective is that of the inventor. If the inventor believed the disclosed "mode" to be the best, the best mode requirement is satisfied even if the inventor was mistaken at the time, or even if other "modes" were later discovered that even the inventor would acknowledge as better than the one disclosed in the patent specification. The patent does not have to be "updated" to disclose later-discovered improvements.[63]

Since satisfaction of the best mode requirement is dependent on the subjective beliefs of the inventor, violation of the requirement may be difficult to prove. However, sometimes in litigation the inventor's contemporaneous documents are used to show that a better mode was recognized but not disclosed.[64] One can also consider the means adopted by the patentee for commercializing the invention. For example, in *Northern Telecom, Inc. v. Datapoint Corp.*,[65] the patent described a system for capturing data on standard audio cassettes. Employees of the patent owner testified that cassettes with special characteristics, different from those of ordinary audio cassettes, had been ordered by the patent owner for its own use.

---

[62] "[T]he best mode requirement . . . ensure[s] that a patent applicant plays 'fair and square' with the patent system. It is a requirement that the *quid pro quo* of the patent grant be satisfied. One must not receive the right to exclude others unless at the time of filing he has provided an adequate disclosure of the best mode known to him of carrying out the invention." *Amgen, Inc. v. Chugai Pharmaceutical Co.*, 927 F.2d 1200, 1209–10 (Fed. Cir. 1991). In some cases, a "better mode" may have been devised by someone other than the inventor, after the date of invention but before the filing of the patent application. If the inventor is aware of this "better mode" before the application is filed, it must be disclosed in the specification, even though it does not represent the inventor's own work, and he could not claim it in the patent. *See Graco, Inc. v. Binks Mfg. Co.*, 60 F.3d 785, 789 (Fed. Cir. 1995).

[63] *See Transco Prods. Inc. v. Performance Contracting, Inc.*, 38 F.3d 551 (Fed. Cir. 1994). Constant changes in patent disclosures, to account for progressive improvements in technology, might cause more administrative difficulties than the benefits would warrant. The addition of new disclosure might also cause difficulty in applying the "new matter" rules. See Section 5.2.

[64] *See, e.g., Dana Corp. v. IPC Ltd. Partnership*, 860 F.2d 415, 418–420 (Fed. Cir. 1988).

[65] 908 F.2d 931 (Fed. Cir. 1990).

This evidence helped to establish a violation of the best mode requirement.[66]

The best mode requirement also has an objective component: was the best mode known to the inventor at the time the patent application was filed *disclosed* in the application in such clear terms that persons skilled in the art, reviewing the patent specification, would recognize it as the best mode and have sufficient information to practice it themselves?[67] Even if the specification includes a general reference to the best mode, the reference may be so lacking in detail that, as a practical matter, the best mode is concealed.[68] Alternatively, the best mode may be disclosed together with so many inferior modes that the best mode is inadequately differentiated.[69] The determination of whether the best mode was adequately disclosed must take into account the level of skill in the art and the extent to which particular information would be understood by those of ordinary skill, even if it were not made explicit.[70]

Although a patent specification must reveal the inventor's best mode of practicing the invention, the level of detail that must be included is not unlimited. The focus is on the invention *as claimed*.[71] The specification need not be equivalent to a "product specification" or a blueprint for mass production. It need not, for example, disclose all of the dimensions, tolerances, drawings and other information that a factory foreman would need to gear up for production. Such detailed information would be impractical to include in every patent, and it would be an unnecessary gift to the patentee's competitors. Still, the line between "best mode" and "product specification" can be a difficult one to draw.

In *Christianson v. Colt Industries*,[72] the court held that patents to various parts of the M-16 rifle were not invalid, even though they failed to disclose the dimensions and tolerances that would have been necessary for others

---

[66] *Northern Telecom*, 908 F.2d at 940.

[67] *See Fonar Corp. v. General Electric Co.*, 107 F.3d 1543, 1548 (Fed. Cir. 1997).

[68] *See, e.g., Spectra-Physics, Inc. v. Coherent, Inc.*, 827 F.2d 1524, 1536 (Fed. Cir. 1987).

[69] *See Randomex, Inc. v. Scopus Corp.*, 849 F.2d 585, 592 (Fed. Cir. 1988) (Mayer, J., dissenting).

[70] *See Chemcast Corp. v. Arco Indus. Corp.*, 913 F.2d 923, 927 (Fed. Cir. 1990). On the other hand, the best mode requirement cannot be satisfied *solely* by reference to information already known in the art. The applicant still must *disclose* the best mode. *See Robotic Vision Sys., Inc. v. View Eng'g, Inc.*, 112 F.3d 1163, 1165 (Fed. Cir. 1997) ("While a disclosure . . . is to be understood from the standpoint of one skilled in the relevant art, a certain basic disclosure is needed of the best mode."). It would not be sufficient, for example, that one skilled in the art could discover the best mode by reviewing technical literature in the field. *See Dana Corp. v. IPC Ltd. Partnership*, 860 F.2d 415, 418 (Fed. Cir. 1988). As is so often the case in patent law, there is only a fine distinction between evaluating the patent disclosure in light of knowledge available to those skilled in the art (which is permitted) and resorting to other sources to supply deficiencies in the patent disclosure (which is not permitted).

[71] *See Engel Indus., Inc. v. Lockformer Co.*, 946 F.2d 1528, 1531–32 (Fed. Cir. 1991).

[72] 822 F.2d 1544, 1562–63 (Fed. Cir. 1987).

to manufacture *interchangeable* parts. Because interchangeability was not a part of the invention claimed, the production details were deemed separable from the "best mode," even though, as a practical matter, the absence of those details would prevent others from competing in the market for rifle parts. The patents were still adequate to allow one to manufacture *a* rifle, even if it was not a rifle that the army, which required interchangeability with M-16 parts, would care to purchase.

For the same reason, a patent applicant is not always required to disclose the details of components that may be used with the claimed invention, but that are not part of the claimed invention itself. To borrow an analogy used by the court in *Randomex, Inc. v. Scopus Corp.*,[73] the inventor of a new engine might have to disclose the kind of fuel that was best for its operation, but the inventor of the engine would not have to disclose the best formula for making that fuel. It would be sufficient to disclose the fuel by brand name, as long as that brand, or its equivalent, were readily available. Engines and fuels are different arts, and a patent claiming only the engine need not disclose how to manufacture the fuel.

One case that put this principle to practice is *DeGeorge v. Bernier*,[74] where the claimed invention was electrical circuitry that would automatically indent paragraphs composed on a word processor. Even though the applicant did not disclose any details of the word processor, the court found no violation of the best mode requirement or the enablement requirement. The applicant did not claim to have invented a word processor, and one could practice the best mode *of the invention* even in conjunction with an inferior word processor.

Whether an inventor is required to disclose such information as the names of companies supplying parts, or the trade names of ingredients used in the inventor's composition, depends on the particular facts of the case.[75] If, for example, only one company sells an ingredient pure enough to produce an effective version of the patented compound, the inventor would probably be required to disclose the name of that company—at least if that information was not already generally known. In other cases, the name of a supplier might be a convenience, but its absence would not prevent others from practicing the inventor's best mode.

Companies that have manufactured a product prior to the filing date of their patent are particularly vulnerable to claims of a best mode violation. Something can always be found in the patentee's product, or in its manufacturing methods, that was not disclosed in the patent. Whatever that thing is, it will be singled out by those challenging the validity of the patent, who will argue that the patentee must have considered that thing

[73] 849 F.2d 585, 590 (Fed. Cir. 1988).
[74] 768 F.2d 1318, 1324–25 (Fed. Cir. 1985).
[75] *See Transco*, 38 F.3d at 560.

the "best" choice, or the patentee would have chosen something else.[76] In the end, the court will have to decide whether that choice is sufficiently related to the claimed invention that it should have been disclosed as the "best mode," or whether it is a choice that has little to do with the invention itself.

Some cases have suggested that the best mode requirement is violated only if the best mode was deliberately concealed.[77] Other cases, while still speaking of "concealment," suggest the "concealment" can be unintentional.[78] The latter view seems to have prevailed.[79] However, whether or not the "concealment" was intentional can still have important consequences. Under some circumstances, intentional concealment of the best mode can be considered "inequitable conduct"[80] that will render all claims of the patent, and possibly those of related patents, unenforceable.[81]

A best mode violation occurs only if the best mode contemplated by *the inventor* is inadequately disclosed in the patent specification. Knowledge of better modes will not be imputed to the inventor through legal fictions. For example, if other engineers working for the same corporation knew of an improvement to the basic invention, but that improvement was not communicated to the inventor before the filing date of the patent, failure to disclose that improvement in the patent specification would not violate the best mode requirement.[82] This result might encourage a "head in the sand" mentality among corporations, who could isolate researchers just to avoid the disclosure of more information than necessary. On the other hand, § 112 literally refers only to the knowledge of the "inventor," not the inventor's colleagues or employer, and it could be difficult to determine whether the inventor had been deliberately shielded from knowledge of improvements to his invention.

8.8 WRITTEN DESCRIPTION REQUIREMENT

Another requirement of a valid patent is the so-called written description requirement, taken from the following language of 35 U.S.C. § 112, Paragraph 1:

---

[76] *See Wahl Instruments, Inc. v. Acvious, Inc.*, 950 F.2d 1575, 1581 (Fed. Cir. 1991).

[77] "Invalidity for violation of the best mode requires intentional concealment of a better mode than was disclosed." *Brooktree Corp. v. Advanced Micro Devices, Inc.*, 977 F.2d 1555, 1575 (Fed. Cir. 1992).

[78] "[O]nly evidence of 'concealment,' whether *accidental* or intentional, is considered." *Spectra-Physics, Inc. v. Coherent, Inc.*, 827 F.2d 1524, 1535 (Fed. Cir. 1987) (emphasis supplied).

[79] *See U.S. Gypsum Co. v. Nat'l Gypsum Co.*, 74 F.3d 1209, 1215–16 (Fed. Cir. 1996).

[80] See Section 9.1.

[81] *See Consolidated Aluminum Corp. v. Foseco Int'l, Ltd.*, 910 F.2d 804 (Fed. Cir. 1990) (application's disclosure was of a "fictitious" and "inoperable" mode).

[82] *See Glaxo Inc. v. Novopharm Ltd.*, 52 F.3d. 1043, 1050 (Fed. Cir. 1995).

The specification shall contain a *written description* of the invention, and of the manner and process of making and using it, in such full, clear, concise, and exact terms as to enable any person skilled in the art to which it pertains, or with which it is most nearly connected, to make and use the same.

The written description requirement is one of the more nebulous concepts in patent law, in part because it is so easily confused with the definiteness and enablement requirements, and in part because its function seems largely redundant of those other tests. It is, after all, the function of the *claims* to "describe" the invention in precise terms.[83] Why should the *specification* be required to "describe" the invention? On the other hand, if the "description" simply means an *enabling disclosure*, as the remainder of the sentence seems to imply, why infer a description requirement as something distinct from the enablement requirement?

The Federal Circuit made some attempt to sort out the confusion in *Vas-Cath Inc. v. Mahurkar.*[84] As the court explained, the written description requirement can be characterized in part as an historical accident, traceable to the late eighteenth century when patents were not required to have claims. In those days, it was the function of the specification not only to enable the practice of the invention, but also to "describe" it so as to warn potential infringers. Today, the written description requirement generally comes into play where the claims have *changed* during prosecution of the patent application.

As discussed in Section 5.1, claim language is regularly changed or "amended" as a normal part of the process of patent prosecution. The patent examiner may object to the language of the claims as filed for any number of reasons, including the applicant's failure to adequately distinguish the invention from the prior art. A common response to such an objection is to modify the language of the claims. An applicant may decide to modify the claims as filed, or add more claims, even without an objection from the examiner, if the applicant thinks of new and better ways to describe the invention. Such changes are allowed as long as the new claims are adequately supported by the specification *as filed.* In most cases, the specification does not change during prosecution.

The filing date of the patent application is often critical to establishing the priority of the invention—in other words, whether the applicant is entitled to a patent because he was the first to invent, or whether the applicant is not entitled to a patent because someone else invented first.[85]

---

[83] According to the second paragraph of § 112, the specification must conclude with "one or more claims particularly pointing out and distinctly claiming the subject matter which the applicant regards as his invention." See Section 8.5.

[84] 935 F.2d 1555, 1560–64 (Fed. Cir. 1991).

[85] A foreign patent application can be of similar importance if the applicant relies on that application for his "filing date." See Section 12.3.

If an application was filed on a particular date, fully describing and enabling the practice of the invention, then the applicant's date of invention is, at the very latest, his filing date. Suppose, however, that the claims are amended during prosecution, so that they describe a new and different invention than what is disclosed in the original specification. In such a case, the date on which the patent application was filed would have no bearing on the actual date of invention. The written description requirement prevents this result by requiring a match between the invention as claimed and the invention as "described" in the specification. In some cases, the test is characterized as whether the claims are "adequately supported" by the specification.[86] The description requirement " 'guards against the inventor's overreaching by insisting that he recount his invention in such detail that his future claims can be determined to be encompassed within his original creation.' "[87]

It may appear that the enablement requirement, discussed in Section 8.6, would prevent an applicant from claiming more than the original application can support. If a modified claim really reflected a new and different invention, it would seem unlikely that the specification as filed would be adequate to enable one to practice that invention. However, according to the Federal Circuit and its predecessor court, " 'it is possible for a specification to *enable* the practice of invention as broadly as it is claimed, and still not *describe* that invention.' "[88]

An example of this distinction can be found in *Martin v. Mayer*,[89] where the invention concerned an electrical cable constructed of various layers, including a conductor, a dielectric and a "high frequency absorption medium." One of the claims at issue concerned a "harness" composed of more than one such cable. The specification as filed disclosed only a single cable. A person skilled in the art might have been *enabled* by the description of the solitary cable to construct a "harness" of several cables, but the specification included no written description of the "harness" to demonstrate that the applicant actually had conceived of that invention when the application was filed.[90]

---

[86] *Vas-Cath*, 935 F.2d at 1560.

[87] *Vas-Cath*, 935 F.2d at 1561. *See also In re Wright*, 866 F.2d 422, 424 (Fed. Cir. 1989) ("When the scope of a claim has been changed by amendment in such a way as to justify an assertion that it is directed to a *different invention* than was the original claim, it is proper to inquire whether the newly claimed subject matter was *described* in the patent application when filed as the invention of the applicant. That is the essence of the so-called 'description requirement'." (emphasis in original)).

[88] *Vas-Cath*, 935 F.2d at 1561 (citation omitted, emphasis in original).

[89] 823 F.2d 500 (Fed. Cir. 1987).

[90] *See also Lockwood v. American Airlines, Inc.*, 107 F.3d 1565, 1572 (Fed. Cir. 1997) (the specification must describe the invention itself, not only so much as necessary to make the invention *obvious*). *Martin* actually arose from an interference. See Section 5.4. Interferences are procedures conducted by the Patent Office to determine which one of two or

The same issue can arise if the specification, as originally filed, discloses a single species of a later-claimed genus. For example, the specification might disclose one example of a chemical compound within the broader group eventually claimed. The specification could enable persons skilled in the art to produce the other compounds in the genus—the single example in the specification, together with the suggestion of a broader genus provided by the claim itself, might be enough guidance to allow production of each compound without "undue experimentation."[91] However, the disclosure of the single species in the specification may be inadequate to show that the applicant had conceived of the broader genus at the time the patent application was filed.[92]

If a claim is broadened by omitting some detail of the preferred embodiment disclosed in the specification, a court may examine whether the omitted detail is "critical." In *In re Peters*,[93] for example, the specification disclosed an improved flat-panel television display, one element of which was tapered. Although the claims originally called for a tapered element, this limitation was later removed as unnecessary. The Patent Office held that the modified claim violated the written description requirement, because the specification as filed did not demonstrate that the applicant was in possession of the broader invention (i.e., tapered *and* untapered elements). The Federal Circuit reversed:

> The broadened claims merely omit an unnecessary limitation that had restricted one element of the invention to the exact and non-critical shape disclosed in the original patent. In sum, nothing in the original disclosure indicates or suggests that the tapered shape of the tips was essential or critical to either the operation or patentability of the invention.[94]

Since the original specification showed that the tapering was not important, the *invention* described by the applicant was not limited to that embodiment.[95]

more applicants claiming the same subject matter is the first and true inventor. The claims (or "counts") addressed in the interference often differ from the claims as originally filed by one or more of the parties to the interference, and one of the issues that may be debated is whether a specification, as filed, shows that the applicant had invented the subject matter of the count.

91 See Section 8.6.

92 *See Regents of the University of California v. Eli Lilly & Co.*, 119 F.3d 1559, 1567–68 (Fed. Cir. 1997); *Vas-Cath*, 935 F.2d at 1561–62.

93 723 F.2d 891 (Fed. Cir. 1983).

94 *Peters*, 723 F.2d at 893–94.

95 The *Martin* opinion does not discuss whether the difference between a single cable and a bundle of cables is "critical." However, the court referred to uncontradicted evidence that "such bundling was not conventional as applied to cables with a conductive outer layer." 823 F.2d at 505.

Thus, a patent satisfies the written description requirement if the specification "conveys with reasonable clarity to those skilled in the art that, as of the filing date [of the application], he or she was in possession *of the invention.* The invention is, for purposes of the 'written description' inquiry, *whatever is now claimed.*"[96] This does not mean that the specification has to describe the later-claimed invention in the very same terms. In *In re Wright,*[97] for example, the claim language "not permanently fixed," as applied to a microcapsule powder used in an imaging process, did not appear in the specification. However, the specification included enough information, including a warning that the powder not be disturbed, to show that the invention as originally contemplated and disclosed included powder that was "not permanently fixed."

It is important that the invention be described in terms adequate to show that the applicant has *invented* the claimed subject matter, not just that he has a plan for doing so. This problem has been known to arise where the patent claims a particular variety of DNA. "An adequate written description of DNA requires more than a mere statement that it is a part of the invention and reference to a potential method for isolating it; what is required is a description of the DNA itself."[98] In these cases it is difficult to disentangle the written description requirement from the enablement requirement. In *Fiers v. Revel,*[99] for example, the court seems to fear that the applicants were claiming an invention much broader than what they had so far achieved: "Claiming all DNA's that achieve a result without defining the means that will do so is not in compliance with the description requirement; it is an attempt to preempt the future before it has arrived."[100] Unless the issue arises from a discrepancy between the originally filed specification and a *modified* claim, this concern should be one that can be adequately addressed by the enablement requirement.[101]

8.9 NOVELTY

An invention can be patented only if it is *new.* Hence, an important part of patent prosecution and patent litigation is comparing the claimed invention to prior inventions to determine if the claims are "novel." Prior inventions, as well as patents, patent applications and publications that disclose prior inventions, are known as "prior art references." The various

---

[96] *Vas-Cath,* 935 F.2d at 1563–64 (emphasis in original); *see also Waldemar Link v. Osteonics Corp.,* 32 F.3d 556, 559 (Fed. Cir. 1994).
[97] 866 F.2d 422, 425 (Fed. Cir. 1989).
[98] *Fiers v. Revel,* 984 F.2d 1164, 1170 (Fed. Cir. 1993).
[99] 984 F.2d 1164 (Fed. Cir. 1993).
[100] *Fiers,* 984 F.2d at 1171.
[101] See Section 8.6.

kinds of prior art references are listed in 35 U.S.C. § 102, a complex provision discussed in detail in the sections that follow. If a claimed invention is identical to one or more prior art references, the claim is said to be "anticipated."[102] If the claimed invention differs from the prior art, but the differences are of the sort that would occur to a person of ordinary skill, the claim is said to be "obvious."[103] Either is sufficient grounds for holding a claim unpatentable or invalid.

8.9.1 Categories of Prior Art

35 U.S.C. § 102 is one of the most important provisions of the Patent Act, but because of its length and structure it is also one of the most difficult to grasp. The provision begins "A person shall be entitled to a patent unless . . ." and the following seven paragraphs (§ 102(a)–§ 102 (g)) list various circumstances under which a patent *cannot* be granted, most of them related to a lack of novelty. If a patent issued even though it violates one of these conditions, the patent can be held invalid by the courts.

8.9.1.1 Prior Knowledge, Use, Patents and Publications (§ 102(a))

Section 102(a) reads as follows:

A person shall be entitled to a patent unless—

(a) the invention was known or used by others in this country, or patented or described in a printed publication in this or a foreign country, before the invention thereof by the applicant for patent. . . .

This section identifies four kinds of prior art reference that might invalidate a patent if they occurred before the applicant's date of invention:[104]

• Prior "knowledge" of the invention by others in *this* country.

• Prior "use" of the invention by others in *this* country.

• A prior patent on the invention in *any* country.

• A prior "printed publication" of the invention in *any* country.[105]

---

[102] See Section 8.9.5.
[103] See Section 8.9.6.
[104] The "date of invention" is discussed in Section 8.9.2.
[105] Prior use or knowledge of the invention in a foreign country is excluded from § 102(a), perhaps because in an earlier era such knowledge or use would have been difficult to verify. However, the increasingly global nature of both commerce and scientific research has spurred some commentators to suggest that the national distinctions embodied in § 102 are out of date.

Patents, printed publications, prior "use" and prior "knowledge" are four common categories of prior art. One feature they share is that, to some degree, they all place the invention in the possession of the public.[106] If an invention has already been the subject of a patent or printed publication, or if the invention is one that has already been known or used, granting a patent on the invention would not "promote the progress of . . . the useful arts."[107] On the contrary, it would take away an invention that the public had already enjoyed. In § 102, "[s]ociety, speaking through Congress and the courts, has said 'thou shalt not take it away.' "[108]

Although prior use, prior knowledge, patents and publications are fairly straightforward concepts, they have been refined through judicial analysis, primarily to clarify the extent to which a reference must be publicly available. For example, while "known or used" could literally refer to secret knowledge or secret use, § 102(a) has been interpreted to require knowledge or use that is accessible to the public.[109] Similarly, the term "patented" means that the invention was *disclosed* in a patent, not merely that it was encompassed within the scope of a broad patent *claim*.[110] "Patented" can refer to the rights granted by foreign countries, even if they differ somewhat from U.S. patent rights,[111] but the foreign "patent" must be "available to the public."[112]

"[D]escribed in a printed publication" may be the language of § 102(a) which has received the most intense judicial scrutiny.[113] The courts have made clear that "printed" is not to be taken too literally. Information that is distributed through other media, such as photographs, CD-ROMs or microfilm, can qualify as "printed publications."[114] The two critical characteristics of a "printed publication" are (1) that it is "accessible" to the public and (2) that it includes an "enabling disclosure."

---

[106] *See Carella v. Starlight Archery & Pro Line Co.*, 804 F.2d 135, 139 (Fed. Cir. 1986). A prior patent at least gives the public *knowledge* of the invention and the expectation of possessing it as soon as the patent has expired.

[107] See Section 1.1.

[108] *Kimberly-Clark Corp. v. Johnson & Johnson*, 745 F.2d 1437, 1453–54 (Fed. Cir. 1984).

[109] *See Carella*, 804 F.2d at 139.

[110] *See In re Benno*, 768 F.2d 1340, 1346 (Fed. Cir. 1985).

[111] *See In re Carlson*, 983 F.2d 1032 (Fed. Cir. 1992).

[112] *See Carlson*, 983 F.2d at 1037. The standard of "availability" is rather low. *See Id.* at 1037–38 (a German Geschmacksmuster can qualify as a "patent" under § 102, even if one must travel to a courthouse in a remote German city in order to see the design to which it applies). Note that a patent document can also constitute a "printed publication."

[113] The same term also appears in the statutory bar provision of 35 U.S.C. § 102(b). See Section 8.10.

[114] *See In re Hall*, 781 F.2d 897, 898 (Fed. Cir. 1986) ("The statutory phrase 'printed publication' has been interpreted to give effect to ongoing advances in the technologies of data storage, retrieval, and dissemination.").

"Accessible" means that "interested members of the public could obtain the information if they wanted to."[115] Most books, technical journals and other materials normally thought of as "publications" are clearly accessible to the public, but inventions are sometimes disclosed in classified documents or documents distributed only on a confidential basis (e.g., documents for the internal use of a corporation). Those do not qualify as "publications."[116] On the other hand, distribution of even a small number of copies without restriction can be considered sufficient.[117]

Some of the most difficult cases arise when a document has not been distributed, but it has been made available in a library or similar collection. In *In re Hall*,[118] for example, the potentially invalidating reference was a doctoral thesis. The thesis had not been "published" in the usual sense, but it had been deposited in a university library in Germany where it was, theoretically, available for review. The court held that "a single catalogued thesis in one university" might "constitute sufficient accessibility to those interested in the art exercising reasonable diligence."[119] On the other hand, in *In re Cronyn*,[120] the court held that three undergraduate theses did not constitute "printed publications." The court held that, in this case, the documents "were not accessible to the public because they had not been either cataloged or indexed in a meaningful way."[121] They could have been located only by sorting through a collection of index cards kept in a shoe box in the university's chemistry department. These cases obviously draw fine, and somewhat arbitrary, distinctions. Although the undergraduate theses in *Cronyn* would have been difficult to track down, as a practical matter the thesis in *Hall* might have been equally elusive. Still, the courts must draw the line somewhere, and they repeatedly emphasize the importance of the particular facts in each case.[122]

The other important requirement of a "printed publication" is that it

---

[115] *Constant v. Advanced Micro-Devices, Inc.*, 848 F.2d 1560, 1569 (Fed. Cir. 1988). If the publication is "accessible," it is irrelevant whether anyone in particular actually reviewed it. *Id.*

[116] *See Northern Telecom, Inc. v. Datapoint Corp.*, 908 F.2d 931, 936–37 (Fed. Cir. 1990). They might, however, serve as evidence of a prior invention under § 102(g). See Section 8.9.1.3

[117] *See Massachusetts Institute of Technology v. A.B. Fortia*, 774 F.2d 1104, 1109 (Fed. Cir. 1985) (paper that was discussed at a conference attended by 50 to 100 interested persons and that was distributed "on request" to at least six persons without restrictions, constituted a "publication"); *but cf. Preemption Devices, Inc. v. Minnesota Mining & Mfg. Co.*, 732 F.2d 903, 906 (Fed. Cir. 1984) (six copies of an article sent to a "friend" were not a "publication").

[118] 781 F.2d 897 (Fed. Cir. 1986).

[119] *Hall*, 781 F.2d at 900.

[120] 890 F.2d 1158 (Fed. Cir. 1989).

[121] *Cronyn*, 890 F.2d at 1161.

[122] *See, e.g., Cronyn*, 890 F.2d at 1161.

include an "enabling disclosure" of the invention.[123] An enabling disclosure is a description of the invention that would allow a person skilled in the art to make and use the invention without undue experimentation.[124] If, for example, a marketing brochure boasts of the advantages of a process, but it does not include enough information to allow the process to be duplicated, the brochure lacks an enabling disclosure.[125] In deciding whether a disclosure is "enabling," the knowledge that would be available to those of skill in the art can be taken into account. In other words, the publication does not have to include information that would already be known to persons of ordinary skill.[126]

8.9.1.2 Prior Applications (§ 102(e))[127]

Another category of prior art reference, not discussed in § 102(a), is a patent *application*. The circumstances under which a patent application can constitute prior art are set forth in § 102(e). The language of the paragraph is rather heavy in legalese:

A person shall be entitled to a patent unless—

(e) the invention was described in a patent granted on an application for patent by another filed in the United States before the invention thereof by the applicant for patent, or on an international application by another who has fulfilled the requirements of paragraphs (1), (2), and (4) of section 371(c) of this title before the invention thereof by the applicant for patent. . . .

The gist of this paragraph is to add the following to the list of potential prior art references:

• A patent application, filed by *another* inventor, before the applicant's date of invention, if that application eventually issued as a patent.

Thus, if Inventor A had a patent application on file before Inventor B had even conceived of the invention, then Inventor A's application would be prior art to Inventor B, even if Inventor's A's application did not issue as a patent until later. The application could be a United States application, or it could be an international application, as long as certain docu-

---

[123] *In re Epstein*, 32 F.3d 1559, 1568 (Fed. Cir. 1994); *Constant v. Advanced Micro-Devices, Inc.*, 848 F.2d 1560, 1569 (Fed. Cir. 1988).

[124] The enabling disclosure requirement also applies to patent specifications. See Section 8.6.

[125] *See Reading & Bates Construction Co. v. Baker Energy Resources Corp.*, 748 F.2d 645, 651–52 (Fed. Cir. 1984).

[126] *In re Donohue*, 766 F.2d 531, 533 (Fed. Cir. 1985).

[127] There is no apparent logic to the ordering of paragraphs in § 102. They will therefore be discussed in the order that seems easiest to understand, rather than in the order in which they appear in the statute.

ments had been deposited and fees paid in the United States. Note that § 102(e) applies only to patent applications that eventually issue.

8.9.1.3 Prior Inventions (§ 102(g))

A final category of prior art reference[128] is embodied in § 102(g):

A person shall be entitled to a patent unless—

(g) before the applicant's invention thereof the invention was made in this country by another who had not abandoned, suppressed, or concealed it. . . .

"Made," in this context, means "invented." Thus, § 102(g) adds the following category of prior art reference to those set forth in §§ 102(a) and (e):

- an invention by another, in this country, which had not been abandoned, suppressed or concealed.

Two inventors, working independently, can conceive of the same invention. The telephone, for example, is said to have been invented independently, and almost simultaneously, by Alexander Graham Bell and Elisha Gray. In most countries, priority is awarded to the first inventor to file a patent application, but in the United States the patent goes to the first to *invent.* Section 102(g) denies a patent to an applicant who was not the first to invent.[129]

There is, however, an important exception. The first invention does not count against a later inventor if the first invention was "abandoned, suppressed, or concealed." An invention is "deemed abandoned, suppressed, or concealed if, within a reasonable time after completion, no steps are taken to make the invention publicly known."[130] Abandonment, suppression and concealment can be inferred if, after a reasonable period of time, the first inventor has not filed a patent application, used the invention in public, embodied the invention in a product for sale or described the invention in a publication.[131] This exception to the "first to invent" rule rewards those who make inventions available to the public, and penalizes those who hide or abandon inventions.[132]

---

[128] Other than those that apply only to the statutory bar provisions discussed in Sections 8.10–8.11.

[129] If the contest for priority occurs in the course of prosecuting a patent application, the result can be an interference proceeding, discussed in Section 5.4. However, § 102(g) can also be invoked in litigation in order to invalidate an issued patent. *New Idea Farm Equip. Corp. v. Sperry Corp.*, 916 F.2d 1561, 1566 (Fed. Cir. 1990).

[130] *Correge v. Murphy*, 705 F.2d 1326, 1330 (Fed. Cir. 1983) (citation omitted).

[131] *See Correge*, 705 F.2d at 1330.

[132] *See Checkpoint Sys., Inc. v. U.S. Int'l Trade Comm'n*, 54 F.3d 765, 761 (Fed. Cir. 1995).

If the delay in publicizing an invention, or applying for a patent, is more than a few years, abandonment may be presumed.[133] This presumption can be overcome by evidence that the delay was caused by efforts to perfect the invention.[134] However, if the delay is caused by efforts to *commercialize* the invention, without altering the invention itself, the presumption still holds.[135] In *Lutzker v. Plet*,[136] where the invention was a device for making canapés, the first inventor (Lutzker) waited more than four years after completing the invention before disclosing it to the public at a trade show. By the time of the trade show, the second inventor (Plet) had invented the device independently and filed a patent application. Lutzker argued that the delay should be excused because it had been due to efforts to perfect the invention. The Patent Office, affirmed by the court, disagreed. The delay was attributed to the development of a recipe book, packaging and other things unrelated to the invention itself. Lutzker was therefore found to have abandoned, suppressed or concealed the invention, and his activities did not prevent the issuance of a patent to Plet.[137]

Two points should be mentioned about the timing of an "abandonment." First, the "abandonment" can be nullified if the first inventor renews his efforts to patent the invention, or to make it available to the public, before the second inventor "enters the field."[138] The first inventor would be credited with the date of renewed activity as his "date of invention." Thus, if Lutzker had begun work on a patent application before Plet entered the field, his earlier inactivity could have been overlooked. Second, § 102(g) refers to prior inventions that "had" not been abandoned, suppressed or concealed, implying that an invention abandoned,

---

[133] *See Lutzker v. Plet*, 843 F.2d 1364, 1367 (Fed. Cir. 1988) (discussing cases in which delays of 29 months to four years were held sufficient to show abandonment, suppression or concealment). However, there is no period of time that is unreasonable *per se*. "Rather a determination of abandonment, suppression or concealment has 'consistently been based on equitable principles and public policy as applied to the facts of each case.' " *Checkpoint*, 54 F.3d at 761 (citation omitted).

[134] *See Lutzker*, 843 F.2d at 1367.

[135] Some cases, however, have held that delays in bringing a product to market which are commensurate with "reasonable business practices" will not be held against the first inventor. *See Checkpoint*, 54 F.3d at 762.

[136] 843 F.2d 1364 (Fed. Cir. 1988).

[137] The court was influenced by the fact that the recipe book and other items accounting for the delay were not related to the disclosure in Lutzker's eventual patent application. *Lutzker*, 843 F.2d at 1367–68. In the later *Checkpoint* case, the court was more inclined to regard commercialization activities as a valid excuse, where the first inventor made no effort to file an application. Rather, the invention would have been first introduced to the public through a product, which the first inventor had developed as expeditiously as possible. *See Checkpoint*, 54 F.3d at 762–63.

[138] *See Lutzker*, 843 F.2d at 1368; *Paulik v. Rizkalla*, 760 F.2d 1270, 1275–76 (Fed. Cir. 1985).

suppressed or concealed *after* the entry into the field of the second inventor would still be effective as prior art.[139]

8.9.2 Date of Invention

To evaluate whether a patent, patent application, publication or other reference is *prior* art under §§ 102(a) or (e), it is necessary to determine the patentee's (or applicant's) "date of invention." In applying § 102(g), it is necessary to determine the "date of invention" of both the patentee (or applicant) and the alleged prior inventor. References *subsequent* to the patentee's (or applicant's) date of invention have no relevance under these statutory provisions.[140]

"Invention," as defined in patent law, involves two steps: "conception" and "reduction to practice." "Conception" is the mental act of invention—the moment of insight when the inventor imagines the thing that ultimately will be claimed. As formally defined by the Federal Circuit, conception requires the formation in the inventor's mind of "a definite and permanent idea of the invention, including every feature of the subject matter sought to be patented."[141] If the inventor has done no more than recognize a problem, the conception of the invention is still incomplete.[142] Conception is complete only when the inventor finds the *solution* to a problem, and the solution is worked out in sufficient detail, in the inventor's mind, that persons of ordinary skill in the art could put the inventor's ideas to practice without extensive research or undue experimentation.[143]

"Reduction to practice" means reducing the idea to a physical embodiment and, in most cases, testing it to confirm that it will work.[144]

---

[139] The language of the statute seems clear. However, the Federal Circuit has not ruled on this issue, and it could be argued that ignoring a later abandonment would hinder the policy of making inventions available to the public.

[140] They may, however, be relevant under the "statutory bar" provisions discussed in Section 8.10.

[141] *Sewall v. Walters*, 21 F.3d 411, 415 (Fed. Cir. 1994); *see also Hybritech Inc. v. Monoclonal Antibodies, Inc.*, 802 F.2d 1367, 1376 (Fed. Cir. 1986).

[142] *See Morgan v. Hirsch*, 728 F.2d 1449 (Fed. Cir. 1994).

[143] *Sewall*, 21 F.3d at 415; *see also Burroughs Wellcome Co. v. Barr Labs., Inc.*, 40 F.3d 1223, 1228 (Fed. Cir. 1994) ("Conception is complete only when the idea is so clearly defined in the inventor's mind that only ordinary skill would be necessary to reduce the invention to practice, without extensive research or experimentation. . . . An idea is definite and permanent when the inventor has a specific, settled idea, a particular solution to the problem at hand, not just a general goal or research plan he hopes to pursue.").

[144] *See Scott v. Finney*, 34 F.3d 1058 (Fed. Cir. 1994) (reduction to practice means demonstrating that the invention is " 'suitable for its intended purpose' " (citation omitted)); *Newkirk v. Lulejian*, 825 F.2d 1581, 1582 (Fed. Cir. 1987) ("proof of actual reduction to practice requires demonstration that the embodiment relied upon as evidence of priority actually worked for its intended purpose").

In the case of an apparatus, reduction to practice means that the apparatus was assembled, at least in prototype. In the case of a method, reduction to practice means that the method was actually performed. A patent claim is not reduced to practice until there is a physical embodiment that includes all of the elements of the claim.[145]

The amount of "testing" of the physical embodiment necessary for reduction to practice varies considerably depending on the nature of the invention. The courts are instructed to employ a "common sense approach."[146] Some devices are considered so simple, and their effectiveness so obvious, that no testing at all is required.[147] On the other hand, some inventions require careful evaluation under conditions that duplicate, or simulate, the intended working environment of the invention. The testing required is whatever is reasonably necessary to demonstrate that the invention will work.[148] Even where testing is required, it is not necessary to demonstrate that the invention is so refined that it is ready to market.[149] A prototype that is not yet of commercial quality may be sufficient to show that the principle of the invention is sound.[150] Moreover, "[t]esting need not show utility beyond a possibility of failure, but only utility beyond a probability of failure."[151]

In a few cases, courts have held the subject matter of an invention to be so unpredictable that the invention could not be fully *conceived* until experiments had been performed and the results evaluated. Conception and reduction to practice are, in these cases, simultaneous. This circumstance is most likely to occur in the fields of chemistry and biotechnology, where useful combinations can sometimes be discovered only by trial and error. In *Smith v. Bousquet*,[152] for example, the court held that the effectiveness of a chemical as an insecticide, on particular species and under particular conditions, could not be predicted until realistic experiments were carried out. Until then, plans to use the

---

[145] *UMC Electronics Co. v. U.S.*, 816 F.2d 647, 652 (Fed. Cir. 1987).

[146] *Scott*, 34 F.3d at 1061.

[147] *See Scott*, 34 F.3d at 1061.

[148] "[The] common sense approach prescribes more scrupulous testing under circumstances approaching actual use conditions when the problem includes many uncertainties. On the other hand, when the problem to be solved does not present myriad variables, common sense similarly permits little or no testing to show the soundness of the principles of operation of the invention." *Scott*, 34 F.3d at 1063.

[149] "Reduction to practice does not require 'that the invention, when tested, be in a commercially satisfactory stage of development.' " *Scott*, 34 F.3d at 1061 (citation omitted); *DSL Dynamic Sciences Ltd. v. Union Switch & Signal, Inc.*, 928 F.2d 1122, 1126 (Fed. Cir. 1991).

[150] *See Scott*, 34 F.3d at 1062.

[151] *Scott*, 34 F.3d at 1062.

[152] 111 F.2d 157 (C.C.P.A. 1940).

chemical as an insecticide were mere hope or speculation, not an invention.[153]

The "reduction to practice" discussed so far is *actual* reduction to practice. The filing of a patent application is considered a *"constructive* reduction to practice."[154] "Constructive" is a word often used in the law when an act is treated as though it were one thing, when it is actually something else.[155] Although filing a patent application is not a reduction to practice at all, it is treated as though it were for purposes of fixing the date of invention. Therefore, an inventor who never produces a physical embodiment of the invention, or who does so only later, will be considered to have reduced to practice on the date the patent application is filed.[156] In any case, the filing date of the application is the presumptive date of invention for any patent, pending proof of earlier conception and reduction to practice.[157]

Both conception and reduction to practice play a role in fixing the "date of invention" for purposes of determining if a reference is *prior* art. Since an invention is complete when it is both conceived and reduced to practice, any reference dated later than the applicant's reduction to practice is not prior art. Thus, if an applicant reduced to practice on December 31, 1990, a printed publication distributed on January 1, 1991, for example, would not be *prior* art under § 102(a). However, in some cases an inventor must rely on his earlier date of conception to prevent a reference from qualifying as prior art. This is allowed if, and only if, the inventor was "diligent" in reducing the invention to practice, beginning on a date prior to the date of the reference.[158]

This principle is usually applied in the context of § 102(g), where the question is whether the applicant (or patentee) was first to invent. The language of the statute makes explicit reference to diligence:

A person shall be entitled to a patent unless—

(g) before the applicant's invention thereof the invention was made in this country by another who had not abandoned, suppressed, or concealed it. *In determining priority of invention, there shall be considered not only the respective date of concep-*

---

[153] More recently, the concept of simultaneous conception and reduction to practice has been applied to inventions involving DNA. *See, e.g., Amgen, Inc. v. Chugai Pharmaceutical Co.*, 927 F.2d 1200, 1206–7 (Fed. Cir. 1991).

[154] *Hazeltine Corp. v. U.S.*, 820 F.2d 1190, 1196 (Fed. Cir. 1987).

[155] See the discussion of "constructive notice" in Section 11.8.3.2.

[156] Treating the filing of a patent application as equivalent to producing a physical embodiment of the invention is not so far-fetched, since the application should include all of the information necessary to allow one skilled in the art to complete such an embodiment without undue experimentation. If it does not include that information, the patent will be invalid for lack of enablement. See Section 8.6.

[157] *Bausch & Lomb, Inc. v. Barnes-Hind/Hydrocurve, Inc.*, 796 F.2d 443, 449 (Fed. Cir. 1986).

[158] *See In re Mulder*, 716 F.2d 1542, 1545 (Fed. Cir. 1983).

tion and reduction to practice of the invention, but also the reasonable diligence of one who was first to conceive and last to reduce to practice, from a time prior to conception by the other.

The easiest cases to resolve are those in which the first inventor to conceive of the invention is also the first to reduce to practice. Suppose, for example, that Inventor A, who has received a patent, sues an infringer. The infringer argues that the invention of Inventor B is prior art to Inventor A's patent under § 102(g). If Inventor A's date of conception precedes Inventor B's date of conception, *and* Inventor's A's date of reduction to practice precedes Inventor B's date of reduction to practice, Inventor B's work is not prior art. If the situation is reversed (Inventor B's dates of conception and reduction to practice precede Inventor A's respective dates), then Inventor B's invention is prior art to Inventor A.

The more complex situations arise if the first inventor to conceive of his invention was the last to reduce to practice. Where this is the case, the first to conceive is regarded as the first to invent if, but only if, he was diligent in reducing to practice. To return to the example, if Inventor A was the first to conceive of the invention, but before he could reduce the invention to practice Inventor B both conceived and reduced to practice, the patent to Inventor A would be valid only if Inventor A had been diligent from a time *prior* to B's date of conception.[159]

The rules can be more easily visualized with the aid of a time-line. In the following examples, C stands for the date of conception and RTP for the date of reduction to practice. Time progresses from left to right. Assume that Inventor A has received a patent. Inventor B developed the same invention independently, and his work is alleged to be prior art under § 102(g). In the first example, B's invention is not prior art because he was last to conceive and last to reduce to practice:

A: C - - - - - - - - - RTP
B: C - - - - - - - - - - - - RTP

In the second example, B's invention is prior art because he was first to conceive and first to reduce to practice:

A: C - - - - - - - - - - - - RTP
B: C - - - - - - - - - RTP

---

[159] The time period that begins just before a rival's conception and ends with one's own reduction to practice is frequently called the "critical period" for diligence. *See, e.g., Bey v. Kollonitsch*, 806 F.2d 1024, 1025–26 (Fed. Cir. 1986). Earlier lapses in diligence can be overlooked.

In the third example, A was first to conceive, but B was first to reduce to practice. B's invention is not prior art *if* A was diligent, though not as swift as B, in reducing his invention to practice:

A: C - - - - - - - - - - - - - - - RTP (diligent?)
B: C - - - - - RTP

In the last example, B was first to conceive, but A was first to reduce to practice. B's invention is prior art *if* B was diligent in reducing his invention to practice:

A: C - - - - - RTP
B: C - - - - - - - - - - - - - - - RTP (diligent?)

The purpose of this rather confusing set of rules is to reward inventors who are the first to conceive of an idea, while at the same time encouraging inventors to bring their ideas to a practical end, or a public disclosure, as soon as possible.

"Diligence" in this context means reasonable efforts to reduce the invention to practice or to file a patent application. "Diligent" effort must be relatively continuous. Some excuses have been recognized for lapses of effort—most notably the need to complete some other invention before the first can be reduced to practice.[160] The courts will also consider "the reasonable everyday problems and limitations encountered by an inventor," including illness, poverty, the need for an occasional vacation or the need to make a living by other means.[161] However, efforts to fund or commercialize the invention, or time devoted to an unrelated invention, are not considered adequate excuses for delay.[162]

8.9.3 Burdens of Proof—Conception, Reduction to Practice and Diligence

If a question of priority turns on the filing date of a patent application or the publication date of a technical journal, the proof is relatively straightforward. The filing date of a patent application is a matter of public record, and the publication date of a journal is usually easy to verify.

---

[160] *See, e.g., Keizer v. Bradley,* 270 F.2d 396 (C.C.P.A. 1959).
[161] *See Griffith v. Kanamaru,* 816 F.2d 624, 626–27 (Fed. Cir. 1987). If the reduction to practice had been a "constructive" reduction to practice, accomplished by filing a patent application, the patent attorney's need to work on other applications can be considered an adequate excuse for delay, if the applications were handled in the order received, or if there was a need to work on related applications as a group. *See Bey,* 806 F.2d at 1028–30.
[162] *See Griffith,* 816 F.2d at 627–28.

If, however, priority depends on dates of conception and reduction to practice, the facts can be much harder to establish. A conception date, in particular, can be a difficult thing to prove because the essential activity occurs entirely in the mind of the inventor.

Whenever there is a successful invention, there are sure to be those who purport to have had the same idea first. By the same token, it is easy for any patentee faced with prior art to claim that his conception occurred even earlier. The courts have therefore established certain rules governing the proof required to establish conception and reduction to practice.

First, the date on which a patent application is filed is presumed to be the applicant's date of invention in the absence of other evidence.[163] During prosecution of a patent application, if the applicant needs to establish an earlier date of invention in order to pre-date a potential prior art reference, this can be accomplished under certain circumstances by means of a sworn affidavit from the inventor establishing prior conception and reduction to practice.[164] This is known as "swearing behind" a reference. In litigation, however, dates of conception and reduction to practice must be demonstrated by "clear and convincing evidence."[165] This is true whether it is the patentee who is trying to disqualify potential prior art, or whether it is the accused infringer who is attempting to establish prior conception and reduction to practice by another, in order to make a case for invalidity under § 102(g).[166]

A date of conception cannot be established entirely by the inventor's own testimony. Such testimony is simply too untrustworthy. Instead, claim to a conception date must be *corroborated,* usually by the testimony of a non-inventor who was made aware of the inventor's work soon after the date in question.[167] For this reason, engineers involved in organized research programs often have their laboratory notebooks periodically reviewed, signed and dated by a colleague.[168] Such a notebook can be the best evidence of what was conceived and when, and it is a practice strongly recommended to anyone pursuing work that may eventually prove patentable. Dates of reduction to practice and allegations of diligence also must be corroborated by evidence independent of the inventor.[169] Al-

---

[163] *Bausch & Lomb, Inc. v. Barnes-Hind/Hydrocurve, Inc.,* 796 F.2d 443, 449 (Fed. Cir. 1986).

[164] *See* 37 C.F.R. § 1.131.

[165] See Section 8.2.

[166] The ultimate burden of proof on validity, however, always remains with the party challenging the patent. *See Innovative Scuba Concepts, Inc. v. Feder Indus., Inc.,* 26 F.3d 1112, 1115 (Fed. Cir. 1994). Dates of conception and reduction to practice can also be critical in interference proceedings. These are discussed in Section 5.4.

[167] *Price v. Symsek,* 988 F.2d 1187, 1194 (Fed. Cir. 1993); *Coleman v. Dines,* 754 F.2d 353, 359 (Fed. Cir. 1985).

[168] The colleague, however, cannot be a co-inventor. See Section 6.1.

[169] *Hahn v. Wong,* 892 F.2d 1028, 1032–33 (Fed. Cir. 1989)

though eye-witness testimony is often best, corroboration is subject to a "rule of reason" which allows the inventor's claims to be substantiated by any evidence that is sufficient to establish credibility.[170] For example, testimony regarding a reduction to practice might be corroborated by dated invoices for the parts that were used to build an embodiment of the invention.[171]

8.9.4 Prior Work by the Same Inventor

The kinds of prior art listed in §§ 102(a), (e) and (g) are limited, expressly or by implication, to prior inventions, patents, patent applications, printed publications, public knowledge or public use attributable to persons *other than the inventor*.[172] This limitation can be difficult to apply in cases where a patent names two or more joint inventors.[173] For example, can a publication by A alone be considered prior art to the joint invention of A and B? In these cases, courts resort to the concept of the "inventive entity," which is simply a way of referring to a specific group of inventors. A reference can be considered prior art to a patent or patent application if it is attributable to a *different inventive entity*. This is true whether the prior inventive entity is composed of entirely different individuals, or whether some individuals are common to both inventive entities. Thus, a publication by A, describing his work alone, could invalidate the subsequent patent of A and B together.[174] A publication describing the work

---

[170] *See Coleman*, 754 F.2d at 360; *Hahn*, 892 F.2d at 1032–33 (corroborating evidence of reduction to practice " 'may consist of the testimony of a witness, other than the inventor, to the actual reduction to practice or it may consist of evidence of surrounding facts and circumstances independent of information received from the inventor' " (citation omitted)); *Holmwood v. Sugavanam*, 948 F.2d 1236, 1239 (Fed. Cir. 1991).

[171] *See Lacotte v. Thomas*, 758 F.2d 611, 613 (Fed. Cir. 1985).

[172] *See In re Katz*, 687 F.2d 450, 454 (C.C.P.A. 1982). Section 102(a) refers to an invention "patented or described in a printed publication . . . before the invention thereof by the applicant." While there is no explicit exception for the applicant's own work, clearly the applicant himself cannot patent or describe an invention in a printed publication before he has invented it. It might be possible for the applicant to produce a patent or publication in comparison to which his later invention is *obvious* (see Section 8.9.6), but the courts have generally ruled out the use of an inventor's own work as the basis for an obviousness challenge. *See Id.* An important exception is created by the *statutory bar* provisions (see Sections 8.10–8.11). A statutory bar, based either on anticipation or obviousness, can be triggered by the inventor's own activities, if they occur more than one year before an application is filed. Also, a prior patent by the same inventor can raise issues of double patenting. See Section 8.12.

[173] See Section 6.1.

[174] This is one occasion on which A and B might reconsider whether B was properly named as a joint inventor. If B's contribution did not rise to the level of invention, and if B was named as an inventor only accidentally, it would be possible to correct the patent to name only A as the inventor, thereby removing the prior publication as a potential prior art reference. See Section 6.1.

of A and B together could invalidate a subsequent patent to A alone. But a publication describing the work of A and B together would not be prior art to the subsequent patent of A and B.[175] Note that the question is not who *wrote* the publication, but rather whose *invention* the publication describes. A publication by A and B describing the work of A alone would not be § 102(a) prior art to A's subsequent patent.[176]

Section 103(c) provides another twist. Even if a prior invention is attributable to a different inventive entity, if the invention is *only* a potential reference under § 102(f) or (g), and if the prior invention and the subsequent application are owned by the *same person* (or both are subject to an obligation to assign to the same person[177]), the prior invention cannot render the subsequent patent invalid for obviousness.[178] This provision applies most often where several people are working on a project for the same corporation,[179] and it prevents the work of one person from invalidating the work of a colleague, recognizing that both are generally working under the same direction and toward the same goal. Note that this provision does not apply to references, such as patents and publications, that would have placed the work of the first inventor before the public.

8.9.5 Anticipation

Establishing that a patent, patent application, publication or other potential reference falls within one of the categories of prior art set forth in § 102 is only a first step. Even if a reference falls within one of the prior art categories, and even if it can be shown to be *prior* art to the patent or application in question, it still must be determined whether or not the invention claimed is novel when compared to the reference. If the claimed invention is identical to subject matter disclosed or embodied in the prior art reference, the claim is "anticipated" and invalid for lack of novelty.

Determining if a claim is anticipated by a prior art reference is a procedure very similar to determining if a product infringes a claim.[180] First, the claim must be "construed" to determine exactly what it means. The rules of claim construction are discussed in Chapter 7. Note that whatever construction is applied to a claim when the issue is infringement is the same construction that must be applied when the issue is validity. A claim can have only one meaning.[181] After the claim has been construed, it must

---

[175] Unless, again, it could suffice for a statutory bar under § 102(b). See Section 8.10.
[176] *See Katz,* 687 F.2d at 455.
[177] See Section 6.2.
[178] See Section 8.9.6.
[179] The law generally treats a corporation as a "person." People are "natural persons."
[180] See Chapter 10.
[181] *Smithkline Diagnostics, Inc. v. Helena Labs.,* 859 F.2d 878, 882 (Fed. Cir. 1988).

be compared to the reference to determine if the reference includes each and every element of the claim. In other words, the claim is used as a "checklist," and every element of the claim must find an exact match in the reference.[182]

Anticipation requires that all of the elements of a claim be found in a *single* reference.[183] This is because combining the teachings of one reference with the teachings of another reference might be sufficiently "inventive" to warrant a patent. The question, in such a case, is whether the combination was "non-obvious." Obviousness is a separate ground of invalidity discussed in the next section. In any event, if the invention represents the combination of features found in more than one reference, it is not invalid on grounds of anticipation.

If the prior art reference is a patent or printed publication, it anticipates only if it discloses or "teaches" each and every element of the claimed invention, when read by a person skilled in the art. A particular claim element can be mentioned *explicitly* in the reference,[184] or it can be *inherent*.[185] Suppose, for example, that a claim to a mousetrap required a "flexible" spring, and a prior publication disclosed a mousetrap with a steel spring of certain dimensions. Even if the publication did not refer to the flexibility of the spring, the spring described might be *inherently* flexible because of its materials and design. In this situation, the "flexible" spring element of the claim would be met by the reference, even though it was not explicit. In fact, inherency is sufficient to meet a claim element even if the persons responsible for the reference were not aware of the inherent trait.[186]

Although anticipation requires that all of the elements of a claim be

---

[182] See *Glaverbel Societe Anonyme v. Northlake Marketing & Supply, Inc.*, 45 F.3d 1550, 1554 (Fed. Cir. 1995) ("Anticipation . . . requires identity of invention: the claimed invention, as described in appropriately construed claims, must be the same as that of the reference, in order to anticipate."). The tests of anticipation and literal infringement (see Section 10.5) are so similar, it is sometimes said that whatever would literally infringe a claim if it came later in time, anticipates if it came before. See *Lewmar Marine, Inc. v. Barient, Inc.*, 827 F.2d 744, 747 (Fed. Cir. 1987). However, since anticipation can be based on references that would not infringe (for example, the description of an invention in a publication), the "infringement test" of anticipation may be more confusing than helpful.

[183] *Glaverbel*, 45 F.3d at 1554; *In re Bond*, 910 F.2d 831, 832 (Fed. Cir. 1990).

[184] The reference, however, does not have to describe a claim element in precisely the same words used in the patent claim. See *Bond*, 910 F.2d at 832 (anticipation is not an "ipsissimis verbis" test).

[185] See *Verdegaal Bros., Inc. v. Union Oil Co.*, 814 F.2d 628, 633 (Fed. Cir. 1987); *Tyler Refrigerator v. Kysor Indus. Corp.*, 777 F.2d 687, 689 (Fed. Cir. 1985). Although anticipation requires that every claim element be found in a single reference, other references can be used to prove the fact of inherency. *Continental Can Co. v. Monsanto Co.*, 948 F.2d 1264, 1268–69 (Fed. Cir. 1991).

[186] *E.I. du Pont de Nemours & Co. v. Phillips Petroleum Co.*, 849 F.2d 1430, 1436 (Fed. Cir. 1988); *Verdegaal*, 814 F.2d at 633.

found in one reference, it may be proper to look to other references as an aid to *understanding* the anticipatory reference.[187] It is not proper to look to other references to fill in claim elements missing in the primary reference.[188] This relatively clear distinction was blurred somewhat by the recent decision in *In re Graves*.[189] There the Federal Circuit held that a reference lacking a claim element could still be held to anticipate, if the missing element was "within the knowledge of a skilled artisan."[190] This sounds suspiciously close to an obviousness test, rather than the classic test of anticipation.

If a patent claims a broad genus, a reference that includes a single species of the genus will anticipate the claim.[191] For example, a claim that specified a fuel composed of (among other things) "10 to 50 percent methane" would be anticipated by a prior fuel that met all of the other claim elements and that was composed of 25 percent methane. The claim is anticipated because it would otherwise prevent the practice of at least one fuel combination already in use. The converse, however, is not true.[192] If a claim called for a fuel composed of exactly 25 percent methane, and a prior publication discussed such a fuel with a methane concentration of anywhere from 10 to 50 percent, the claim requiring exactly 25 percent would not be anticipated. It might or might not be invalid for obviousness.

8.9.6 Obviousness (§ 103)

Obviousness is a concept drawn from the following language of 35 U.S.C. § 103(a):

A patent may not be obtained though the invention is not identically disclosed or described as set forth in section 102 of this title, if the differences between the subject matter sought to be patented and the prior art are such that the subject matter as a whole would have been obvious at the time the invention was made to a person having ordinary skill in the art to which said subject matter pertains.

Like anticipation, obviousness is a ground for rejecting a patent claim in the course of prosecution or invalidating a patent claim in the course

---

[187] *See In re Baxter Travenol Labs.*, 952 F.2d 388, 390 (Fed. Cir. 1991).
[188] *Scripps Clinic & Research Foundation v. Genentech, Inc.*, 927 F.2d 1565, 1576 (Fed. Cir. 1991).
[189] 69 F.3d 1147 (Fed. Cir. 1995).
[190] *Graves*, 69 F.3d at 1152.
[191] *Chester v. Miller*, 906 F.2d 1574, 1577 (Fed. Cir. 1990).
[192] *See Minnesota Mining & Mfg. Co. v. Johnson & Johnson Orthopaedics, Inc.*, 976 F.2d 1559, 1572 (Fed. Cir. 1992) (although patentee's claims were "subsumed" in a prior reference's "generalized disclosure," this did not constitute "literal identity" of invention).

of infringement litigation. Obviousness, however, does not require that the claimed invention be identical to the prior art. Instead, obviousness focuses on the differences between the claim and the prior art, and asks whether those differences are really inventive, or whether they are differences that might have occurred to anyone of ordinary skill. Like § 102, § 103 prevents a patent claim from taking from the public what, in a sense, it already possesses.[193]

Obviousness is judged from the perspective of the "person of ordinary skill in the art" at the time the invention was made.[194] The "person of ordinary skill in the art" is a mythical everyman whose perspective is often called upon in patent law, not only in context of obviousness but also, for example, in deciding whether a patent specification enables the practice of the claimed invention.[195] The person of ordinary skill is a more technically minded cousin of John Q. Public. The person of ordinary skill is not an inventor or innovator, but a person of ordinary competence who does the expected thing.[196] The level of expertise and education required of the "person of ordinary skill" varies depending on the art. In a very sophisticated art, a person of "ordinary skill" might have a Ph.D. and years of hands-on experience. In a less sophisticated art, the person of "ordinary skill" might be a shade tree mechanic. If a court is called upon to decide whether or not a claimed invention is obvious, it first must decide what level of skill represents "ordinary" skill in the art at the time the invention was made.[197]

---

[193] Obviousness looks to the differences between the claimed invention and the prior art, *Ryko Mfg. Co. v. Nu-Star, Inc.*, 950 F.2d 714, 717 (Fed. Cir. 1991), but the invention still must be viewed "as a whole." *See Id.; Para-Ordnance Mfg., Inc. v. SGS Imports Int'l, Inc.*, 73 F.3d 1085, 1087 (Fed. Cir. 1995).

[194] *See Ryko*, 950 F.2d at 718; *Custom Accessories, Inc. v. Jeffrey-Allan Indus., Inc.*, 807 F.2d 955, 962 (Fed. Cir. 1986) (The question is whether the invention would have been obvious to one of ordinary skill in the art of the invention—"not to the judge, or to a layman, or to those skilled in remote arts, or to geniuses in the art.").

[195] See Section 8.6.

[196] *Standard Oil Co. v. American Cyanamid Co.*, 774 F.2d 448, 454 (Fed. Cir. 1985) ("A person of ordinary skill in the art is . . . presumed to be one who thinks along the lines of conventional wisdom in the art and is not one who undertakes to innovate, whether by patient, and often expensive, systematic research or by extraordinary insights, it makes no difference which.").

[197] *See Custom Accessories*, 807 F.2d at 962. Factors that may be considered include "[the] type of problems encountered in the [the] art; prior art solutions to those problems; [the] rapidity with which innovations are made; [the] sophistication of the technology; and [the] educational level of active workers in the field." *Id.* An invention may be obvious to a person of "ordinary skill" even if it would not be obvious to a layperson. On the other hand, an invention that would be obvious to a person of *extraordinary* skill can still be patentable. Inventors and patentees are often assumed to be persons of extraordinary skill.

Non-obviousness should not be confused with complexity. Sometimes the simplest inventions are the most innovative.[198] Moreover, the invention need not have been the result of a "flash of genius"—the kind of sudden inspiration that led Archimedes to shout "Eureka!" An invention that is the product patient experimentation, or that is discovered entirely by accident, is just as patentable as one that arises from pure mental effort.[199] The only requirement is that the invention would not have occurred to a person of ordinary skill. This principle accounts for the last sentence of § 103(a), which provides, rather cryptically, that "[p]atentability shall not be negatived by the manner in which the invention was made."

The standard of patentability is not whether the invention would have been "obvious to *try*."[200] If, for example, there were a long list of compounds that might prove to be an effective treatment for a disease, any one of which would be obvious to try, the discovery that a particular compound on that list is an effective treatment might still be a non-obvious invention.[201] The deciding factor is whether a person skilled in the art, contemplating that particular compound, would have had a "reasonable expectation of success" before the discovery had been made.[202] Although it is a confusing approach to distinguish between "obvious to do" and "obvious to try," it at least acknowledges that important and non-obvious inventions can arise from laborious trial and error. This particularly seems to be the case in the fields of chemistry and biotechnology.

Sometimes an invention would have been obvious from a *technological* point of view, but not from a *business* point of view. Suppose, for example, that a patent claimed a mousetrap of a prior design, but with certain parts made of solid gold. The patentee might argue that the mousetrap was non-obvious because no one would have believed a solid gold mousetrap

---

[198] *See In re* Oetiker, 877 F.2d 1443, 1447 (Fed. Cir. 1992) ("Simplicity is not inimical to patentability."); *Demaco Corp. v. F. Von Langsdorff Licensing Ltd.*, 851 F.2d 1387, 1390–91 (Fed. Cir. 1988) ("Nor does the patent statute require that an invention be complex in order to be nonobvious.").

[199] *See Graham v. John Deere Co.*, 383 U.S. 1, 15, 86 S. Ct. 684, 692 (1966); *Vandenberg v. Dairy Equipment Co.*, 740 F.2d 1560, 1565 (Fed. Cir. 1984).

[200] *In re Fine*, 837 F.2d 1071, 1075 (Fed. Cir. 1988); *Hybritech Inc. v. Monoclonal Antibodies, Inc.*, 802 F.2d 1367, 1380 (Fed. Cir. 1986).

[201] *See In re Baird*, 16 F.3d 380, 382 (Fed. Cir. 1994) ("A disclosure of millions of compounds does not render obvious a claim to three compounds, particularly when the disclosure indicates a preference leading away from the claimed compounds.").

[202] *See In re O'Farrell*, 853 F.2d 894, 903–4 (Fed. Cir. 1988); *In re Merck & Co.*, 800 F.2d 1091, 1097 (Fed. Cir. 1986). Another "obvious to try" situation might occur if a publication included "a general disclosure [to] pique the scientist's curiosity, such that further investigation might be done as a result of the disclosure, but the disclosure itself [did] not contain a sufficient teaching of how to obtain the desired result." *In re Eli Lilly & Co.*, 902 F.2d 943, 945 (Fed. Cir. 1990).

to be a profitable item. Perhaps the inventor was a marketing genius, who realized that a solid gold mousetrap would be a successful novelty gift for the wealthy. Patents, however, are meant to encourage the *technological* arts. Therefore, even if the mousetrap was ingenious from a marketing standpoint, it would be unpatentable if obvious from a technological standpoint.[203]

While anticipation requires that all the elements of the claimed invention be found in a single prior art reference, obviousness can be based on the *combination* of more than one reference. For example, if some elements of the claimed invention were found in one technical journal, and the remaining elements were found in another journal, it could be argued that the combination of one with the other would have been obvious to a person of ordinary skill who was aware of both.

It is not necessary that any person skilled in the art actually considered such a combination before the claimed invention was made. Instead, courts often imagine the hypothetical "person of ordinary skill in the art" standing in a workshop, surrounded by all of the relevant patents, publications and other prior art references.[204] The question then becomes, would such a person, confronting the problem solved by the invention and aware of all of these references, have found it obvious to make the claimed combination?

The references that may be considered include any of the kinds of prior art set forth in § 102, as long as they are in "the field of the inventor's endeavor" or an "analogous art." An "analogous art" is one that is "reasonably pertinent to the particular problem with which the inventor is involved"—in other words, an art that an inventor would look to for solutions or ideas.[205] For example, in *In re Paulsen*,[206] the claimed invention concerned a case for a portable computer, hinged in such a way that it could be closed tight for carrying or latched in an upright position for viewing the display screen. The court found it appropriate to consider references concerning hinges and latches, even if they were not in the portable computer field:

---

[203] *See Orthopedic Equipment Co. v. U.S.*, 702 F.2d 1005, 1013 (Fed. Cir. 1983) ("[T]he fact that the two disclosed apparatus would not be combined by businessmen for economic reasons is not the same as saying that it could not be done because skilled persons in the art felt that there was some technological incompatibility that prevented their combination. Only the latter fact is telling on the issue of nonobviousness.").

[204] *See Para-Ordnance Mfg. v. SGS Imports Int'l, Inc.*, 73 F.3d 1085, 1088 (Fed. Cir. 1995). However, the visual image of the art "tableau" has been criticized by the judge who first created it, perhaps because it suggests the use of hindsight in selecting the references to "hang in the workshop." *See Standard Oil Co. v. American Cyanamid Co.*, 774 F.2d 448, 454 n.3 (Fed. Cir. 1985) (referring to the "unfortunate popularity" of the tableau imagery).

[205] *See Wang Labs., Inc. v. Toshiba Corp.*, 993 F.2d 858, 864 (Fed. Cir. 1993); *In re Clay*, 966 F.2d 656, 659 (Fed. Cir. 1992).

[206] 30 F.3d 1475 (Fed. Cir. 1994).

The problems encountered by the inventors . . . were problems that were not unique to portable computers. They concerned how to connect and secure the computer's display housing to the computer while meeting certain size constraints and functional requirements. . . . We agree with the Board that given the nature of the problems confronted by the inventors, one of ordinary skill in the art "would have consulted the mechanical arts for housings, hinges, latches, springs, etc."[207]

In *In re Oetiker*,[208] on the other hand, the court found insufficient evidence that a person working on hose clamps would have been motivated to consider fasteners used in clothing.[209]

In judging whether a claimed invention would have been obvious, it is important to avoid the use of hindsight.[210] After an invention has been made, it may be all too easy to claim that it was obvious. Obviousness must be judged from the perspective of one of ordinary skill in the art "at the time the invention was made." Accordingly, one cannot prove obviousness by simply canvassing the prior art, using the patent itself as a guide, until all the elements of the invention have been found.[211] Rather, one must show some pre-existing "suggestion" or "motivation" to combine the references in the manner claimed.[212] This does not mean that one reference must include an explicit reference to the other, but it does mean there must be something, either in the references themselves or in the general knowledge available in the art, that would have led a person of ordinary skill to combine those particular references in the manner claimed, and with a reasonable expectation of success.[213]

Sometimes a prior reference "teaches away" from the claimed invention. To "teach away" means to suggest that the claimed combination should be avoided as undesirable or ineffective.[214] This is one factor to consider in deciding whether certain references render a claimed invention obvious.[215] Nevertheless, sufficient disclosure can render an invention

---

[207] *Paulsen*, 30 F.3d at 1481–82.

[208] 977 F.2d 1443 (Fed. Cir. 1992).

[209] *Oetiker*, 977 F.2d at 1447.

[210] *Para-Ordnance*, 73 F.3d at 1087; *In re Fine*, 837 F.2d 1071, 1075 (Fed. Cir. 1988).

[211] *See In re Gorman*, 933 F.2d 982, 987 (Fed. Cir. 1991) ("It is impermissible . . . simply to engage in a hindsight reconstruction of the claimed invention, using the applicant's structure as a template and selecting elements from references to fill the gaps.").

[212] *See Oetiker*, 977 F.2d at 1447; *Interconnect Planning Corp. v. Feil*, 774 F.2d 1132, 1143 (Fed. Cir. 1985).

[213] *See In re Jones*, 958 F.2d 347, 351 (Fed. Cir. 1992); *In re Dow Chemical Co.*, 837 F.2d 469, 473 (Fed. Cir. 1988).

[214] *See In re Gurley*, 27 F.3d 551, 553 (Fed. Cir. 1994) ("A reference may be said to teach away when a person of ordinary skill, upon reading the reference, would be discouraged from following the path set out in the reference, or would be led in a direction divergent from the path that was taken by the applicant.").

[215] *See Gurley*, 27 F.3d at 553.

obvious and unpatentable, even if the reference suggests that the invention is an inferior approach.[216]

It seems easier to conclude that the claimed invention was an obvious one if there are a large number of similar ideas found in the prior art. However, one can reach the opposite conclusion, reasoning that where so many inventors came so close to the claimed invention, but still managed to be different, there must be something about the claimed invention that everyone else missed.[217] A defendant in a patent case who is attempting to prove obviousness must decide whether it is more persuasive to weigh in with every reference available or to select only a few that are most similar to the claimed invention.

Although obviousness determinations are highly fact-specific,[218] a pair of examples will give the reader some flavor for how the decisions are made. In *In re Gorman*,[219] the claimed invention was a novelty lollipop in the shape of a thumb. The elements of the claimed invention included a thumb-shaped candy core; a protective covering, also thumb-shaped, which served first as a mold for the candy core and then as a "toy and novelty item for placement upon the thumb of the user"; a lollipop stick; a plug of chewing gum or similar edible material to seal the bottom of the candy; and a plastic or cardboard disk at the base of the "thumb."

The prior art located by the Patent Office included thirteen references. Some showed candy or ice cream formed in a rubbery mold, which served double-duty as a wrapper for the product. One ice cream product on a stick included a similar cardboard base. Other references (believe it or not) disclosed thumb-shaped candies and confections. Edible plugs also had been disclosed for sealing liquid inside of candy and ice cream products. Although Gorman's claim was very detailed, and none of the references included all of the things that Gorman claimed, the Patent Office found that the combination still would have been obvious to any person of ordinary skill. The Federal Circuit affirmed: "The various elements Gorman combined . . . are all shown in the cited references in various subcombinations, used in the same way, for the same purpose as in the claimed invention."[220]

In *Moleculon Research Corp. v. CBS, Inc.*,[221] on the other hand, the Federal Circuit upheld the determination of the trial court that the claimed in-

---

[216] *See Gurley*, 27 F.3d at 553 ("A known and obvious composition does not become patentable simply because it has been described as somewhat inferior to some other product for the same use.").

[217] *See In re Gorman*, 933 F.2d at 986.

[218] Even though the ultimate determination of obviousness is a "question of law." See Section 11.4.

[219] 933 F.2d 892, 897 (Fed. Cir. 1991).

[220] *Gorman*, 933 F.2d at 987.

[221] 793 F.2d 1261 (Fed. Cir. 1986).

vention was not obvious. There the invention was a cube-puzzle of the kind popularized by Rubik's Cube. In fact, Rubik's Cube was the product accused of infringement. The claims described a puzzle in the shape of a subdivided cube, the pieces of which could be scrambled and restored by rotating the facets of the cube. CBS, which owned the rights to Rubik's Cube, argued that the claims were obvious in light of a prior patent, to one Gustafson, disclosing a spherical puzzle with a subdivided, rotatable shell. Although a person skilled in the art might have *considered* converting Gustafson's sphere puzzle into a cube with rotating faces, nothing in the art suggested that such a change would have been desirable. On the contrary, the evidence showed that Gustafson, while considering other shapes, had dismissed a cube as inadequate.[222] Moreover, one expert described the cube as a "quantum leap" from the sphere.[223] On the basis of this evidence, the lower court properly concluded that even someone aware of Gustafson's sphere would not have found it obvious to make the cube.

Even these two examples are enough to prove the Federal Circuit's observation that "[t]he obviousness standard, while easy to expound, is sometimes difficult to apply."[224] An obviousness analysis requires a difficult act of the imagination in that the decision maker, whether a patent examiner or judge, must view the situation from the perspective of another person (a person of ordinary skill in the art), at a different time (the time the invention was made), while ignoring information that is foremost in the decision maker's mind (the disclosure of the invention in the patent itself).[225] And even if the decision maker can manage this feat, obviousness can still seem a matter of opinion. It is not hard to imagine a *Gorman* or *Moleculon* opinion reaching an opposite conclusion.

8.9.6.1 Secondary Considerations

Because the obviousness determination is such a difficult and subjective one, courts in recent years have increasingly emphasized the importance of "secondary considerations." "Secondary considerations" are factors that are believed to provide objective evidence of obviousness or non-obviousness. A leading case on secondary considerations is *Graham v. John Deere Co.*,[226] one of the Supreme Court's infrequent opinions in the area of patent law. The court suggested that in deciding the fundamental question of obviousness, it might be appropriate to consider "secondary considerations" such as "commercial success, long felt but unsolved needs,

---

[222] *Moleculon*, 793 F.2d at 1268.
[223] *Moleculon*, 793 F.2d at 1268.
[224] *Uniroyal, Inc. v. Rudkin-Wiley Corp.*, 837 F.2d 1044, 1050 (Fed. Cir. 1988).
[225] *See Uniroyal*, 837 F.2d at 1050–51.
[226] 383 U.S. 1, 86 S. Ct. 684 (1966).

failure of others, etc."[227] Under subsequent Federal Circuit precedent, consideration of these factors has become mandatory.[228]

"Secondary considerations" include the following:

- Commercial success.
- Long-felt need.
- Failure of others.
- Industry recognition.
- Expressions of skepticism or disbelief.
- Unexpected results.
- Copying.
- Near-simultaneous invention.

The secondary consideration most frequently encountered is "commercial success." "Commercial success" means evidence that a product covered by a patent claim has earned substantial profits in the marketplace. In theory, an invention that has been successful in the marketplace could not have been an obvious one. Otherwise, someone else would have stepped ahead of the inventor in order to reap the available rewards.

There are at least three possible objections to this theory. First, the theory works only if the success of the invention had been foreseeable.[229] Second, *someone* has to be first to invent, even if the invention is an obvious one and the rewards are substantial. Finally, commercial success can be due to any number of factors other than the claimed invention, including marketing know-how, advertising, manufacturing techniques, quality control, price or features of the product other than those covered by the claim. In order to meet this last objection, a patentee or applicant offering evidence of commercial success must demonstrate a "nexus" between that success and the claimed invention. "Nexus" means a logical, cause-and-effect relationship between the success of the product and the claimed

---

[227] *Graham*, 383 U.S. at 17–18, 86 S. Ct. at 694.

[228] *See In re GPAC Inc.*, 57 F.3d 1573, 1580 (Fed. Cir. 1995); *Hybritech, Inc. v. Monoclonal Antibodies, Inc.*, 802 F.2d 1367, 1380 (secondary considerations are more than "icing on the cake"); *Stratoflex, Inc. v. Aeroquip Corp.*, 713 F.2d 1530, 1539 (Fed. Cir. 1983).

[229] *See Dickey-John Corp. v. Int'l Tapetronics Corp.*, 710 F.2d 329, 346–47 (7th Cir. 1983) ("If individuals believe there is 'a fortune waiting in the wings' for the person who solves the problem, we infer that with such an incentive, many artisans were actually attempting to find the solution. The longer they failed to do so, the stronger the inference that it took extraordinary skill to solve the problem.").

invention.[230] Such a connection might be shown in a number of ways, including consumer surveys, comparisons to similar products or testimony concerning the relative advantages of the claimed invention.[231]

Commercial success is useful as a secondary consideration to patentees or applicants who have marketed a product covered by the claim. However, commercial success can also be premised on a product marketed by someone else—even an infringer—as long as there is a nexus between the success of the product and the invention claimed.[232] Success in licensing[233] may also be offered as evidence of commercial success.[234]

The other secondary considerations are relatively straightforward. If there had been a "long-felt need" for an invention, or if others had tried and failed to solve the problem addressed by the invention, it is reasonable to infer that the invention was not an obvious one. Otherwise the problem would have been solved before, and the need already satisfied.[235] Reactions to the invention by persons skilled in the art can also be important. If experts in the field praised the invention or, even better, if they expressed skepticism or disbelief that anyone had solved the problems overcome by the invention, this also serves as evidence of non-obviousness.[236] "Unexpected results" can be useful in showing that an invention was not an obvious one, particularly where the results are unexpectedly good.[237] Finally, since imitation is the sincerest form of flattery, copying of the invention can be taken as objective evidence that the invention was not obvious.[238]

---

[230] *In re Paulsen*, 30 F.3d 1475, 1482 (Fed. Cir. 1994); *Demaco Corp. v. F. Von Langsdorff Licensing Ltd.*, 851 F.2d 1387, 1392 (Fed. Cir. 1988); *Sjoland v. Musland*, 847 F.2d 1573, 1582 (Fed. Cir. 1988).

[231] *See Demaco*, 851 F.2d at 1392–93. A patentee is required to produce evidence of a causal link between the commercial success and the claimed invention, but need not, as an initial matter, affirmatively prove that the claimed invention is the sole cause of the success, to the exclusion of every other possible factor, such as advertising and marketing. If the patentee meets the initial burden of proof, it is up to the challenger to prove that the commercial success should be attributed to one of those other factors. *See Id.* at 1392–94.

[232] *See Syntex Inc. v. Paragon Optical Inc.*, 7 U.S.P.Q.2d 1001, 1005 (D. Az. 1987); *Truswal Sys. Corp. v. Hydro-Air Eng'g, Inc.*, 813 F.2d 1207, 1215 (Fed. Cir. 1987) (Judge Rich dissenting).

[233] See Section 6.3.

[234] *See GPAC*, 57 F.3d at 1580.

[235] *See In re Dow Chemical Co.*, 837 F.2d 469, 472 (Fed. Cir. 1988) ("Recognition of need, and difficulties encountered by those skilled in the field, are classical indicia of unobviousness."); *In re Piasecki*, 745 F.2d 1468, 1475 (Fed. Cir. 1984).

[236] *See Environmental Designs, Ltd. v. Union Oil Co.*, 713 F.2d 693, 697–98 (Fed. Cir. 1983); *Burlington Indus., Inc. v. Quigg*, 822 F.2d 1581, 1582–84 (Fed. Cir. 1987).

[237] *See Medtronic Inc. v. Intermedics, Inc.*, 799 F.2d 734, 738 (Fed. Cir. 1986); *Ashland Oil, Inc. v. Delta Resins & Refractories, Inc.*, 776 F.2d 281, 307 (Fed. Cir. 1985).

[238] *Diversitech Corp. v. Century Steps, Inc.*, 850 F.2d 675, 679 (Fed. Cir. 1988); *Panduit Corp. v. Dennison Mfg. Co.*, 776 F.2d 1082, 1099 (Fed. Cir. 1985).

All of the secondary considerations discussed so far are potential evidence of *non-obviousness*.[239] "Near-simultaneous invention" is the only secondary consideration that is positive evidence of *obviousness*. If an invention is made independently by another inventor, at nearly the same time as the applicant or patentee, this is evidence that the invention was not the result of uncommon effort or insight. Rather, the art may simply have progressed to the point where the claimed invention was the obvious next step.[240] Note that an independent near-simultaneous invention can serve as objective evidence of obviousness, even if that invention occurred shortly after the invention by the patentee or applicant, thereby disqualifying it as potential prior art under § 102.

8.9.7 Derivation (§ 102(f))

One rule of patentability that almost goes without saying is that an applicant cannot claim someone else's invention. This rule is embodied in 35 U.S.C. § 102(f), which states that a patent cannot be obtained if the applicant "did not himself invent the subject matter sought to be patented." If the purported inventor took the idea from someone else, the claim is unpatentable or, if already issued, invalid. A defense based on § 102(f) is usually referred to as a "derivation" defense, because the claim is said to be "derived" from someone else's invention.[241]

A derivation defense requires proof, by clear and convincing evidence, (1) that the invention was fully conceived by another person before it had been conceived by the purported inventor, and (2) that the conception was communicated to the purported inventor.[242] The information communicated must have been an "enabling disclosure" of the invention,[243] not merely information that could have made the invention obvious.[244]

8.10 SECTION 102(b) STATUTORY BARS

The previous discussion of § 102 concerned the effect of events occurring before the applicant's *date of invention*. The portions of § 102 that

---

[239] The absence of commercial success, long-felt need, and the other indicia of non-obviousness has generally been held a "neutral factor," rather than positive evidence of obviousness. *See Medtronic*, 799 F.2d at 739 n.13.

[240] *See In re Merk & Co.*, 800 F.2d 1091, 1098 (Fed. Cir. 1986).

[241] *See Price v. Symsek*, 988 F.2d 1187, 1190 (Fed. Cir. 1993).

[242] *Gambro Lundia AB v. Baxter Healthcare Corp.*, 110 F.3d 1573, 1576 (Fed. Cir. 1997). The claim of prior conception must be corroborated. *Id.* See Section 8.9.3

[243] See Section 8.6.

[244] *Gambro*, 110 F.3d at 1577–78. *Gambro* suggests that one could never base a finding of obviousness on the kind of disclosure contemplated in § 102(f). However, the Federal Circuit recently decided that a § 102(f) disclosure, combined with other references, *can* lead to a finding of obviousness. *Oddzon Prods., Inc. v. Just Toys, Inc.*, 122 F.3d 1396, 1403–4 (Fed. Cir. 1997).

deal with these events (paragraphs (a), (e) and (g)) ensure that on the date of the applicant's invention, the invention was new. Paragraph (b) of § 102 serves a different purpose. Section 102(b) ensures that the applicant did not delay too long in filing a patent application, after the occurrence of certain key events.

Section 102(b) provides as follows:

A person shall be entitled to a patent unless—

(b) the invention was patented or described in a printed publication in this or a foreign country or in public use or on sale in this country, more than one year prior to the date of the application for patent in the United States. . . .

Section 102(b) is similar to 102(a) in that both refer to prior patents, printed publications and public use.[245] However, § 102(b) differs fundamentally from § 102(a) in three respects. First, § 102(b) adds the "on sale" language. Second, a § 102(b) reference often arises from the actions of the applicant himself, whereas a § 102(a) reference can only arise from the acts of a third party.[246] Finally, the important date for § 102(b) is not the date of the invention, but a date exactly *one year before the patent application was filed.*[247] This date is known as the application's "critical date."

Imagine the following scenario. On January 1, 1990, an inventor conceives of a better mousetrap, and on January 2, 1990, the inventor reduces the invention to practice by constructing a prototype in his workshop. January 2, 1990 is the "date of the invention," and that date is corroborated by a witnessed laboratory notebook. On January 3, 1990, the inventor submits a complete description of the mousetrap to the *Inventor's Newsletter,* which publishes the description on February 1, 1990. On February 2, 1991, the inventor files a patent application. The "critical date" of the application, under § 102(b), is February 2, 1990. The publication in the *Inventor's Newsletter* on February 1, 1990 is not prior art under § 102(a) because it did not occur before the applicant's date of invention. However, the publication did occur before the "critical date." Consequently, if the publication included a complete and enabling description of the invention, the patent application would be rejected under § 102(b).

---

[245] The definition of "printed publication" under § 102(a) also applies under § 102(b). See Section 8.9.1.1.

[246] An applicant can use an invention publicly, patent it or describe in a printed publication more than one year before the application filing date, but could hardly do so before his own date of invention, as would be required under § 102(a). A § 102(a) reference, at least in terms of anticipation, logically has to be the work of another.

[247] When the process of prosecution results in a chain of related applications, a later application may be entitled to the effective filing date of a preceding application for purposes of § 102(b). See Section 5.2.

In essence, § 102(b) provides a one-year "grace period" after the first patent, publication, public use or offer to sell that relates to the claimed invention. An inventor has that long to file a patent application, or the right to a patent is lost. Any problems that might arise from the inventor's own activities can be avoided simply by ensuring that a patent application is on file within one year of the date of invention. This practice should be adopted by all inventors, though frequently it is not.

The rationale for § 102(b) is threefold. First, and most generally, it encourages diligence by penalizing inventors who are lazy, or inclined to suppress their inventions, or who for some other reason delay in filing a patent application.[248] Second, it prevents the public from being misled where the availability of the invention to the public, without evidence that the inventor intends to obtain a patent, might create the impression that the invention is up for grabs.[249] Finally, it prevents what could be an unwarranted extension of the inventor's monopoly powers beyond the 20 years contemplated by the patent system.[250] If there were no § 102(b), an inventor might delay seeking patent protection indefinitely, and the mere threat that he would do so eventually could prevent potential competitors from daring to compete. On the other hand, an inventor does need a certain amount of time to perfect the invention and prepare a patent application. Section 102(b) establishes one year as the period that most effectively balances the needs of the inventor against the needs of the public.

The prohibitions of § 102(b) are commonly known as "statutory bars." A "statutory bar" can prevent the issuance of a claim in a patent application, or it can be used to challenge the validity of an issued patent claim in subsequent infringement litigation. A reference that qualifies under § 102(b) can also be used as the basis for a finding of obviousness.[251] In some cases, a reference can qualify as prior art under either § 102(a) or § 102(b). If so, § 102(b) can provide the simpler analysis since it relies on the easily determined "critical date" of the patent application, rather than the often difficult to determine "date of invention."

---

[248] *See La Bounty Mfg., Inc. v. U.S. Int'l Trade Comm'n*, 958 F.2d 1066, 1071 (Fed. Cir. 1992) ("The general purpose behind [the] section 102(b) bars is to require inventors to assert with due diligence their right to a patent through the prompt filing of a patent application."); *Intel Corp. v. U.S. Int'l Trade Comm'n*, 946 F.2d 821, 830 (Fed. Cir. 1991); *RCA Corp. v. Data General Corp.*, 887 F.2d 1056, 1062 (Fed. Cir. 1989).

[249] *See Envirotech Corp. v. Westech Eng'g, Inc.*, 904 F.2d 1571, 1574 (Fed. Cir. 1990).

[250] *See Ferag AG v. Quipp, Inc.*, 45 F.3d 1562, 1566 (Fed. Cir. 1995); *Envirotech*, 904 F.2d at 1574; *RCA*, 887 F.2d at 1062.

[251] *See Elmer v. ICC Fabricating, Inc.*, 67 F.3d 1571, 1574 (Fed. Cir. 1995); *Baker Oil Tools, Inc. v. Geo Vann, Inc.*, 828 F.2d 1558, 1563 (Fed. Cir. 1987).

8.10.1 "On Sale Bar"

The most frequently encountered statutory bar is probably the "on sale bar" created when the inventor, or a third party, takes steps to commercialize the claimed invention more than one year before the filing date of the patent application. An "on sale bar" arises if a product embodying the claimed invention, or rendering it obvious, was sold or offered for sale before the "critical date."[252] A single sale, or a single offer to sell, is sufficient to invoke the statutory bar.[253]

Disputes frequently arise over whether certain activity did or did not constitute a sale or definite offer to sell. For example, an inventor may contend that a commercial relationship with a potential customer was not related to a bona fide sale of patented product, but rather to joint development effort. In *Continental Can Co. v. Monsanto Co.*,[254] for example, a plastics company entered into an agreement with the Coca-Cola Company to develop a plastic bottle. Under the agreement, the companies would work together to produce a suitable bottle, with the plastics company making the bottles and Coca-Cola testing them. If a satisfactory bottle were developed, Coca-Cola would purchase the bottles from the plastics company, under terms that were partially negotiated. The plastics company produced bottles in a variety of shapes, including one that allegedly embodied the patent claim in question, but the project was abandoned when tests proved unsuccessful.[255] Although the trial court found that the relationship had placed the patented bottle "on sale" before the critical date, the Federal Circuit disagreed and reversed:

Although Admiral Plastic's hope was surely commercial sales, and the record shows that prices and quantities were discussed, this does not of itself place the subject matter "on sale" in the sense of § 102(b). The . . . bottle was a part of a terminated development project that never bore commercial fruit and was cloaked in confidentiality. While the line is not always bright between development and being on sale . . . in this case the line was not crossed.[256]

---

[252] *See Keystone Retaining Wall Sys., Inc. v. Westrock, Inc.*, 997 F.2d 1444, 1451 (Fed. Cir. 1993).

[253] *Intel Corp. v. U.S. Int'l Trade Comm'n*, 946 F.2d 821, 830 (Fed. Cir. 1991). However, the sale must be to a separate entity. A transaction between related corporations which was completed purely for accounting purposes would not constitute a genuine "sale," at least if the "selling" entity "so controls the purchaser that the invention remains out of the public's hands." *See Ferag AG v. Quipp, Inc.*, 45 F.3d 1562, 1567 (Fed. Cir. 1995). The offer must also be a "definite offer," rather than "nebulous discussion about a possible sale." *RCA Corp. v. Data General Corp.*, 887 F.2d 1056, 1062 (Fed. Cir. 1989).

[254] 948 F.2d 1264 (Fed. Cir. 1991).

[255] *See Continental Can*, 948 F.2d at 1269.

[256] *Continental Can*, 948 F.2d at 1270.

Whether a product embodying the invention was genuinely offered for sale is determined under the "totality of the circumstances" and with a view to the policies underlying § 102(b).[257] One factor to consider is whether the invention had been reduced to practice[258] prior to the "offer." Although reduction to practice is not absolutely necessary before an invention can be offered for sale, when the invention is still in a nebulous state prior to reduction to practice, it is more likely that any discussion of a sale was hypothetical, rather than a definite offer.[259] Recently, the Federal Circuit has suggested that an invention must be "substantially completed," and there must be "reason to expect that it will work for its intended purpose," before it can be placed "on sale."[260]

Similarly, a transaction does not constitute a bar under § 102(b) if it is part of an "experimental use"—that is, if the object of the "sale" was not to profit from the invention, but to test it in the field.[261] To qualify under this exception, the "sale" must be "merely incidental to the primary purpose of experimentation."[262] Although a court will consider a variety of factors in deciding if a sale was for purposes of commerce or of experiment, including the subjective intent of the seller, at a minimum the seller must inform the purchaser that the goods are experimental, and the seller must retain sufficient control over the goods to conduct the required monitoring or tests.[263]

A court will also consider whether the seller kept the kind of records that would suggest experimentation, whether the seller required the purchaser to keep the activities confidential, whether payment was received and whether the sale was accompanied by promotional efforts.[264] Keeping track of customer responses and complaints after sale of a new product is not sufficient to show that the sales were primarily experimental.[265] Moreover, the experiments have to relate to the *claimed invention*. If the experiments relate to some other aspect of a product, or if they are nothing more than marketing tests to gauge consumer demand, the sale is not within the experimental use exception.[266]

---

[257] *Envirotech Corp. v. Westech Eng'g, Inc.*, 904 F.2d 1571, 1574 (Fed. Cir. 1990).

[258] See Section 8.9.2.

[259] *See Keystone*, 997 F.2d at 1452; *UMC Electronics Co. v. U.S.*, 816 F.2d 647, 656 (Fed. Cir. 1987).

[260] *Micro Chemical, Inc. v. Great Plains Chemical Co.*, 103 F.3d 1538, 1545 (Fed. Cir. 1997).

[261] *See Kolmes v. World Fibers Corp.*, 107 F.3d 1534, 1540 (Fed. Cir. 1997).

[262] *Paragon Podiatry Lab., Inc. v. KLM Labs., Inc.* 984 F.2d 1182, 1185 (Fed. Cir. 1993).

[263] *See Paragon*, 984 F.2d at 1186–87; *La Bounty Mfg., Inc. v. U.S. Int'l Trade Comm'n*, 958 F.2d 1066, 1071–72 (Fed. Cir. 1992).

[264] *See U.S. Environmental Prods. Inc. v. Westall*, 911 F.2d 713, 717 (Fed. Cir. 1990).

[265] *See Paragon*, 984 F.2d at 1187–88.

[266] *In re Smith*, 714 F.2d 1127, 1135–36 (Fed. Cir. 1983).

8.10.2 Public Use Bar

Public use of the claimed invention before the application's critical date can also operate as a bar under § 102(b), but it is subject to the same experimental use exception. Some inventions must be tested in a more-or-less public environment, and if it is clear that the use is experimental it will not invalidate a claim.[267] Because only "public" use is proscribed by § 102(b), a use that is observed only by persons under an obligation of secrecy does not invoke the statutory bar.[268]

When the inventor demonstrates his invention to a few friends or associates, the determination of whether such use was "public" can be difficult. In *Moleculon Research Corp. v. CBS, Inc.*,[269] the inventor displayed a model of his cube puzzle to a few university colleagues. However, the "personal relationships and surrounding circumstances" were sufficient for the court to find that the inventor had retained control over the invention and the distribution of information concerning it, even though there was no express agreement of confidentiality.[270] In contrast, a jury in *Beachcombers v. Wildwood Creative Products, Inc.*[271] found that a demonstration of an improved kaleidoscope to 20–30 party guests was a "public use," and the Federal Circuit affirmed. The purpose of the demonstration was "getting feedback on the device," and the host made no efforts toward secrecy.[272]

Although efforts to commercialize an invention are often sufficient to warrant imposition of both an "on sale bar" and a "public use bar," the former can exist even if the commercialization did not make the invention public.[273] For example, if a patent claim describes a process, and a product made by that process was sold by the applicant before the critical date, an on sale bar can apply even if the process itself was not revealed.[274] Similarly, if a product that *embodies* the claimed invention is offered for sale before the critical date, the statutory bar will apply even if the product did not *disclose* the claimed invention.[275]

---

[267] See *Allied Colloids Inc. v. American Cyanamid Co.*, 64 F.2d 1570, 1574 (Fed. Cir. 1995) ("the inventor may test the invention, in public if that is reasonably appropriate to the invention, without incurring a public use bar"); *Manville Sales Corp. v. Paramount Sys., Inc.*, 917 F.2d 544, 550–51 (Fed. Cir. 1990).

[268] See *In re Smith*, 714 F.2d 1127, 1134 (Fed. Cir. 1983).

[269] 793 F.2d 1261 (Fed. Cir. 1986).

[270] *Moleculon*, 793 F.2d at 1266.

[271] 31 F.3d 1154 (Fed. Cir. 1994).

[272] *Beachcombers*, 31 F.3d at 1160.

[273] In the paradoxical words of *Kinzenbaw v. Deere & Co.*, 741 F.2d 383, 390 (Fed. Cir. 1984), "[a] commercial use is a public use even if it is kept secret."

[274] See *D.L. Auld Co. v. Chroma Graphics Corp.*, 714 F.2d 1144, 1147–48 (Fed. Cir. 1983).

[275] *In re Epstein*, 32 F.3d 1559, 1568 (Fed. Cir. 1994); *J.A. LaPorte, Inc. v. Norfolk Dredging Co.*, 787 F.2d 1577, 1583 (Fed. Cir. 1986). This rule applies whether the product was sold by

8.11 OTHER STATUTORY BARS (§§ 102(c), (d))

A similar type of "statutory bar" is created by 35 U.S.C. § 102(d), which provides as follows:

A person shall be entitled to a patent unless—

(d) the invention was first patented or caused to be patented, or was the subject of an inventor's certificate, by the applicant or his legal representatives or assigns in a foreign country prior to the date of the application for patent in this country on an application for patent or inventor's certificate filed more than twelve months before the filing of the application in the United States. . . .

Simply put, an inventor who applies for a patent in a foreign country, waits more than twelve months before filing in the United States and receives the foreign patent before filing in the United States will be denied a United States patent. As in the case of § 102(b), § 102(d) promotes diligence in filing and prevents the extension of the patent monopoly.[276] Anyone who applies for a patent in a foreign country and plans to obtain a United States patent is well advised to file in the United States no more than twelve months later, thereby avoiding the risk that the foreign patent will be granted sooner than expected.

Finally, one other rarely used form of "statutory bar" arises from § 102(c), which provides that an inventor is not entitled to a patent if "he has abandoned the invention." "Abandoning the invention" means abandoning the right to *patent* the invention. Mere delay in filing a patent application does not show that the invention was "abandoned,"[277] although it can have important consequences in a priority contest under § 102(g),[278] and it can allow the imposition of an "on sale" or similar bar under § 102(b). However, if an inventor were to announce to the public that he would not patent his invention, such an announcement might constitute an abandonment.[279]

---

the applicant or by a third party. *J.A. LaPorte,* 787 F.2d at 1583. However, selling a product made by a patented process, without revealing that process, operates as a bar only if the product was sold by the applicant or the applicant's assignee. *See W.L. Gore & Assoc., Inc. v. Garlock, Inc.,* 721 F.2d 1540, 1550 (Fed. Cir. 1983). The reason for this distinction is unclear.

[276] *See In re Kathawala,* 9 F.3d 942, 947 (Fed. Cir. 1993).

[277] *See Paulik v. Rizkalla,* 760 F.2d 1270, 1272 (Fed. Cir. 1985) (" 'the mere lapse of time' will not prevent the inventor from receiving a patent").

[278] See Section 8.9.1.3.

[279] An *application* can be "abandoned" and then re-filed, without abandoning the invention in terms of § 102(c). The abandonment could, however, sacrifice the early filing date of the application for purposes of § 102(b).

8.12 DOUBLE PATENTING

An inventor is entitled to one patent on one invention.[280] If more than one patent could be obtained on the same invention, an inventor could extend the period of exclusivity that a patent is supposed to provide. For example, an inventor could apply for one patent in 1998 and a second on the same invention in 2008, thereby obtaining the equivalent of a 30-year patent. To prevent this result, a claim can be held unpatentable or invalid if it duplicates the subject matter of a claim in an earlier patent to the same inventor. This is referred to as "double patenting." Double patenting can also be found where the claims are attributable to different "inventive entities"[281] but are owned by a common assignee.[282]

Double patenting comes in two forms. The first is "same invention" double patenting, which means that the later claim is identical in scope to the earlier claim.[283] The prohibition against "same invention" double patenting is said to have a statutory basis in 35 U.S.C. § 101, which states that "[w]hoever invents or discovers any new and useful process . . . may obtain *a* patent therefor."[284] The more common form of double patenting is "obviousness-type double patenting," which means that the later claim, though not identical, is only an "obvious variation" of the earlier claim.[285] The reasoning behind this prohibition is that once a patent has expired, the public should be at liberty to use not only the precise invention claimed, but also variations that would be obvious to one of ordinary skill.[286]

Issues of obviousness-type double patenting often arise where an inventor seeks to patent both a broad genus and a narrow species of that genus. For example, an inventor might conceive of both a generic design for a new mousetrap and a specific variation of that design using a particularly sensitive trigger. If the inventor obtained a patent on the broad invention first and then sought a patent on the variation or improvement, the question would be whether the variation was obvious in light of the more general design. If not, the inventor would be entitled to both patents.[287]

---

[280] *See In re Goodman,* 11 F.3d 1046, 1053 (Fed. Cir. 1993).

[281] See Section 8.9.4.

[282] *See In re Longi,* 759 F.2d 887, 893 (Fed. Cir. 1985).

[283] *See Goodman,* 11 F.3d at 1052; *Longi,* 759 F.2d at 892.

[284] *See Longi,* 759 F.2d at 892.

[285] *See Goodman,* 11 F.3d at 1052; *Longi,* 759 F.2d at 892.

[286] *Longi,* 759 F.2d at 892–93.

[287] It is true that the combination of both patents, issued at different times, might prevent anyone from making the specific mousetrap for a period of more than 20 years. However, this is not considered improper. If one product embodies several distinct patentable inventions, each such invention can result in a patent. When a particular patent expires, that invention is available to the public *as long as* it is practiced in a way that does not violate some other patent. *See In re Kaplan,* 789 F.2d 1574, 1577–78 (Fed. Cir. 1986).

On the other hand, if the inventor obtained the narrower patent first and the broader patent second, the second patent would almost certainly be held "obvious" in light of the first. This result conforms with the rule derived in the context of § 102 that a claim to a genus is anticipated if a single species of that genus is found in the prior art.[288]

On rare occasions the inventor actually filed the application for the broader patent *first,* and it issued second only because of delays in prosecution over which the inventor had no control. Under these circumstances, the second patent has been denied only if each claimed invention would be obvious in light of the other—a so-called two-way test of obviousness. While this can result in an extension of the patent monopoly beyond the contemplated period, where it was not the patentee's fault the extension is not considered "unjustified."[289] Note that the term of patents applied for after June 7, 1995 runs from their filing date rather than their issue date, as was previously the case, so this particular concern will eventually be eliminated.

Obviousness-type double patenting can be "cured," in a sense, by the filing of a "terminal disclaimer" with the Patent Office.[290] A terminal disclaimer is a binding statement that (1) a later patent will expire at the same time as a prior patent, and (2) the later patent will be enforceable only as long as it and the prior patent are commonly owned.[291] The voluntary curtailment of the term of the second patent removes any concern that the existence of two similar patents will improperly extend the duration of the patent monopoly. The requirement of common ownership eliminates the additional risk that the two similar patents might be assigned to different parties, each of whom could press duplicative and harassing claims against a potential infringer.[292]

The terminal disclaimer mechanism provides inventors with some incentive to further develop their patented ideas, even in ways that might be considered "obvious," and to disclose those developments to the public through additional patents.[293] However, this procedure applies only to obviousness-type double patenting; "same invention" double patenting

---

[288] See Section 8.9.5. Although this is classified as an instance of "obviousness-type" double patenting, *see Goodman,* 11 F.3d at 1052–53, one can conceive of cases in which the full scope of a genus is not "obvious" merely from the disclosure of a species of the genus. Perhaps this would be better classified as "anticipation-type" double patenting.

[289] *In re Braat,* 937 F.2d 589, 595 (Fed. Cir. 1991). The same "two-way" approach for obviousness-type double patenting is adopted when one of the patents at issue is a utility patent and the other is a design patent. *See Carman Indus., Inc. v. Wahl,* 724 F.2d 932, 940 (Fed. Cir. 1983).

[290] *See Goodman,* 11 F.3d at 1052; *Longi,* 759 F.2d at 894; 35 U.S.C. § 253.

[291] *See* 37 C.F.R. § 1.321(c); *In re Van Ornum,* 696 F.2d 937, 944–48 (C.C.P.A. 1982).

[292] *See Van Ornum,* 686 F.2d at 944–45.

[293] *See Quad Environmental Technologies Corp. v. Union Sanitary Dist.,* 946 F.2d 870, 873 (Fed. Cir. 1991).

cannot be remedied by a terminal disclaimer. A terminal disclaimer is also no protection against grounds of invalidity other than double patenting.[294] Consider, for example, the case of a prior patent and a subsequent application by different inventors but assigned to the same corporation. A terminal disclaimer would eliminate any question of obviousness-type double patenting, but it would not prevent the prior patent to "another" inventor from invalidating the later application under § 102(e).[295]

Sometimes related patents will issue as the result of a "restriction requirement."[296] A restriction requirement results when the patent examiner, during prosecution, finds that an application claims two or more distinct inventions. The applicant must elect which invention to pursue in the pending application, and if the applicant wishes to pursue one of the other inventions, the applicant must file a "divisional" application. That application, and the original application, may each result in a patent. Because, in this case, the existence of two separate patents is attributable to the Patent Office's determination that each application represents a distinct invention, the patents are immune from a challenge of double patenting.[297] A different result would be unfair to the applicant. But if the claims of the separate applications evolve during the course of prosecution, as they sometimes do, the applicant must maintain "consonance"— that is, the claims cannot be changed in such a way that what was formerly patentably distinct is no longer so. If "consonance" is lost, so is the immunity from double patenting.[298]

---

[294] *See Quad*, 946 F.2d at 874.
[295] See Section 8.9.1.2. Corporations sometimes avoid this kind of problem by filing applications to related inventions, but attributed to different inventive entities, on the same day, thereby ensuring that no application is prior art to another.
[296] See Section 5.3.
[297] *See* 35 U.S.C. § 121; *Gerber Garment Technology, Inc. v. Lectra Sys., Inc.*, 916 F.2d 683, 687 (Fed. Cir. 1990).
[298] *See Gerber*, 916 F.2d at 688.

CHAPTER 9

Enforceability Defenses

Certain defenses to a claim of patent infringement produce, if successful, a holding that the patent is "unenforceable" rather than "invalid." The most important of these are the "inequitable conduct" and "misuse" defenses.[1] If a patent is "unenforceable," it cannot be the basis of an infringement claim.

9.1 INEQUITABLE CONDUCT

In a court proceeding, the presence of an adversary helps to keep the litigants honest. If one party shades the truth or withholds important evidence from the court, the other party will expose the error, if it can. However, as discussed in Section 5.1, patent prosecution is *ex parte*, meaning that persons who might oppose the issuance of a patent have no opportunity to participate. If the applicant shades the truth, there is no one to contradict him. Moreover, the Patent Office often relies heavily on information provided by the applicant. The applicant's sales activities, for example, might be enough to raise a statutory bar under § 102(b),[2] but the patent examiner generally knows about those activities only what the applicant chooses to tell. Nevertheless, every issued patent enjoys a presumption of validity.

Because an applicant could take unfair advantage of this situation, ap-

---

[1] Another "unenforceability" defense might be raised where ownership of a patent subject to a terminal disclaimer had been transferred, contrary to the requirement that patents linked by a terminal disclaimer remain commonly owned. See Section 8.12.

[2] See Section 8.10.1.

plicants are charged with a duty of candor more demanding than what is normally expected of parties in an adversarial proceeding. Applicants are required to disclose to the patent examiner any information that is "material" to the issuance of the patent under consideration.[3] Applicants are not affirmatively required to *search* for such information. They are not, for example, required to search the prior art for potentially invalidating references.[4] But any such information that the applicant is aware of must be divulged. This duty extends to the applicant, the applicant's attorneys and to anyone else who has substantial involvement in the application process.[5] A failure to meet the required duty of candor is known as "inequitable conduct."

Inequitable conduct may be raised as a defense in patent infringement litigation, and, if it is proven, the patent will be held "unenforceable."[6] Although technically the patent may not be *invalid*, the effect is much the same, with one important exception. If a single claim of a patent is invalid (for example, because it is anticipated by a prior art reference), the remaining claims of the patent can be enforced if they do not suffer the same defect.[7] In contrast, if an applicant obtained a single patent claim through inequitable conduct, the *entire patent* is unenforceable.[8] This result often makes inequitable conduct a more attractive defense than, for example, anticipation, even though both defenses could be based on the same prior art reference.

An inequitable conduct defense can be based on a misrepresentation made to the Patent Office, or a withholding of information. In either case, two elements must be proven: *materiality* and *intent*.[9] Both standards have been subject to conflicting definitions over the years, suggesting that the courts have had difficulty in defining the conduct that should be considered "inequitable."

"Materiality" means that the information withheld or misrepresented was of sufficient importance to warrant the penalties associated with in-

---

[3] 37 C.F.R. § 1.56.

[4] *See FMC Corp. v. Hennessy Indus., Inc.*, 836 F.2d 521, 526 n.6 (Fed. Cir. 1987). Yet an applicant should not cultivate ignorance if there are sufficient warnings that invalidating prior art does exist. *See Id; Hewlett-Packard Co. v. Bausch & Lomb Inc.*, 882 F.2d 1556, 1562 (Fed. Cir. 1989) (evidence of "studied ignorance" can lead to an inference of wrongful intent).

[5] *Molins PLC v. Textron, Inc.*, 48 F.3d 1172, 1178 7 n.6 (Fed. Cir. 1995); *Fox Indus., Inc. v. Structural Preservation Sys., Inc.*, 922 F.2d 801, 804 (Fed. Cir. 1990); 37 C.F.R. § 1.56(a).

[6] *Minnesota Mining & Mfg. Co. v. Johnson & Johnson Orthopaedics, Inc.*, 976 F.2d 1559, 1569 (Fed. Cir. 1992).

[7] 35 U.S.C. § 288.

[8] *Kingsdown Medical Consultants, Ltd. v. Hollister, Inc.*, 863 F.2d 867, 874 (Fed. Cir. 1988). Unenforceability can even extend to another patent if the patents are found sufficiently related. This is sometimes referred to as "infectious unenforceability." *See Baxter Int'l, Inc. v. McGaw, Inc.*, 958 F. Supp. 1313, 1315–16 (N.D. Ill. 1997).

[9] *Kingsdown*, 863 F.2d at 872.

equitable conduct. One test of materiality is whether the patent would have issued if the correct information had been known to the examiner. This is sometimes called the "but for" test—in other words, "but for" the misrepresentation, would the patent have issued?[10] Another, less restrictive test is whether there is a *substantial likelihood* that a *reasonable patent examiner* would have considered the information *important* in deciding whether the application should issue as a patent.[11] Information can be material as defined by this test even if, ultimately, the examiner would have decided that the patent should issue.[12]

The latter test has been adopted by the Federal Circuit as the *threshold* test of materiality.[13] If the withheld or misrepresented information does not meet this threshold, the inequitable conduct defense necessarily fails. The source of the threshold standard was the Patent Office's own Rule 56, but that rule was amended in 1992 to adopt a new definition of materiality. According to the new definition, information is material if, by itself or in combination with other information, it is inconsistent with a position taken by the applicant, or it is sufficient to establish a *prima facie* case of unpatentability.[14] The latter means that the information initially compels a conclusion of unpatentability (under a preponderance-of-the-evidence burden of proof), before any evidence in favor of patentability is considered.[15] It remains to be seen how or if the new standard changes the Federal Circuit's threshold of materiality.

Under any standard, information cannot be material if it is cumulative of other information available to the examiner. For example, if the information is a withheld prior art reference, it is not material if the examiner considered prior art that was just as pertinent, or more pertinent, than the reference in question.[16] Also, if information was withheld by the applicant but the examiner discovered it on his own, the applicant's action could not be considered inequitable conduct.[17]

---

[10] This test comes in two flavors—the "subjective but for" test, and the "objective but for" test. The subjective test is whether the particular examiner involved would have allowed the application to issue as a patent if not for the challenged conduct. *See American Hoist & Derrick Co. v. Sowa & Sons, Inc.*, 725 F.2d 1350, 1362–63 (Fed. Cir. 1984). This can only be determined if the examiner testifies, a practice that the Patent Office does not endorse. The more practical "objective but for" test asks whether a reasonable examiner would have allowed the patent to issue. *See Id.*

[11] *Molins*, 48 F.3d at 1179.

[12] *See A.B. Dick Co. v. Burroughs Corp.*, 798 F.2d 1392, 1397 (Fed. Cir. 1986).

[13] *Molins*, 48 F.3d at 1179 n.8.

[14] 37 C.F.R. § 1.56(b).

[15] 37 C.F.R. § 1.56(b).

[16] *Molins*, 48 F.3d at 1179.

[17] *Molins*, 48 F.3d at 1185; *Scripps Clinic Research Foundation v. Genentech, Inc.*, 927 F.2d 1565, 1582 (Fed. Cir. 1991) ("When a reference was before the examiner, whether through the examiner's search or the applicant's disclosure, it cannot be deemed to have been withheld from the examiner.").

The *intent* threshold of inequitable conduct is as important as the materiality threshold. If information was withheld or misrepresented by the applicant because of an innocent mistake, the applicant did not commit inequitable conduct, no matter how material the information may have been. At one time, some courts considered *gross negligence* to be sufficient "intent" to warrant a finding of inequitable conduct.[18] However, in *Kingsdown Medical Consultants v. Hollister Inc.*,[19] the Federal Circuit, resolving conflicting precedent, held that inequitable conduct can only occur if the applicant or attorney deliberately attempted to deceive the Patent Office.[20] Hence, a lapse that is the result of carelessness, even gross carelessness, does not amount to inequitable conduct.

Note that intent to deceive can be proven by indirect evidence. It is rare that inequitable conduct will be proven by an applicant's admission or a "smoking gun" document referring to a planned deception. Rather, the proof is likely to be found in circumstances where the information was so important, and the situation so devoid of any possibility of an excuse, that one must conclude that the deception was deliberate.[21]

If the information withheld or misrepresented meets the threshold test of materiality, and if there is also proof of intent to deceive, the ultimate decision of whether there was inequitable conduct is left to the discretion of the judge,[22] who must balance the materiality of the information against the seriousness of the intent.[23] The more important the information, the less the required showing of intent before the patent will be held unenforceable.[24]

Charges of inequitable conduct have become so routine in patent litigation that the Federal Circuit has referred to them as "an absolute

---

[18] *See, e.g., Driscoll v. Cebalo*, 731 F.2d 878, 885 (Fed. Cir. 1984).

[19] 863 F.2d 867 (Fed. Cir. 1988) (resolution of conflicting precedent decided *en banc*).

[20] *Kingsdown*, 863 F.2d at 876 ("We adopt the view that a finding that particular conduct amounts to 'gross negligence' does not of itself justify an inference of intent to deceive; the involved conduct, viewed in light of all of the evidence, including evidence indicative of good faith, must indicate sufficient culpability to require a finding of intent to deceive.").

[21] " '[S]moking gun' evidence is not required in order to establish an intent to deceive. . . . Rather, this element of inequitable conduct must generally be inferred from the facts and circumstances surrounding the applicant's overall conduct." *Paragon Podiatry Lab., Inc. v. KLM Labs., Inc.*, 984 F.2d 1182, 1189–90 (Fed. Cir. 1993); *see also Molins*, 48 F.3d at 1180–81; *General Electro Music Corp. v. Samick Music Corp.*, 19 F.3d 1405 (Fed. Cir. 1994).

[22] *Molins*, 48 F.3d at 1178.

[23] *See Molins*, 48 F.3d at 1178 ("Once threshold findings of materiality and intent are established, the court must weigh them to determine whether the equities warrant a conclusion that inequitable conduct has occurred. . . . In light of all the circumstances, an equitable judgment must be made concerning whether the applicant's conduct is so culpable that the patent should not be enforced.").

[24] *See Halliburton Co. v. Schlumberger Technology Corp.*, 925 F.2d 1435, 1439–40 (Fed. Cir. 1991); *Demaco Corp. v. F. Von Langsdorff Licensing Ltd.*, 851 F.2d 1387, 1394–95 (Fed. Cir. 1988).

plague."[25] It is difficult to say whether this reflects a low standard of ethics among applicants and prosecuting attorneys, or just the readiness of accused infringers to raise every conceivable defense.

9.2 MISUSE

The patent system strikes a delicate balance between, on the one hand, the desire to encourage innovation by rewarding inventors with exclusive rights to their inventions and, on the other hand, the desire to promote healthy competition in the marketplace. While the essence of the patent system is the grant of a monopoly, it is still a monopoly of limited scope and duration. If a patent owner attempts to leverage the advantage of a patent into something beyond its intended boundaries, the patent owner may be held to have committed "misuse."[26] Like the inequitable conduct defense, the misuse defense leads, if successful, to a holding that the patent is unenforceable.

An early example of overreaching by a patent owner can be found in *Morton Salt Co. v. G.S. Suppiger.*[27] Suppiger obtained a patent on a machine used in the canning industry for adding salt tablets to the contents of the cans. Only the machine was patented; the salt tablets were not. Nevertheless, when Suppiger leased its machines to canneries, it licensed the canneries to use the machines only if they agreed to buy all of their salt tablets from a Suppiger subsidiary. The Supreme Court viewed this extension of the patent grant as improper and held that a patent owner guilty of such practices could not look to a court for relief.[28] Today such conduct would be characterized as "misuse."

Although there is no exhaustive list of the kinds of behavior that might constitute misuse, the following often raise questions:

- A patent license, such as that discussed in *Morton Salt,* which compels the licensee to purchase separate, unpatented goods from the patent owner. This is called a "tying" arrangement.[29]

---

[25] *Burlington Indus., Inc. v. Dayco Corp.,* 849 F.2d 1418, 1422 (Fed. Cir. 1988).

[26] *See Atari Games Corp. v. Nintendo of America, Inc.,* 897 F.2d 1572, 1576 (Fed. Cir. 1990) ("a patent owner may not take the property right granted by a patent and use it to extend his power in the marketplace improperly, i.e. beyond the limits of what Congress intended to give in the patent laws"); *Windsurfing Int'l, Inc. v. AMF, Inc.,* 782 F.2d 995, 1001 (Fed. Cir. 1986) (a misuse defense "requires that the alleged infringer show that the patentee has impermissibly broadened 'the physical or temporal scope' of the patent grant with anticompetitive effect" (citation omitted)).

[27] 314 U.S. 488, 62 S. Ct. 402 (1941).

[28] *Morton Salt,* 314 U.S. at 492–94, 62 S. Ct. at 405–6.

[29] *See Senza-Gel Corp. v. Seiffhart,* 803 F.2d 661(Fed. Cir. 1986). Note that it is not misuse to demand that licensees purchase from the patent owner goods which, if purchased from someone else, could supply the basis of a claim of contributory infringement—for

- A patent license that forbids the licensee from dealing with the patent owner's competitors. This is sometimes called "tying-out" in contrast the "tying-in" found in *Morton Salt.*

- A patent license granted only on the condition that *other* patents are also licensed, even though the other patents may be undesired or even invalid.[30]

- A patent license that attempts to fix downstream prices.

The misuse defense covers some of the same territory as the federal antitrust laws,[31] at least where the challenged activity takes the form of a threat to competition. Conduct may rise to the level of misuse without violating the antitrust laws,[32] but similar considerations of "market power," anticompetitive effects and business justifications appear in either context,[33] particularly after recent changes to 35 U.S.C. § 271. The latter now states that it is misuse to condition a patent license on the sale of a separate, unpatented product only if the patent owner has "market power" in the relevant market.[34] The same limitation applies to patent licenses offered only as a group.[35]

"Market power" is a concept developed in the setting of antitrust law, and perhaps only an economist could provide a thorough definition. In general terms, "market power" means the ability to alter the conditions of trade, and in particular to raise prices, beyond what could be accomplished in a competitive market. Whether a company has market power depends on the availability of acceptable substitutes for whatever goods or services that company controls. Thus, if *Morton Salt* had applied the current version of § 271, the court might have considered whether Suppiger's patented salt depositing machines were so superior that it could compel canneries to obtain a patent license, even at the cost of having to purchase unpatented salt tablets from Suppiger's subsidiary. If the can-

example, goods useful only in practicing the patented invention. *See* 35 U.S.C. § 271(d). Contributory infringement is discussed in Section 10.4.

[30] It is common for patent owners to license a group of related patents as a package—an arrangement that may be convenient for the licensee as well as for the patent owner. The potential of misuse exists only if the patent owner refuses to license individual patents on reasonable terms.

[31] The federal antitrust laws (e.g., the Sherman Antitrust Act, 15 U.S.C. §§ 1–7) are designed to protect competition in the marketplace. Because a patent is a *legal* form of monopoly, efforts to enforce a patent within its legitimate scope do not violate the antitrust laws. *See Atari,* 897 F.2d at 1576. On the other hand, it can be a violation of the antitrust laws to enforce a patent obtained by fraud or known to be invalid. *See Id.* at 1576.

[32] *Morton Salt,* 314 U.S. at 494, 62 S. Ct. at 406; *Senza-Gel,* 803 F.2d at 668.

[33] *See Windsurfing,* 782 F.2d at 1002 (unless conduct has been deemed *per se* anticompetitive, there must be a showing that it "tends to restrain competition unlawfully in an appropriately defined market").

[34] 35 U.S.C. § 271(d).

[35] 35 U.S.C. § 271(d).

neries could easily have chosen another machine without such restrictions, Suppiger would not have had the "power" to restrain competition.

Even where a misuse defense is dependent on a demonstration of anticompetitive effects, it is not necessary that the party raising the defense have suffered those anticompetitive effects personally. Protection of the public from abusive practices, and denial of relief to those undeserving of the court's protection, are reasons enough to hold a patent unenforceable, no matter what effect the challenged conduct has had on the litigants in a particular case.[36]

Some conduct that might seem anticompetitive is not considered misuse. For example, it is not misuse to grant only a limited number of licenses to a patent, to grant no licenses to a patent or to completely suppress an invention by neither practicing it nor licensing it.[37] It is up to the patentee to decide whether the invention will be exploited during the term of the patent. In only a few cases have courts found this result so injurious to the public welfare that they have refused to enjoin infringement, a decision that is tantamount to granting a compulsory license.[38]

Unlike invalidity, or unenforceability resulting from inequitable conduct, unenforceability resulting from misuse is reversible. The patent can be enforced again as soon as the objectionable conduct has ceased and any lingering effects have "dissipated."[39]

[36] *Morton Salt,* 314 U.S. at 493–94, 62 S. Ct. at 405–6.

[37] *See* 35 U.S.C. § 271(d) (stating that "refus[al] to license or use any rights to the patent" is not an act of misuse); *Rite-Hite Corp. v. Kelley Co.,* 56 F.3d 1538, 1547 (Fed. Cir. 1995).

[38] *See Rite-Hite,* 56 F.3d at 1547–48.

[39] *Morton Salt* 314 U.S. at 493, 62 S. Ct. at 405; *see also Senza-Gel,* 803 F.2d at 668 n.10.

CHAPTER 10

Infringement

The owner of a patent has the exclusive right to make, use, sell, offer to sell or import into the United States the invention described by the claims. Anyone else who engages in those activities, without the permission of the patent owner, is an "infringer."[1] An infringer can be sued for money damages[2] and can be compelled by a court to cease the infringing activities.

10.1 PATENT TERM

A patent can be infringed only during the period of time when the patent is in force. A patent becomes effective on its *issue* date and expires 20 years after the *filing* date of the application.[3] Thus, the term of a patent will vary depending on how long it takes for the application to make its way through the Patent Office. A patent issued in 2002 on an application filed in 1997 would last only fifteen years, expiring in 2017.[4]

Until recently, the term of a patent was seventeen years from the date of *issue*.[5] However, long delays in prosecution, sometimes due to maneu-

---

[1] *See* 35 U.S.C. § 271.

[2] See Section 11.8.

[3] 35 U.S.C. § 154. If the patent issued from an application that was a "continuation" of a prior application or applications (see Section 5.2), the term is measured from the filing date of the earliest application in the chain.

[4] The 20-year term applies to utility patents. "Design patents," discussed in Section 12.1, have a term of 14 years from the date of issue. 35 U.S.C. § 173.

[5] Due to the change from a 17-year to a 20-year term, patents applied for prior to June 8, 1995 are entitled to the greater of the 20-year term provided by the current statute, or the term of 17 years from issue provided by the former statute. 35 U.S.C. § 154(c).

vering by the applicant, occasionally resulted in patents issuing on inventions that had already been in public use for decades. In 1990, for example, computer chip manufacturers learned that a patent had been issued to one Gilbert Hyatt claiming the basic concept of the microprocessor—already the subject of a long-established and lucrative industry. This patent appeared at such a late date because it took 21 years and the prosecution of a long chain of related applications before the patent issued. Since the application process is conducted in secret, none of the chip manufacturers knew of the patent before it issued. The current practice of measuring the effective term of a patent from its filing date reduces the incentive for applicants to delay prosecution and surprise an industry with a so-called submarine patent.[6]

Until a patent issues it cannot be infringed, even by someone who knows that an application is "pending." Yet once the patent does issue, the patent owner can force any infringing activity to cease, even if that activity has already begun.[7]

10.2 GEOGRAPHIC LIMITATIONS

United States patent law does not apply to activities that take place entirely in another country. The sale or use of a patented product in Japan, for example, is not an infringement of a United States patent, although it could be an infringement of a corresponding Japanese patent. The law also provides an explicit exception for inventions built into vehicles, such as aircraft, that may enter the United States temporarily. If a United States patent covered a design for landing gear, and a Japanese airliner with the claimed landing gear flew into the United States to deliver passengers, the "use" of the patented landing gear in the United States would not infringe the patent.[8]

In two respects, United States patent law does take notice of activities occurring in another country. First, delivering the *components* of a patented invention from the United States to a foreign country, where they will be assembled into the claimed combination, can be an infringement of a United States patent.[9] The legal analysis mirrors that of "contributory

---

[6] Because delays in prosecution can sometimes be beyond the applicant's control, the law allows for an extension of the patent term for up to five years under certain circumstances, including where the application was the subject of an interference proceeding (see Section 5.4) or delayed by appellate review of a patent examiner's decision. *See* 35 U.S.C. § 154(b). Term extensions are also available in certain situations where marketing of the invention was delayed because of an FDA review. *See* 35 U.S.C. §§ 155–156.

[7] However, see Section 5.5 regarding "intervening rights" that may arise in the context of patents that are *reissued*.

[8] *See* 35 U.S.C. § 272. The exception applies to countries offering reciprocal privileges.

[9] *See* 35 U.S.C. § 271(f).

infringement" or "inducement" of infringement in the United States, topics discussed in Section 10.4. Second, it can be an infringement of a United States patent to import, use, sell or offer to sell in the United States a product made in a foreign country by a *process* patented in the United States.[10] This prevents the evasion of United States patents by moving production overseas.[11]

The latter provision does not apply if the product is "materially changed by subsequent processes," or if the product "becomes a trivial and nonessential component of another product."[12] So, for example, if the patent claimed a process for refining aluminum, it would probably not be an infringement to import an automobile having an aluminum ashtray, even if the material from which the ashtray was made could be traced back to the patented process. At some point, the imported product becomes too far removed from the claimed process to regard the importation of that product as an infringement.

10.3 STATE OF MIND

Generally speaking, the intentions of the infringer are irrelevant to infringement. A patent can be infringed even by someone who is unaware that the patent exists.[13] However, infringement which *is* intentional, referred to as "willful infringement," can result in an award of increased damages, up to three times the amount of damages that could be recovered from an "innocent infringer," together with attorneys' fees. These increased awards, intended as a penalty or deterrent, are discussed in Section 11.8.2.

"Indirect" infringement, discussed in Section 10.4, is an exception to the general rule. "Inducement" of infringement and "contributory infringement," both forms of indirect infringement, do require an awareness of the patent and knowledge of the infringing acts.

10.4 DIRECT AND INDIRECT INFRINGEMENT

One who, without authority, makes, uses, sells, offers to sell or imports into the United States a product covered by a patent is a "direct in-

---

[10] 35 U.S.C. § 271(g).

[11] *See Eli Lilly & Co. v. American Cyanamid Co.*, 82 F.3d 1568, 1571–72 (Fed. Cir. 1996).

[12] 35 U.S.C. § 271(g); *see also Eli Lilly*, 82 F.3d at 1572; *Bio-Technology General Corp. v. Genentech, Inc.*, 80 F.3d 1553, 1560 (Fed. Cir. 1996). Of course, whether the product of a patented process has been "materially changed" is a matter of degree and can be a difficult question. Because the statute is relatively new, there have been few opportunities so far for the courts to clarify how the rule will be applied.

[13] *Hilton Davis Chemical Co. v. Warner-Jenkinson Co.*, 62 F.3d 1512, 1519 (Fed. Cir. 1995) ("Intent is not an element of infringement. . . . A patent may exclude others from practicing the claimed invention, regardless of whether the infringers even know of the patent."); *Warner-Jenkinson, Inc. v. Hilton Davis Chemical Co.*, 117 S. Ct. 1040, 1052 (1997).

fringer." One who is not a "direct infringer" may be held equally liable for encouraging or contributing to infringement by *someone else.* This is sometimes referred to as "indirect" or "dependent" infringement.[14]

Indirect infringement comes in two forms—"inducement" of infringement and "contributory infringement." The concept of inducement is the simpler one. Anyone who "actively induces" the infringement of a patent by another may be held liable as an infringer.[15] Consider the case of *Moleculon Research Corp. v. CBS, Inc.*[16] CBS sold the popular toy known as Rubik's Cube, a product that Moleculon believed to infringe its patent on a rotating-cube puzzle. Some of the claims, rather than describing the puzzle as a physical object, instead claimed a method of solving the puzzle by rotating the facets of the cube. These method claims could be directly infringed only by someone performing the steps of the method—that is, by someone using the puzzle. However, it would have been impractical to file suit against every consumer who purchased Rubik's Cube. Even though CBS did not directly infringe those method claims, the court found that it could be held liable for inducing infringement by purchasers, largely because it sold puzzles and instruction sheets that would lead purchasers to practice the method.[17]

Although a direct infringer can be completely innocent of the existence of the patent, one who induces infringement must know of the patent and must intend to cause the infringing acts.[18] Where such intent is found, it is even possible to hold officers or directors of a corporation liable for an infringement by their corporation, if they "actively assisted" in that infringement.[19] This is one instance in which the corporate form will not shield officers or directors from personal liability for the acts of their corporation. Such liability still is comparatively rare since it is seldom possible to prove the necessary intent.

A "contributory infringer" is one who imports, sells or offers to sell a *component* of a patented combination, or a material or apparatus to be used in a patented process, if all of the following conditions are met:[20]

---

[14] In any case of indirect infringement, there must be evidence of a related *direct* infringement by someone else. *Sage Prods., Inc. v. Devon Indus., Inc.,* 45 F.3d 1575, 1577 (Fed. Cir. 1995). However, that direct infringement can be shown by circumstantial evidence. *See Moleculon Research Corp. v. CBS, Inc.,* 793 F.2d 1261, 1272 (Fed. Cir. 1990).

[15] 35 U.S.C. § 271(b).

[16] 793 F.2d 1261 (Fed. Cir. 1986).

[17] *Moleculon,* 794 F.2d at 1272.

[18] *See Manville Sales Corp. v. Paramount Sys., Inc.,* 917 F.2d 544, 553 (Fed. Cir. 1990); *Hewlett-Packard Co. v. Bausch & Lomb Inc.,* 909 F.2d 1464, 1469 (Fed. Cir. 1990). Some courts may impose a "knew *or should have known*" standard of knowledge. *See Manville,* 917 F.2d at 553.

[19] *See Manville,* 917 F.2d at 553; *Orthokinetics, Inc. v. Safety Travel Chairs, Inc.,* 806 F.2d 1565, 1578–79 (Fed. Cir. 1986).

[20] 35 U.S.C. § 271(c).

- The item is a "*material part* of the patented invention."

- The item is imported, sold or offered for sale with *knowledge* that the item was "*especially made or especially adapted*" for use in an infringing manner.[21]

- The item is *not* a "staple article or commodity of commerce suitable for substantial noninfringing use."

Many patented combinations include individual elements that themselves are common and unpatentable. The Oviatt mousetrap design (see Appendix A) includes an ordinary ping-pong ball. The Oviatt patent cannot prevent anyone from making, using, importing, selling or offering to sell ping-pong balls, which have obvious uses unrelated to the mousetrap invention. The inventor's legitimate monopoly extends only to the claimed combination. Suppose, however, that someone sold the remaining components of the Oviatt mousetrap, without the ping-pong ball. Since all of the claims of the Oviatt patent require a ball, selling the remaining pieces would not directly infringe the patent.[22] However, it is likely that anyone who purchased the incomplete trap would eventually supply the missing ball, thereby forming an infringing combination. If the patent owner were forced to sue only those who formed that combination—consumers who purchased an incomplete trap and supplied their own ping-pong ball—enforcement of the Oviatt patent would be impractical.

Patent law treats as contributory infringement the importation, sale or offer to sell a component of a claimed combination if the component is "especially made" for use in the patented combination (like the tubed structure depicted in the Oviatt patent) and not a "staple article or commodity of commerce suitable for substantial noninfringing use" (like a ping-pong ball). Originally, the law made no distinction between contributory infringement and inducement, and it is still useful to consider contributory infringement in the inducement context. The sale of a ping-pong ball could not, by itself, be legitimately regarded as an inducement to infringe the Oviatt patent, since the ping-pong ball could be used for something else. The sale of the single-purpose apparatus could, how-

---

[21] Although it is not apparent on the face of the statute, contributory infringement requires both knowledge that the component is adapted to a particular use and knowledge of the patent that proscribes that use. *Hewlett-Packard Co. v. Bausch & Lomb Inc.*, 909 F.2d 1464, 1469 (Fed. Cir. 1990). Someone who is not aware of a patent cannot be a contributory infringer, at least until notified that the patent exists. However, in contrast to inducement, contributory infringement does not require intent to cause the infringing acts. *See Id.* Although the courts have drawn these distinctions, it remains conceptually difficult to separate *knowledge* of the infringing acts, *intent* to cause the infringing acts and *intent to infringe.*

[22] See Section 10.5.

ever, be viewed as an inducement to infringe, since the apparatus has no other plausible use.

The concept of a "staple article of commerce" most obviously applies to basic materials sold in large quantities and useful in numerous applications. Ordinary nuts and bolts and common chemicals would be considered "staples," and their sale would not trigger contributory infringement.[23] But in this context "staple" also applies to goods having even one "substantial" noninfringing use.[24] If it did not, in practical effect the patentee's monopoly would extend to unpatented uses and combinations. If Oviatt could prevent the unlicensed sale of ping-pong balls, he would have an effective monopoly not only on his own invention, but also on the game of ping-pong.

Issues of contributory infringement often arise in the context of replacing worn or broken parts in a patented device. One who obtains a patented device from a legitimate source is permitted to repair that device, or replace a broken or exhausted part, without further obligation to the patent owner.[25] On the other hand, one cannot "reconstruct" the patented device to such an extent that one is, in effect, building a new and unlicensed device.[26] If the substitution of a part effects a "reconstruction" rather than a repair of the patented device, that "reconstruction" can constitute an infringement, and whoever supplied the part may be found liable as a contributory infringer.[27]

The line between "repair" and "reconstruction" is a difficult one to draw,[28] but courts generally have taken a broad view of what it is permissible to repair or replace.[29] If it is simply a matter of replacing a spent component, the replacement will probably not be considered an infringement, as long as the component is not the subject of a patent in its own right. For example, the Federal Circuit held that supplying replacement liners for a biohazard disposal system was not an infringement of the

---

[23] There might be a legitimate claim of inducement, however, if the sale were accompanied by instructions telling the purchaser how to use the goods in an infringing manner.

[24] *See Preemption Devices, Inc. v. Minnesota Mining & Mfg. Co.*, 803 F.2d 1170, 1174 (Fed. Cir. 1986) (a non-staple article is one that has no substantial noninfringing use).

[25] This is true whether or not the replaced part is one "essential" to the combination and whether or not the replaced part is the thing that distinguished the invention from the prior art. *See Porter v. Farmers Supply Service, Inc.*, 790 F.2d 882, 885–86 (Fed. Cir. 1986).

[26] *See Aro Mfg. Co. v. Convertible Top Replacement Co.*, 365 U.S. 336, 346, 81 S. Ct. 599, 604 (1961).

[27] *See FMC Corp. v. Up-Right, Inc.*, 21 F.3d 1073, 1076 (Fed. Cir. 1994).

[28] One court, in a passage cited with approval by the Federal Circuit, declined to adopt any bright-line test to distinguish between repair and reconstruction, placing its reliance instead on " 'the exercise of sound common sense and an intelligent judgment.' " *FMC*, 21 F.3d at 1079 (quoting *Goodyear Shoe Machinery Co. v. Jackson*, 112 F. 146, 150 (1st Cir. 1901)).

[29] *See Sage Prods.*, 45 F.3d at 1578.

related patent because the liners, only a component of the patented combination, were meant to be replaced after a single use.[30] In fact, though it defies logic, one may be allowed to replace an entire device over a period of time, by the successive replacement of worn out or spent parts, as long as in no single instance are the replacements so extensive that they amount to "reconstruction."[31]

10.5 LITERAL INFRINGEMENT

Determining if a patent is infringed is a two-step process.[32] First, one must examine the language of the claims at issue and determine what the claims *mean*. This step, referred to as "claim construction" or "claim interpretation," proceeds according to the rules discussed in Chapter 7. Although it is a principle difficult to apply in practice, claims are supposed to be "construed" without any reference to the thing that has been accused of infringing.[33] Once the claims have been properly construed, they must be *compared* to the accused product or method to see if the claims are infringed. A patent is said to be "literally infringed" if the claims literally or "exactly" describe the thing accused of infringement.[34]

A claim cannot be literally infringed if any claim element is missing entirely from the accused product.[35] This is so even if the missing element seems insignificant in comparison to the invention as a whole. If a mousetrap claim refers to a hook for hanging the trap on a wall when the trap

---

[30] *Sage Prods.*, 45 F.3d 1575 (Fed. Cir. 1995). However, the Federal Circuit recently held that replacement of a carbide drill tip constituted reconstruction, rather than repair, of the patented drill, even though the tip was only a component of the claimed combination. *Aktiebolag v. E.J. Co.*, 121 F.3d 669 (Fed. Cir. 1997). A number of factors influence the court, including the elaborate procedures necessary to replace the tip, the long useful life of the tip compared to other components of the drill, the lack of any substantial industry in replacement tips and the lack of any evidence that the patentee intended for the drill tip to be replaced before the entire drill was disposed of. It is too early to tell whether this case represents a new trend.

[31] *See FMC*, 21 F.3d at 1077. An extreme instance of "reconstruction" appears in one very old case, where patented metal fasteners for cotton bales were melted down after use to form new fasteners. *See Aro*, 365 U.S. at 365, 81 S. Ct. at 610 (Justice Black, concurring).

[32] *Roton Barrier, Inc. v. Stanley Works*, 79 F.3d 1112, 1125 (Fed. Cir. 1996).

[33] *SRI Int'l v. Matsushita Electric Corp.*, 775 F.2d 1107, 1118 (Fed. Cir. 1985) (en banc) ("[C]laims are not construed 'to cover' or 'not to cover' the accused device. That procedure would make infringement a matter of judicial whim. It is only *after* the claims have been *construed without reference to the accused device* that the claims, as so construed, are applied to the accused device to determine infringement." (emphasis in original)). *But see Scripps Clinic & Research Found. v. Genentech, Inc.*, 927 F.2d 1565, 1580 (Fed. Cir. 1991) ("Of course the particular accused product (or process) is kept in mind, for it is efficient to focus on the construction of only the disputed elements or limitations of the claims.").

[34] *Southwall Technologies, Inc. v. Cardinal IG Co.*, 54 F.3d 1570, 1575 (Fed. Cir. 1995).

[35] *See London v. Carson Pirie Scott & Co.*, 946 F.2d 1534, 1539 (Fed. Cir. 1991).

is not in use, a trap that has no hook does not literally infringe. This principle is often called the "all elements" rule. It can be helpful to think of a patent claim as a kind of checklist of features, every one of which must be found in the accused product in order for the claim to be infringed.

On the other hand, infringement is not avoided by adding things that are not described in the claim.[36] Suppose, for example, that a first inventor claimed a mousetrap comprising the combination of a spring, a latch, a mouse-trapping jaw and a trigger which, when disturbed by the mouse, releases the latch and closes the jaw. A later inventor improves the combination by adding an audible alarm that sounds when the trap has sprung. The improved trap would still literally infringe, as long as it had the spring, latch, jaw and trigger claimed.

Some accused infringers mistakenly believe that if they have obtained a patent covering their own product, they are immune from charges of infringing another patent. This is simply not the case. A patent only conveys the right to *exclude others*; it does not convey a right to produce or sell the invention claimed.[37] Even if the inventor of the trap-with-alarm had obtained a patent on the improvement (which is perfectly proper as long as the improvement is "non-obvious"), the product would still infringe.[38] However, the new patent would prevent the first inventor from adding an alarm to his invention, without a license from the second inventor.

The concept of literal infringement is relatively straightforward—a patent is literally infringed if the accused product is exactly what the claims describe. But this is not the end of the infringement inquiry. Even if the accused product is *not* exactly what the claims describe, it can still be found infringing under the "doctrine of equivalents." Alternatively, if an accused product *is* exactly what the claims describe, it can still theoretically be found non-infringing under the "reverse doctrine of equivalents." These doctrines are discussed in the Sections that follow.

---

[36] *Northern Telecom, Inc. v. Datapoint Corp.*, 908 F.2d 931, 945 (Fed. Cir. 1990) ("The addition of features does not avoid infringement, if all the elements of the patent claims have been adopted. . . . Nor is infringement avoided if a claimed feature performs not only as shown in the patent, but also performs an additional function."). There is an exception if the claim is limited by its terms to the recited elements *and no others*. When a claim preamble ends with the words "consisting of" (rather than the more common "comprising"), the claim is understood to be limited to *only* the elements recited. See Section 7.6.

[37] *Atlas Powder Co. v. E.I. Du Pont de Nemours & Co.*, 750 F.2d 1569, 1580 (Fed. Cir. 1984).

[38] *See Atlas Powder*, 750 F.2d at 1580 ("if Atlas patents A+B+C and Du Pont then patents the improvement A+B+C+D, Du Pont is liable to Atlas for any manufacture, use, or sale of A+B+C+D because the latter directly infringes claims to A+B+C"). Note however, that a second patent can bear on whether an improvement is "equivalent" to the original, if there is no literal infringement. See Section 10.6.

10.6 THE DOCTRINE OF EQUIVALENTS

The "doctrine of equivalents" is one of the most important doctrines in patent law, and one of the most perplexing. It is not based on the patent statutes passed by Congress, but is entirely a product of judicial reasoning. Some critics view the doctrine as inconsistent with other fundamental principles of patent law. However, the doctrine has a long history, and, having survived recent criticisms, it is clearly here to stay.

10.6.1 *Winans v. Denmead*

A good introduction is provided by *Winans v. Denmead*,[39] a seminal case in the evolution of the doctrine of equivalents. Winans obtained a patent on a coal-carrying railroad car shaped like the base (or "frustum") of a cone, with the smaller end extending below the level of the axles. The circular cross-section and tapered dimensions of the car equalized the pressures on the load-bearing surfaces, with the result that a lighter car could carry a relatively larger burden without damage. Winans' patent claim specifically referred to a car "in the form of a frustum of a cone." The car accused of infringing Winans' patent was similarly tapered, but it had an octagonal rather than a circular cross-section. Rather than the "frustum of a cone," the shape of the car was closer to an octagonal pyramid. The accused car did not fall within the literal language of the claim, but it provided similar (though reduced) benefits in equalizing the pressures exerted by the load.

Even though the accused car was outside of the literal language of the claim, the court found that it employed the principle of Winans' invention. The differences were merely differences of "form," and the court held these differences insufficient to avoid infringement.

The exclusive right to the thing patented is not secured, if the public are at liberty to make substantial copies of it, varying its form or proportions. And, therefore, the patentee, having described his invention, and shown its principles, and claimed it in that form which most perfectly embodies it, is, in contemplation of law, deemed to claim every form in which his invention may be copied, unless he manifests an intention to disclaim some of those forms.[40]

The dissenting justice rejected this "substance over form" approach to infringement and emphasized the importance of definite claims in informing the public of the limits of the patentee's monopoly. In his view, a patentee should be held to the limitations made explicit in the claims.

[39] 56 U.S. 330 (1853).
[40] *Winans,* 56 U.S. at 343.

He also warned that nothing could be "more mischievous, more productive of oppressive and costly litigation, or exorbitant and unjust pretentions and vexatious demands" than any relaxation of the requirement that patentees be bound by definite claims.[41]

10.6.2 *Graver Tank*

The modern history of the doctrine of equivalents begins in 1950 with *Graver Tank & Mfg. Co. v. Linde Air Prods. Co.*[42] The patent at issue claimed a material to be used in an electric welding process, including as a principal ingredient an "alkaline earth metal" such as magnesium. The accused product used manganese instead of magnesium, and while the names of the ingredients are nearly the same, manganese is *not* an "alkaline earth metal" as specifically required by the patent claims. Nevertheless, invoking the doctrine of equivalents as expressed in *Winans v. Denmead*, the court found the patent infringed. The following paragraph summed up the majority's support for the doctrine:

[T]o permit imitation of a patented invention which does not copy every literal detail would be to convert the protection of the patent grant into a hollow and useless thing. Such a limitation would leave room for—indeed encourage—the unscrupulous copyist to make unimportant and insubstantial changes and substitutions in the patent which, though adding nothing, would be enough to take the copied matter outside the claim, and hence outside the reach of law. . . . Outright and forthright duplication is a dull and very rare type of infringement. To prohibit no other would place the inventor at the mercy of verbalism and would subordinate substance to form.[43]

The court declined to establish any definite test of whether something outside of the literal scope of a patent claim is still "equivalent." "Equivalence," said the court, "is not the prisoner of a formula."[44] Rather, the judgment must be made in the context of the particular invention, the functions performed by the claimed and the substituted element, and the knowledge available to those skilled in the art. In addition, "[a]n important factor is whether persons reasonably skilled in the art would have known of the interchangeability of an ingredient not contained in the patent with one that was."[45] The court also referred to an earlier case inquiring whether the accused product performs " 'substantially the same

---

41 *Winans*, 56 U.S. at 347 (Justice Campbell, dissenting).
42 339 U.S. 605, 70 S. Ct. 854 (1950).
43 *Graver Tank*, 339 U.S. at 607, 70 S. Ct. at 856.
44 *Graver Tank*, 339 U.S. at 609, 70 S. Ct. at 856–57.
45 *Graver Tank*, 339 U.S. at 609, 70 S. Ct. at 857.

function in substantially the same way to obtain the same result,' "[46] reasoning that " 'if two devices do the same work in substantially the same way, and accomplish substantially the same result, they are the same, even though they differ in name, form or shape.' "[47]

Applying these principles to the case before it, the court found the patent infringed, even though the accused welding material did not include the "alkaline earth metal" apparently required by the claim. The manganese served the same purpose as an "alkaline earth metal," and persons skilled in the art knew the two ingredients to be interchangeable. The substitution was nothing more than a slight and obvious variation of the invention literally described.[48]

10.6.3 Challenges to the Doctrine

The doctrine of equivalents is intended to free the infringement inquiry from excessive literalism and elevate substance over form. From that perspective, the doctrine seems an enlightened policy. On the other hand, the doctrine is at odds with the requirement of claims "particularly pointing out and distinctly claiming the subject matter which the applicant regards as his invention."[49] Ideally, claims notify the public of what can or cannot be done without risk of infringing the patent.[50] But when the doctrine of equivalents is applied, claims can be positively misleading, by seeming to include restrictions that, in the end, a court will disregard. By attempting to honor the "competitor's need for precise wording as an aid in avoiding infringement," while avoiding "the risk of injustice that may result from a blindered focus on words alone,"[51] *Graver Tank* committed courts to a narrow and difficult path.

Recognizing the tension between the doctrine of equivalents and fair notice to potential infringers, the Federal Circuit has warned that

[a]pplication of the doctrine of equivalents is the exception . . . not the rule, for if the public comes to believe (or fear) that the language of patent claims can never be relied on, and that the doctrine of equivalents is simply the second prong of every infringement charge, regularly available to extend protection beyond the

---

[46] *Graver Tank*, 339 U.S. at 608, 70 S. Ct. at 856 (quoting *Sanitary Refrigerator Co. v. Winters*, 280 U.S. 30, 42, 50 S. Ct. 9, 13 (1929)).

[47] *Graver Tank*, 339 U.S. at 608, 70 S. Ct. at 856 (quoting *Union Paper-Bag Machine Co. v. Murphy*, 97 U.S. 120, 125 (1877)).

[48] *Graver Tank*, 339 U.S. at 612, 70 S. Ct. at 858.

[49] 35 U.S.C. § 112.

[50] *See Slimfold Mfg. Co., Inc. v. Kinkead Indus., Inc.*, 932 F.2d 1453, 1457 (Fed. Cir. 1991) ("Inherent in our claim-based patent system is also the principle that the protected invention is what the claims say it is, and thus that infringement can be avoided by avoiding the language of the claims.").

[51] *Laitram Corp. v. Cambridge Wire Cloth Co.*, 863 F.2d 855, 856–57 (Fed. Cir. 1988).

scope of the claims, then claims will cease to serve their intended purpose. Competitors will never know whether their actions infringe a granted patent.[52]

Yet in practice, allegations of infringement under the doctrine of equivalents have become the rule, not the exception. Wherever there is any doubt as to literal infringement, the doctrine of equivalents is routinely invoked as a fall-back position. Indeed, attorneys representing patent owners would be remiss if they failed to take advantage of the opportunities the doctrine provides. The principle that "the protected invention is what the claims say it is,"[53] appears increasingly "utopian."[54]

Eventually, critics began to suggest ways in which application of the doctrine of equivalents might be limited. For example, because *Graver Tank* had alluded to the "pirating" of an invention, or a "fraud on the patent" by an "unscrupulous copyist," some critics suggested that the doctrine of equivalents ought to be applied only in such egregious circumstances.[55] Had this approach been adopted, it would have significantly changed the prevailing practice of applying the doctrine even against "innocent infringers."

However, in *Warner-Jenkinson Co., Inc. v. Hilton Davis Chemical Co.*,[56] the Supreme Court stepped into the debate for the first time since *Graver Tank*. Although the court "share[d] the concern . . . that the doctrine of equivalents . . . has taken on a life of its own, unbounded by the patent claims,"[57] it declined the invitation to abolish the doctrine of equivalents or limit it to "unscrupulous copyists."[58] Instead, it reaffirmed the principles of *Graver Tank* and the generalized application of the doctrine, with some refinements discussed below. Unless Congress enacts new legislation, the doctrine of equivalents will be with us for the foreseeable future.

---

[52] *London v. Carson Pirie Scott & Co.*, 946 F.2d 1534, 1538 (Fed. Cir. 1991).

[53] *Slimfold*, 932 F.2d at 1457.

[54] *Paper Converting Machine Co. v. Magna-Graphics Corp.*, 745 F.2d 11, 19 (Fed. Cir. 1984).

[55] *See, e.g., International Visual Corp. v. Crown Metal Mfg. Co.*, 991 F.2d 768, 773–75 (Fed. Cir. 1993) (Lourie, J., concurring). Note, however, that one person's "piracy" is another person's "designing around" a patent claim. The latter, which refers to the deliberate avoidance of a patent claim when engineering a product, is encouraged as a means of furthering the "useful arts" promoted by patent law. *See State Indus., Inc. v. A.O. Smith Corp.*, 791 F.2d 1226, 1235–36 (Fed. Cir. 1985) ("One of the benefits of a patent system is its so-called 'negative incentive' to 'design around' a competitor's products, even when they are patented, thus bringing a steady flow of innovations to the marketplace."). "[O]ne wonders how ever to distinguish between the intentional copyist making minor changes to lower the risk of legal action, and the incremental innovator designing around the claims, yet seeking to capture as much as is permissible of the patented advance." *Warner-Jenkinson Co. v. Hilton Davis Chemical Co.*, 117 S. Ct. 1040, 1052 (1997).

[56] 117 S. Ct. 1040 (1997).

[57] *Warner-Jenkinson*, 117 S. Ct. at 1048–49.

[58] *Warner-Jenkinson*, 117 S. Ct. at 1051–52.

10.6.4 Tests of Equivalence

One of the most intractable problems raised by the doctrine of equivalents is that of how a court, or in many cases a jury, can decide what is "equivalent" and what is not. Fulfilling the prophecy of the dissenting justice in *Winans v. Denmead*, the issue of equivalence has been as "productive of oppressive and costly litigation" as any other, primarily because the results are unpredictable.[59] In virtually any case where literal infringement is absent, the patentee can produce evidence of similarities between what is literally described by the patent claims and what is found in the accused product, seemingly leading to a conclusion of equivalence. At the same time, the defendant can produce evidence of dissimilarities, seemingly leading to a conclusion of non-equivalence. How is a judge or jury to decide? What Justice Story observed as long ago as 1818 remains true today:

In all my experience I can scarcely recollect a single instance, in which the general question, whether the principles of two machines were the same or different, has not produced from different witnesses, equally credible and equally intelligent, opposite answers.[60]

Although the *Graver Tank* court declined to reduce "equivalence" to a formula, its reference to equivalence based on performing "substantially the same function in substantially the same way to obtain the same result" was adopted in many subsequent decisions as the touchstone of infringement.[61] Indeed, this function-way-result test of equivalence (also referred to as the "three-prong" test of equivalence) has been the dominant test for the past 45 years, taking on a significance that the *Graver Tank* court may not have intended or foreseen. The Federal Circuit, for example, has gone so far as to require that a patentee produce independent evidence on *each* part of the three-prong test—in other words, evidence that the substituted ingredient or apparatus (1) performs substantially the same function, in (2) substantially the same way, to (3) achieve substantially the same result as that which is literally claimed.[62] Without such close adherence to the three-prong test, it was feared that juries would be "put to sea without guiding charts."[63] All the same, the debate commonly boils

---

[59] *See Paper Converting Machine Co. v. Magna-Graphics Corp.*, 745 F.2d 11, 19 (Fed. Cir. 1984) ("In view of [the doctrine of equivalents], a copier rarely knows whether his product 'infringes' a patent or not until a district court passes on the issue.").

[60] *Barrett v. Hall*, 2 F. Cas. 914, 923 (C.C.D. Mass. 1818).

[61] *See, e.g., Malta v. Schulmerich Carillons, Inc.*, 952 F.2d 1320, 1327 (Fed. Cir. 1991); *Lear Siegler, Inc. v. Sealy Mattress Co.*, 873 F.2d 1422, 1425 (Fed. Cir. 1989).

[62] *See Malta*, 952 F.2d at 1327; *Lear Siegler*, 873 F.2d at 1425.

[63] *Lear Siegler*, 873 F.2d at 1426–27.

down to the second prong of the test—whether the accused product and the claimed invention function in "substantially the same way"[64]—and the answer to that question is rarely straightforward.

Another important consideration is whether the item found in the accused product is known to be interchangeable with the item literally claimed. This is not, however, a definitive test of equivalence.[65] Things may be "interchangeable" in the broadest sense if they produce similar results, but still operate in substantially different ways. A word processor may be interchangeable with a ballpoint pen for the purpose of preparing a grocery list, but it would be rare that the two would be considered "equivalent" in any infringement analysis.[66]

More recently, the trend has been to downplay the function-way-result test as the conclusive test of equivalency.[67] Instead, the three-prong test has been described as just one approach to the fundamental inquiry, which is whether the differences between the claimed and the accused product are "insubstantial."[68] Under this test, an "equivalent" is "an insubstantial change which, from the perspective of one of ordinary skill in the art, adds nothing of significance to the claimed invention."[69] Yet to ask whether a difference is "substantial" seems only a rephrasing of the equivalence question, not a clarification.[70] For its part, the Supreme Court in *Warner-Jenkinson* declined to endorse any particular "linguistic framework" for deciding the ultimate question of equivalence.[71] In short, the question of "equivalence" is likely to remain a perennial source of confusion and difficulty.

---

[64] *See Slimfold Mfg. Co., Inc. v. Kinkead Indus., Inc.*, 932 F.2d 1453, 1457 (Fed. Cir. 1991).

[65] *See Warner-Jenkinson Co. v. Hilton Davis Chemical Co.*, 117 S. Ct. 1040, 1053 (1997) (known interchangeability "is not relevant for its own sake, but rather for what it tells the factfinder about the similarities or differences between those elements"); *Key Mfg. Gp., Inc. v. Microdot, Inc.*, 925 F.2d 1444, 1449 (Fed. Cir. 1991) ("an interchangeable device is not necessarily an equivalent device"); *Perkin-Elmer Corp. v. Westinghouse Electric Corp.*, 822 F.2d 1528, 1535 (Fed. Cir. 1987) (interchangeable devices "still must perform substantially the same function in substantially the same way to obtain the same result").

[66] *See Perkin-Elmer*, 822 F.2d at 1535 (devices were "interchangeable" only in "entirely different and unrelated environments" and were not interchangeable for performing certain functions).

[67] *See Hilton Davis Chemical Co. v. Warner-Jenkinson Co.*, 62 F.3d 1512, 1518 (Fed. Cir. 1995) (en banc) ("It goes too far . . . to describe the function-way-result test as 'the' test for equivalency announced in *Graver Tank*.").

[68] *See Hilton Davis*, 62 F.3d at 1518.

[69] *Valmont Indus., Inc. v. Reinke Mfg. Co.*, 983 F.2d 1039, 1043 (Fed. Cir. 1993).

[70] *See Warner-Jenkinson*, 117 S. Ct. at 1054 ("the insubstantial differences test offers little additional guidance as to what might render a given difference 'insubstantial' ").

[71] *Warner-Jenkinson*, 117 S. Ct. at 1054.

10.6.5 Improvements

Equivalency is measured from the perspective of one of ordinary skill in the art *at the time of the alleged infringement.*[72] As a result, variations that the patentee had not even imagined, much less enabled, can be held infringing under the doctrine of equivalents. For example, if a transistor were substituted for a vacuum tube referenced in a patent claim, that claim might still be infringed under the doctrine of equivalents even if, when the patent application was filed, transistors had not been invented yet. If the rule were otherwise, technological advancements would allow competitors to take the substance of an invention but still avoid infringement. However, this does not mean that technological advancements are irrelevant when judging equivalency. A transistor might be such an advancement over a vacuum tube that, in the context of a particular invention, the differences between the two would be thought "substantial" even at the time of infringement.

Texas Instruments, Inc. v. U.S. Int'l Trade Comm'n[73] is a case that illustrates the difficulty of applying the concept of equivalency in fields subject to rapid technological change.[74] Texas Instruments obtained the first patent ever issued on a pocket calculator. The court acknowledged it as a "pioneering invention"[75] and noted that the prototype had become part of the permanent collection at the Smithsonian's Museum of History and Technology. In essence, the claims of the patent called for the basic combination of a keyboard, a processing circuit, a memory and a display, but because the claims were drafted in "means-plus-function" format,[76] the claims literally incorporated only the particular keyboard, processing circuit, memory and display described in the patent specification, and their "equivalents."

About seventeen years after its patent application was filed, and ten years after the patent issued, Texas Instruments brought an action to prevent the importation of pocket calculators by foreign manufacturers. During those years, the field had advanced in significant ways. MOS transistors had replaced bipolar transistors, liquid crystal displays had replaced ther-

---

[72] *Warner-Jenkinson,* 117 S. Ct. at 1053; *Texas Instruments, Inc. v. United States Int'l Trade Comm'n,* 805 F.2d 1558, 1563 (Fed. Cir. 1986); *see also Atlas Powder,* 750 F.2d at 1581 (whether an item is known to be interchangeable with another is judged as of the time of the infringement).

[73] 805 F.2d 1558 (Fed. Cir. 1986). Also see the opinion on denial of rehearing en banc, 846 F.2d 1369 (Fed. Cir. 1988).

[74] The opinion deals with equivalence under 35 U.S.C. § 112(6), discussed in Section 10.7, and under the doctrine of equivalents, but the court treats the two issues as essentially the same. *See Texas Instruments,* 805 F.2d at 1571.

[75] See Section 10.6.4.

[76] See Section 7.7.4.

mal printer displays, and so forth. The Federal Circuit found that each substitution, by itself, might be considered the substitution of an "equivalent," but when considered *as a whole*, all of the technological changes were sufficient to take the accused devices beyond the protection of the doctrine of equivalents.[77] The decision was a controversial one, even among the judges of the Federal Circuit.

One factor that bears on whether an improvement is still an "equivalent" is whether the improvement is itself the subject of a patent. If an "equivalent" is really something that "adds nothing of significance to the claimed invention,"[78] a change worthy of a patent would seem to be beyond the reach of the doctrine of equivalents. However, while it is a factor to be considered and given "due weight,"[79] it cannot be said categorically that a patented improvement is never "equivalent."[80]

Just as an improvement is sometimes still an "equivalent," the same is true of an inferior variation of the invention literally claimed. As the Federal Circuit has observed, "inferior infringement is still infringement."[81] The question, as before, is whether or not the differences are "substantial."

10.6.6 Impact of the All Elements Rule on Equivalence

One of the most important refinements of the principles announced in *Graver Tank* involves the "all elements" rule, which states that each and every element of the claimed invention must be found in an infringing product.[82] In *Pennwalt Corp. v. Durand-Wayland, Inc.*,[83] the court considered whether the doctrine of equivalents could be applied if the claimed invention and the accused product were similar *as a whole*, even though individual claim elements were entirely absent in the accused product.

The invention in *Pennwalt* was a machine used to sort fruit by color and weight. One of the claimed components of the machine was a "position indicating means," which kept track of the physical location of a piece of fruit as it passed through the sorter. The accused product was also a sorting device, and it produced comparable results. However, it did so without

---

[77] *Texas Instruments*, 805 F.2d at 1570–72.

[78] *Valmont Indus., Inc. v. Reinke Mfg. Co.*, 983 F.2d 1039, 1043 (Fed. Cir. 1993).

[79] *National Presto Indus., Inc. v. West Bend Co.*, 76 F. 3d 1185, 1192 (Fed. Cir. 1996); *see also Zygo Corp. v. Wyko Corp.* 79 F.3d 1563, 1570 (Fed. Cir. 1996) ("The nonobviousness of the accused device, evidenced by the grant of a United States patent, is relevant to the issue of whether the change therein is substantial.").

[80] *National Presto*, 76 F.3d at 1192; *Atlas Powder Co. v. E.I. Du Pont de Nemours & Co.*, 750 F.2d 1569, 1580 (Fed. Cir. 1984). See Section 10.5 regarding the effect of a separate patent on the question of literal infringement.

[81] *Whapeton Canvas Co. v. Frontier, Inc.*, 870 F.2d 1546, 1548 n.2 (Fed. Cir. 1989).

[82] See Section 10.5.

[83] 833 F.2d 931 (Fed. Cir. 1987) (*en banc*).

any means for keeping track of the physical location of a piece of fruit. Although a number of judges dissented, the majority held that an accused product cannot infringe a claim under the doctrine of equivalents unless each and every claim element, or its equivalent, can be found in the accused product. Overall similarity is insufficient if any claim element is entirely missing.[84] In *Warner-Jenkinson*, the Supreme Court reaffirmed the rule established in *Pennwalt*, stating that a strict, element-by-element application of the doctrine would ensure fair notice to potential infringers.[85]

Note, however, that there need not be a "one-to-one correspondence" between the claim and the accused product. A single component of an accused product can perform the functions of several components described in the claim, and the single component can be considered the equivalent of *each* claimed component.[86] This principle allows somewhat greater flexibility in applying the doctrine of equivalents than the *Pennwalt* rule might suggest.

10.6.7 Impact of the Prior Art on Equivalence

While the doctrine of equivalents extends the patent monopoly beyond the literal language of the claims, there are limits to how far the patentee can go. One of these limits is a function of the prior art.[87] The doctrine of equivalents cannot expand the scope of a claim so far that it encompasses the prior art.[88] One method of analyzing the problem (though it is not an exclusive method) is to imagine a "hypothetical claim" that would be *literally* infringed by the product at issue.[89] If no such claim could have been validly obtained from the Patent Office, because it would have been anticipated by the prior art or rendered obvious,[90] then the accused product cannot be held to infringe under the doctrine of equivalents.[91] The purpose of this limitation is to ensure that patentees do not achieve

---

[84] *Pennwalt*, 833 F.2d at 935, 939; *see also Lear Siegler*, 873 F.2d at 1425 (" 'a court may not, under the guise of applying the doctrine of equivalents, erase a plethora of meaningful structural and functional limitations of the claims[s] on which the public is entitled to rely in avoiding infringement.' "). Similarly, one cannot claim as an equivalent a structure that is specifically excluded by the language of the claim. *See Weiner v. NEC Electronics, Inc.*, 102 F.3d 534, 541 (Fed. Cir. 1996).

[85] *Warner-Jenkinson, Inc. v. Hilton Davis Chemical Co.*, 117 S. Ct. 1040, 1049 (1997).

[86] *Dolly, Inc. v. Spalding & Evenflo Co.*, 16 F.3d 394, 398 (Fed. Cir. 1994); *Sun Studs, Inc. v. ATA Equipment Leasing, Inc.*, 872 F.2d 978, 989 (Fed. Cir. 1989) ("elements or steps may be combined without *ipso facto* loss of equivalency").

[87] The concept of "prior art" is discussed in Section 8.9.

[88] *We Care, Inc. v. Ultra-Mark Int'l Corp.*, 930 F.2d 1567, 1571 (Fed. Cir. 1991).

[89] *Wilson Sporting Goods Co. v. David Geoffrey & Assoc.*, 904 F.2d 677, 684 (Fed. Cir. 1990); *see also Conroy v. Reebok Int'l, Ltd.*, 14 F.3d 1570, 1576–77 (Fed. Cir. 1994).

[90] See Sections 8.9.5–8.9.6.

[91] *We Care*, 930 F.2d at 1571.

indirectly, through the doctrine of equivalents, a monopoly that could not have been obtained directly by prosecution of a broader claim.[92]

The restrictions imposed by the prior art create, in effect, a "safe haven" insofar as the doctrine of equivalents is concerned, if the accused product in all relevant respects is identical to an invention in the prior art. No "hypothetical claim" could encompass such a product, yet avoid invalidity. The restriction applies only to the claim as a whole, so there is no immunity from infringement by equivalence unless all of the relevant features of the accused product are found in the prior art, either in one reference or in several that, together, made the combination obvious.[93] Because patents are often granted to novel combinations of known elements, one cannot escape infringement, either literal or under the doctrine of equivalents, merely by identifying isolated features of the accused product in the prior art.[94]

The prior art also influences the doctrine of equivalents in a subtler fashion, through the concept of the "pioneer patent." Whereas most patents are granted to incremental improvements of inventions that have gone before, a "pioneer patent" is one that breaks with the past so distinctly that it creates an entirely new field. Patents such as Bell's on the telephone, or the Texas Instruments calculator patent, have staked claims to "pioneering" status. Some cases have held that a "pioneer patent," as a very basic advancement in technology, should be given a correspondingly broad scope of equivalence. A patent on a narrow improvement, on the other hand, should be held more strictly to the language of the claims.[95] Of course, whether or not a patent deserves to be called "pioneering" will often be a subject for debate.[96]

For the most part, the Federal Circuit has declined to divide patents into "pioneering" and "non-pioneering" categories. Instead, it has

---

[92] *Wilson Sporting Goods*, 904 F.2d at 684 ("The doctrine of equivalents exists to prevent fraud on a patent . . . *not* to give a patentee something which he could not lawfully have obtained from the PTO had he tried.").

[93] *See Conroy*, 14 F.3d at 1577; *Corning Glass Works v. Sumitmo Electric U.S.A., Inc.*, 868 F.2d 1251, 1261 (Fed. Cir. 1989) ("Nothing is taken from the 'public domain' when the issue of equivalency is directed to a limitation only, in contrast to the entirety of the claimed invention.").

[94] *See Corning*, 868 F.2d at 1261.

[95] *See Sun Studs*, 872 F.2d at 987 ("The concept of the 'pioneer' arises from an ancient jurisprudence, reflecting judicial appreciation that a broad breakthrough invention merits a broader scope of equivalents than does a narrow improvement in a crowded technology.").

[96] "That an improvement enjoys commercial success and has some industry impact, as many do, cannot compel a finding that an improvement falls within the pioneer category." *Perkin-Elmer*, 822 F.2d at 1532. Even the pioneering status of Texas Instruments' calculator patent was challenged. *See Texas Instruments, Inc. v. U.S. Int'l Trade Comm'n*, 846 F.2d 1369, 1370 (Fed. Cir. 1988).

treated pioneering patents as just one end of a spectrum that embraces various degrees of inventiveness.[97] Moreover, it has emphasized that pioneer patents are not subject to different legal standards than other patents, as a reward for merit or otherwise. A pioneering patent merely enjoys a potentially broader scope of equivalence because it is not hemmed in by large numbers of similar inventions in the prior art, as is generally true of an incremental improvement in an already crowded field.[98]

10.6.8 Prosecution History Estoppel

One of the most important limitations of the doctrine of equivalents is the doctrine of "prosecution history estoppel." The "prosecution history" is the written record of an applicant's dealings with the Patent Office, including any actions taken by the examiner, and any statements, arguments or modifications of the claims made by the applicant.[99] "Estoppel" means a claim is barred, because the claimant's prior actions are inconsistent with that claim. Simply put, prosecution history estoppel prevents a patent owner from contradicting the prosecution history, by claiming as an "equivalent" subject matter that was *given up* during prosecution in order to obtain the patent.[100]

Brenner v. United States[101] provides a good example of prosecution history estoppel. The patented invention concerned a system for coding and sorting mail. The claims described a means for applying a "codable" material, such as a magnetic strip, to an article of mail. The material would carry the information needed for the sorting. When the patent application was filed, the claims referred to a "coded" rather than "codable" material, implying that the information was encoded beforehand. However, the applicant changed the claim language to "codable," telling the examiner

---

[97] *See Sun Studs*, 872 F.2d at 987 ("'[T]he 'pioneer' is not a separate class of invention, carrying a unique body of law. The wide range of technological advance between pioneering breakthrough and modest improvement accommodates gradations in scope of equivalency."); *Texas Instruments*, 846 F.2d at 1370 ("'[t]here is not a discontinuous transition from 'mere improvement' to 'pioneer' '").

[98] *See Texas Instruments*, 846 F.2d at 1370 (the "liberal" scope of equivalency afforded to pioneer patents "flows directly from the relative sparseness of prior art in nascent fields of technology").

[99] See Section 5.1.

[100] *See Hogannas AB v. Dresser Indus., Inc.*, 9 F.3d 948, 951–52 (Fed. Cir. 1993) ("The essence of prosecution history estoppel is that a patentee should not be able to obtain, through the doctrine of equivalents, coverage of subject matter that was relinquished during prosecution to procure issuance of the patent."). While the clearest cases of estoppel arise after a claim is narrowed by *amendment*, even where a claim is unchanged estoppel can result from an applicant's *arguments* in favor of a narrow claim interpretation. *See Texas Instruments, Inc. v. U.S. Int'l Trade Comm'n*, 988 F.2d 1165, 1174 (Fed. Cir. 1993).

[101] 773 F.2d 306 (Fed. Cir. 1985).

that the new language more accurately described the invention " 'since when the material is placed on the mail it is not yet coded.' "[102] When compelled to distinguish certain prior art, the applicant stressed this distinction and also emphasized that the material could be erased after encoding.

The system accused of infringing used an ink jet printer to spray bar codes directly on the mail to be sorted. The only article applied to the mail was the ink itself, and the ink was not literally "codable." By the time the ink hit the paper, it was fixed in a predetermined pattern, and it could not be altered or erased afterward. The trial court, affirmed by the Federal Circuit, found that the accused system could not be held "equivalent" to the system claimed because the applicant, during prosecution, had clearly limited the invention to "codable material."[103]

Prosecution history estoppel checks the inclination of some patent owners to treat claims as the proverbial "nose of wax," to be twisted in one direction to avoid invalidity and another to ensure infringement. An applicant who represents the invention as one thing in prosecution must be prepared to live with that interpretation in litigation.[104] There can be no "second bite at the abandoned apple."[105] The doctrine also provides better notice to a patentee's competitors of the scope of the patented invention, at least in those cases where the competitors have an opportunity to review the prosecution history.[106] Most importantly, the doctrine of prosecution history estoppel prevents applicants from circumventing the process of patent examination. If the scope of equivalence were not limited by the prosecution history, an applicant could narrow the claims as much as necessary to satisfy the examiner, while resorting to the doctrine of equivalents to preserve what amounts to a broader claim. Prosecution history estoppel helps to ensure that a patent claim is no broader in scope than the examiner understood it to be.[107]

Yet prosecution history estoppel cannot be applied unthinkingly wherever claim language was altered during prosecution. Careful consid-

---

[102] *Brenner,* 773 F.2d at 307.

[103] *Brenner,* 773 F.2d at 308.

[104] *See Southwall Technologies, Inc. v. Cardinal IG Co.,* 54 F.3d 1570, 1576 (Fed. Cir. 1995) ("The prosecution history limits the interpretation of claim terms so as to exclude any interpretation that was disclaimed during prosecution.").

[105] *Lemelson v. General Mills, Inc.,* 968 F.2d 1202, 1208 (Fed. Cir. 1992).

[106] *See Lemelson,* 968 F.2d at 1208 ("Other players in the marketplace are entitled to rely on the record made in the Patent Office in determining the meaning and scope of the patent.").

[107] *See Genentech, Inc. v. Wellcome Foundation Ltd.,* 29 F. 3d 1555, 1564 (Fed. Cir. 1994) ("An applicant should not be able deliberately to narrow the scope of examination to avoid during prosecution scrutiny by the PTO of subject matter . . . and then, obtain in court, either literally or under the doctrine of equivalents, a scope of protection which encompasses that subject matter.").

eration must be given to exactly how the claim was changed, and why.[108] Claim language may be altered for reasons that have nothing to do with patentability, or at least nothing to do with avoiding the prior art. For example, language may be added to a claim solely for the sake of clarity.[109] In these cases, the change does not limit the scope of equivalence because it was never the intention of the applicant to narrow the claim, nor would the examiner have understood that to be the effect. Unless the claim was narrowed, and the purpose of the narrowing was to support patentability, prosecution history estoppel does not apply.[110]

Naturally, this leads to disputes over the reasons for altering claim language, and those reasons are often poorly documented in the prosecution history. In *Warner-Jenkinson*, the Supreme Court introduced a *presumption* that claim amendments required by the Patent Office during prosecution were occasioned by a "substantial reason related to patentability."[111] The burden is on the patent owner to rebut that presumption by showing that the amendment had another explanation "sufficient to overcome prosecution history estoppel."[112] This new procedural framework raises two still-unanswered questions: what type of evidence can the patentee present to overcome the presumption, and when is the reason "sufficient"?

The concurring Justices in *Warner-Jenkinson* warned of the potential unfairness to patentees who had prosecuted their patents before the presumption was announced and who may not have made it their practice to record the reasons for amending a claim.[113] On remand of the same case, the Federal Circuit echoed this concern but declined to characterize the evidence that a patentee might submit to rebut the presumption. The court merely stated that "where the prosecution history is silent or unclear the . . . court should give a patentee the opportunity to establish the reason, if any, for a claim change," and the trial court should determine suitable procedures for conducting the inquiry.[114] Courts may eventually decide that the "reason" for an amendment must be found in the prosecution history itself, but this is unlikely given the intention to protect patentees from the retroactive effect of the presumption. Or courts may

---

[108] *Insta-Foam Prods., Inc. v. Universal Foam Sys., Inc.*, 906 F.2d 698, 703 (Fed. Cir. 1990) (" 'a close examination must be made as to, not only what was surrendered, but also the reason for such a surrender' "); *Environmental Instruments, Inc. v. Sutron Corp.*, 877 F.2d 1561, 1566 (Fed. Cir. 1989).

[109] *See, e.g., Andrew Corp. v. Gabriel Electronics, Inc.*, 847 F.2d 819, 825 (Fed. Cir. 1988); *Moeller v. Ionetics, Inc.*, 794 F.2d 653, 659–60 (Fed. Cir. 1986).

[110] *Pall Corp. v. Micron Separations, Inc.*, 66 F.3d 1211, 1219 (Fed. Cir. 1995) ("[C]laims are often amended and rewritten and added and subtracted. A non-substantive change or a change that did not in fact determine patentability does not create an estoppel.").

[111] *Warner-Jenkinson, Inc. v. Hilton Davis Chemical Co.*, 117 S. Ct. 1040, 1051 (1997).

[112] *Warner-Jenkinson*, 117 S. Ct. at 1051.

[113] *Warner-Jenkinson*, 117 S. Ct. at 1055.

[114] *Hilton Davis Chemical Co. v. Warner-Jenkinson Co.*, 114 F.3d 1161, 1163 (Fed. Cir. 1997).

allow reliance on contemporaneous documents, such as attorney notes, or even testimony from the patent examiner, though the Patent Office usually takes a dim view of attempts to obtain such testimony. A third alternative is that patentees will be permitted simply to explain what was intended by an amendment, without any documentation or other corroborating evidence. However, such after-the-fact explanations are often unreliable because of the incentive of litigants to remember events in a favorable light. Worse, they are nearly unrebuttable, because no one except the patentee can explain what his intentions really were. Until these evidentiary questions are sorted out, it is difficult to predict what effects the new presumption will have.

A question no less important than the *reason* a claim was narrowed is the *extent* to which it was narrowed. In other words, what exactly did the patent applicant give up, and how far must the scope of equivalents be restricted? It is not true that after a claim has been narrowed in prosecution, nothing can later be argued as an "equivalent."[115] Prosecution history estoppel only prevents an assertion of equivalency that recaptures what was surrendered.

An amendment may have " 'a limiting effect within a spectrum ranging from great to small to zero,' "[116] depending, to some extent, on the reasons for the amendment and, in particular, the nature of the prior art.[117] Where there is ambiguity, one might infer that the claim was meant to be narrowed only as much as necessary to avoid the prior art. However, when an amendment clearly excludes an entire category of items (such as the change from "coded" to "codable"), a patentee will be held to that limitation, whether or not it was strictly "necessary."[118]

One of the difficulties in judging the scope of an estoppel is knowing from whose perspective the prosecution history should be judged. How relevant are the subjective intentions of the applicant? Recently, the Federal Circuit has endorsed the viewpoint of the "reasonable competitor" as the deciding factor in judging how much the applicant surrendered.[119] Although in reality it is probably rare that a "reasonable competitor" would consult a prosecution history, at least until charged with infringing

---

[115] *Durango Assoc., Inc. v. Reflange, Inc.*, 843 F.2d 1349, 1358 (Fed. Cir. 1988).

[116] *Pall Corp.*, 66 F.3d at 1219 (citation omitted).

[117] *See Festo Corp. v. Shoketsu Kinzoku Kogyo Kabushiki Co.*, 72 F.3d 857, 864 (Fed. Cir. 1995) ("The scope of any asserted estoppel is determined in light of the prior art in the field of art relevant to the change, the statements made to the patent examiner as to the reason for the change, and the purpose of the change as it relates to the allowance of the claims.").

[118] *See Southwall*, 54 F.3d at 1580 (unambiguous surrender of subject matter creates an estoppel, regardless of the characteristics of the prior art); *Prodyne Enterprises, Inc. v. Julie Pomerantz, Inc.*, 743 F.2d 1581, 1583 (Fed. Cir. 1984) (a court will not undertake the "speculative inquiry" of whether a limitation was necessary to avoid the prior art).

[119] *See, e.g., Mark I Marketing Corp. v. Donnelley & Sons Co.*, 66 F.3d 285, 291 (Fed. Cir. 1995); *Hogannas*, 9 F.3d at 952.

the patent, the standard is at least an objective one that promotes more predictable results.[120]

10.6.9 Disclosure of Unclaimed Embodiments

Sometimes the variation claimed as an "equivalent" by the patentee is discussed in the patent specification, even though it is beyond the literal scope of the *claims*. In some ways this seems to bolster the patentee's argument in favor of equivalence. At least it shows that the patentee was aware of the "equivalent," and it suggests the possibility of substituting the "equivalent" for the matter literally claimed. However, the effect of the disclosure can be quite the opposite, as illustrated in the case of *Maxwell v. J. Baker, Inc.*[121]

Maxwell was a store employee who invented a system for tying together pairs of shoes for display. Previous systems had relied on plastic filaments strung through the eyelets of the shoes, but this only worked for shoes that *had* eyelets. This led some retailers to puncture holes in the shoes, just to provide a way of tying them together. Maxwell's idea was to anchor plastic tabs inside of the shoes and use holes or loops in the tabs as the attachment point for the filament. The figures in Maxwell's patent specification showed the tabs anchored between the inner and outer soles of the shoes, and the claims explicitly referred to this construction, but the specification also observed that the tabs could be stitched into the lining of the shoes.

The court held that shoes having tabs sown into the lining did not infringe Maxwell's patent under the doctrine of equivalents, precisely because that option had been disclosed, but not claimed, in Maxwell's patent. Such disclosures are "dedicated to the public."[122]

A patentee may not narrowly claim his invention and then, in the course of an infringement suit, argue that the doctrine of equivalents should permit a finding of infringement because the specification discloses the equivalents. Such a result would merely encourage a patent applicant to present a broad disclosure in the specification of the application and file narrow claims, avoiding examination of broader claims that the applicant could have filed consistent with the specification.

The court's position tends to penalize applicants for making their disclosures more thorough and informative. If Maxwell had kept silent about

---

[120] Note that if courts are willing to accept evidence of a patentee's undocumented reasons for an amendment, this will tend to undermine the use of the "reasonable competitor's" viewpoint for judging the effects of the prosecution history.

[121] 86 F.3d 1098 (Fed. Cir. 1996).

[122] *Maxwell*, 86 F.3d at 1106–7; *see also Unique Concepts, Inc. v. Brown*, 939 F.2d 1558, 1562–63 (Fed. Cir. 1991). *But c.f., YBM Magnex, Inc. v. Int'l Trade Comm'n*, 145 F.3d 1317 (Fed. Cir. 1998) (holding that *Maxwell* creates no "blanket rule" regarding disclosed but unclaimed embodiments, but offering little to clarify the limits of the *Maxwell* principle).

the unclaimed alternative, it might well have been found infringing. On the other hand, if viewed from the perspective of a competitor trying to determine what would infringe, it might be reasonable to conclude that things discussed in the patent, but specifically excluded from the claims, were not meant to be covered by the patent.

10.7 EQUIVALENCE IN THE CONTEXT OF MEANS-PLUS-FUNCTION CLAIMS

Patent law would be less confusing if equivalence were an issue arising solely in connection with the doctrine of equivalents, but in fact equivalence is an issue affecting *literal* infringement if the claim is a means-plus-function claim drafted in accordance with Paragraph 6 of 35 U.S.C. § 112.[123] Means-plus-function claims are discussed in Section 7.7.4, but to summarize, a claim element described as a "means" for performing a specific function is literally infringed only if (1) the accused product performs that function, and (2) the function is performed by a structure that is identical or "equivalent" to the corresponding structure disclosed in the patent specification.[124]

Suppose that a claim to a mousetrap had, as one claim element, a "means for snapping the trap shut," and in the patent specification the structure disclosed for performing that function was a steel spring. The first step in determining if the claim was infringed would be to see if the accused mousetrap had *any* means for "snapping the trap shut." If that function was not performed by any component of the accused mousetrap, the claim would not be literally infringed.[125] If the accused mousetrap did have some means for performing that function, one would then ask whether the structure performing that function was identical or "equivalent" to the steel spring. If the accused mousetrap used, for example, a rubber band to perform the same function, one would have to decide whether a rubber band and a steel spring were "equivalent" in the context of the invention.

Paradoxically, this is one case in which literal infringement is not based on taking the language of the claims literally. Literally, a claim requiring a "means for snapping the trap shut" would be satisfied by *any* means for

---

[123] "An element in a claim for a combination may be expressed as a means or step for performing a specified function without the recital of structure, material, or acts in support thereof, and such claim shall be construed to cover the corresponding structure, material or acts described in the specification and equivalents thereof."

[124] *Pennwalt Corp. v. Durand-Wayland, Inc.*, 833 F.2d 931, 934 (Fed. Cir. 1987) (*en banc*); *King Instruments Corp. v. Perego*, 65 F.3d 941, 945–46 (Fed. Cir. 1995); *Intellicall, Inc. v. Phonometrics, Inc.*, 952 F.2d 1384, 1388–89 (Fed. Cir. 1992).

[125] One might inquire, however, whether it performed an equivalent function that might be sufficient for a finding of infringement under the doctrine of equivalents.

snapping the trap shut. The compromise embodied in § 112(6) is that patentees are allowed to express a claim element as a "means" (which otherwise might be considered indefinite), but literal infringement is restricted to equivalents of the corresponding structure shown in the specification.[126]

The Federal Circuit has cautioned that equivalency for purposes of § 112(6) is not to be confused with equivalency for purposes of the doctrine of equivalents.[127] The contexts are different, since the latter is a specialized subset of the *literal* infringement inquiry.[128] The basis for comparison is also different. Section 112(6) requires comparison of the accused product to the structures disclosed in the *specification,* while the doctrine of equivalents requires comparison of the accused product to the *claims.* Nevertheless, the tests of equivalence are similar. Both "invoke[] the familiar concept of an insubstantial change which adds nothing of significance."[129]

The Federal Circuit has not taken a consistent position on whether the function-way-result test of the doctrine of equivalents can also be applied to equivalence under § 112(6). In the *Texas Instruments* case, the court stated that in either instance "the test is the same three-part test of history: does the asserted equivalent perform substantially the same function in substantially the same way to accomplish substantially the same result."[130] More recently, the court has stated that "[a] determination of section 112 equivalence does not involve the . . . tripartite test of the doctrine of equivalents."[131] Perhaps the most that can really be said is that equivalence under § 112(6), like the equivalence discussed in *Graver Tank,* is "not the prisoner of a formula," but depends on the circumstances of each case.[132]

One difference between § 112(6) and the doctrine of equivalents that has been noted by the Federal Circuit, though perhaps overstated, involves the prior art. As discussed previously, the prior art limits the subject matter that a patentee can claim as "equivalent" under the doctrine of equivalents.[133] Otherwise a patentee could obtain, in effect, a broader claim than

---

[126] *See Johnston v. IVAC Corp.,* 885 F.2d 1574, 1580 (Fed. Cir. 1989) (§ 112(6) "operates to *cut back* on the types of *means* which could literally satisfy the claim language" (emphasis in original)).

[127] *See Valmont Indus., Inc. v. Reinke Mfg. Co.,* 983 F.2d 1039, 1043 (Fed. Cir. 1993).

[128] *See Valmont,* 983 F.2d at 1043 ("The doctrine of equivalents has a different purpose and application than section 112.").

[129] *Valmont,* 983 F.2d at 1043.

[130] *Texas Instruments, Inc. v. United States Int'l Trade Comm'n,* 805 F.2d 1558, 1571 (Fed. Cir. 1986)

[131] *Valmont,* 983 F.2d at 1043.

[132] "[A]ids for determining a structural equivalent to the structure disclosed in the patent specification are the same as those used in interpreting any other type of claim language, namely, the specification, the prosecution history, other claims in the patent, and expert testimony." *Intel Corp. v. U.S. Int'l Trade Comm'n,* 946 F.2d 821, 842–43 (Fed. Cir. 1991).

[133] See Section 10.6.7.

would have been allowed by the Patent Office. But in *Intel Corp. v. U.S. Int'l Trade Comm'n*,[134] the court held that "[i]t is not necessary to consider the prior art in applying section 112, paragraph 6."[135] Section 112(6) applies only to individual claim *elements*, and such elements are often found in the prior art, without affecting the patentability of the claimed *combination*. To return to the mousetrap example, the existence of rubber bands in the prior art would not prevent the patentee from arguing that a rubber band is equivalent to a steel spring when employed as a "means for snapping the trap shut."

The distinction may have been overstated because the doctrine of equivalents also applies to claim elements—a point reemphasized in *Warner-Jenkinson*.[136] If a mousetrap claim explicitly referred to a "steel spring," one could conclude that a rubber band was an equivalent, even if rubber bands were found in the prior art. The prior art would prevent a finding of equivalence only if the *combination* of a rubber band with all of the other claim elements could be found in the prior art.[137] Conversely, one can conceive of a situation in which the only novelty to be found in a means-plus-function claim was derived from the unique structures disclosed in the specification.[138] If the accused product substituted other structures already known in the art, so that the accused product *as a whole* was indistinguishable from the prior art, then perhaps this fact ought to prevent a finding of equivalence under § 112(6). However, this scenario does not appear to have arisen so far.

10.8 THE REVERSE DOCTRINE OF EQUIVALENTS

The doctrine of equivalents has a judicially devised counterpart known as the "reverse doctrine of equivalents." The source of the "reverse doctrine" is the following language in *Graver Tank*:[139]

---

[134] 946 F.2d 821 (Fed. Cir. 1991).

[135] *Intel*, 946 F.2d at 842.

[136] *See Warner-Jenkinson, Inc. v. Hilton Davis Chemical Co.*, 117 S. Ct. 1040, 1049 (1997).

[137] *See Corning Glass Works v. Sumitmo Electric U.S.A., Inc.*, 868 F.2d 1251, 1261 (Fed. Cir. 1989).

[138] This should not have been the case until recently because it was the practice of the Patent Office to ignore the structures disclosed in the specification when deciding if a claim could be granted. In other words, the Patent Office would treat a means-plus-function claim element as though it covered *all* means for performing the specified function. Any novelty supporting patentability would have to be found in the claim itself. However, the Federal Circuit put a stop to this practice in *In re Donaldson Co.*, 16 F.3d 1189, 1193 (Fed. Cir. 1994). Now it is possible to allow a claim solely because the structures disclosed in the specification are novel.

[139] *Graver Tank & Mfg. Co. v. Linde Air Prods. Co.*, 339 U.S. 605, 608–9, 70 S. Ct. 854, 856 (1950); *see also Scripps Clinic & Research Found. v. Genentech, Inc.*, 927 F.2d 1565, 1581 ("the purpose of the 'reverse' doctrine is to prevent unwarranted extension of the claims beyond a fair scope of the patentee's invention"); *SRI Int'l v. Matsushita Electric Corp.*, 775 F.2d 1107, 1123 (Fed. Cir. 1985) (*en banc*).

The wholesome realism of [the doctrine of equivalents] is not always applied in favor of a patentee but is sometimes used against him. Thus, where a device is so far changed in principle from a patented article that it performs the same or a similar function in a substantially different way, but nevertheless falls within the literal words of the claim, the doctrine of equivalents may be used to restrict the claim and defeat the patentee's action for infringement.

Thus, a product literally described by a claim can be held non-infringing, if it is "so far changed in principle" that it functions in a "substantially different way" when compared to what the patentee actually invented.

The language in *Graver Tank* suggests that the doctrine of equivalents is a two-way street, but in practice the "reverse doctrine" has proven to be far less potent than its counterpart. Cases won on the reverse doctrine of equivalents are exceedingly rare.[140] If a court finds that an accused product is literally described by a patent claim, it is difficult to convince that court that the accused product is still "changed in principle" compared to the patentee's invention.[141]

10.9 EXPERIMENTAL USE EXCEPTION TO INFRINGEMENT

A rarely invoked defense to a charge of infringement is that the challenged activity was done for purposes of experimentation rather than profit. This defense finds some support in a number of older cases in which a patented device was constructed not to sell it, but to test its advantages. For example, in *Akro Agate Co. v. Master Marble Co.*,[142] the court held that the use of a patented machine to make glass marbles was not an infringement because the marbles had been made only as an experiment, the results were unsatisfactory and the marbles themselves were not sold. In *Kaz Mfg. Co. v. Chesebrough-Ponds, Inc.*,[143] a patented vaporizor was constructed solely for the purpose of a television commercial in which the design was compared unfavorably to a rival (with the slogan "steam is dangerous"). The court did not view this as an infringement either.

The Federal Circuit has viewed the experimental use exception as a narrow one, applicable only when the experiments were conducted solely "for amusement, to satisfy idle curiosity, or for strictly philosophical inquiry."[144] In other words, a kitchen experimenter amusing himself on a

---

[140] *See, e.g., Precision Metal Fabricators Inc. v. Jetstream Sys. Co.*, 6 U.S.P.Q.2d 1704 (N. D. Cal. 1988); *Lesona Corp. v. United States*, 530 F.2d 896, 905–6 (Ct. Cl. 1976).

[141] *See SRI*, 775 F.2d at 1123 n.19.

[142] 318 F. Supp. 305, 315, 333 (N.D.W. Va. 1937).

[143] *Akro*, 317 F.2d 679 (2d Cir. 1963).

[144] *Roche Prods. v. Bolar Pharmaceutical Co.*, 733 F.2d 858, 863 (Fed. Cir. 1984).

rainy afternoon might practice a patent without infringing, but experiments conducted for *commercial* purposes are likely to violate a patent, if they involve making or using the claimed invention.[145] In the former instance, the infringement is excused primarily on the legal principle of "de minimis non curat lex," or "the law does not concern itself with trifles."[146]

In 35 U.S.C. § 271(e), Congress established a narrow "experimental use" exception to cover the testing of patented pharmaceuticals.[147] When a patent on a particular drug expires, rival manufacturers are, of course, permitted to market their own versions of the drug. However, before this can happen, the new drug must undergo extensive government-required tests of safety and effectiveness. If manufacturing and using the drug for purposes of such tests were held to be an infringement, the tests could not *begin* until after the patent had expired. Consequently, there would be a considerable delay between the expiration of the patent and the opportunity to market a competitive drug. The patent owner would have, in effect, a patent of longer duration than the patent laws intend. Section 271(e) prevents this by allowing these tests to occur prior to the expiration of the patent, without fear of liability.

---

[145] *See Douglas v. United States*, 181 U.S.P.Q. 170, 176–77 (Ct. Cl. 1974).

[146] *See Roche*, 733 F.2d at 863; *Douglas*, 181 U.S.P.Q. at 177.

[147] Although the statute is not clear on this point, it has been held to cover both drugs and *medical devices* that must undergo government-required tests. *Eil Lilly & Co. v. Medtronic, Inc.*, 496 U.S. 661, 110 S. Ct. 2683 (1990).

CHAPTER 11

Patent Litigation

A patent owner whose rights have been infringed can file a lawsuit in a Federal District Court.[1] If the suit is successful, the infringer can be compelled to stop its infringing activity and pay the patent owner for any infringement that has already occurred. Litigation, or the threat of litigation, is what gives a patent its "teeth."

A typical lawsuit concerns three issues:

- Is the patent valid and enforceable?
- Are the claims infringed?
- If the claims are infringed, what damages should be awarded?

The patent owner can prevail only if the patent is valid *and* infringed. On occasion, the defendant[2] will concede that the patent is valid and challenge only the charge of infringement, or it will concede infringement and argue invalidity, but it is far more common for the defendant to make war on both fronts. A patent suit may also involve other related claims

---

[1] A suit for patent infringement cannot be filed in a state court, because the federal courts have "exclusive jurisdiction." *See* 28 U.S.C. § 1338(a). However, if the infringing goods are being imported, it is possible to initiate a proceeding in the International Trade Commission in lieu of, or in addition to, a suit in a District Court. See Section 11.9. Infringement suits against the United States government must be brought in the Court of Claims. *See* 28 U.S.C. § 1498.

[2] It is convenient to use the term "defendant" interchangeably with "accused infringer," but in a declaratory judgment action (see Section 11.2) the accused infringer may technically be the plaintiff.

(e.g., breach of contract, unfair competition or antitrust claims) if they arise from the same factual situation.

Infringement litigation is often a complicated, time-consuming and costly process. Patent cases typically involve both subtle issues of law and complex questions of technology. In order to try such a case, both parties have to acquire a thorough understanding of, at a minimum, the patent and its file history, the accused products and any prior art that might be used to challenge the validity of the patent. As a result, just the "discovery" phase of the litigation, in which both parties gather the evidence needed to try the case, often takes more than a year. It is not unusual for an infringement suit to take several years from the day it is filed until the final disposition of the case, and worse examples can be found.[3]

Patent cases are difficult for courts and juries, both because the law is unfamiliar and because an understanding of complex technology is often critical to deciding the case. Imagine how difficult it would be for an average juror to determine, for example, whether one complex procedure in genetic engineering is "equivalent" to another. Simply mastering the vocabulary can be a daunting task. These difficulties contribute to a certain level of unpredictability in the outcome of patent litigation.

11.1 JURISDICTION AND VENUE

The geographical location where a suit for patent infringement must be filed (for example, in the Northern District of California or in the Eastern District of New York) depends on the rules of "in personam jurisdiction" and "venue." A federal court has "in personam jurisdiction" (or jurisdiction over the person) only if the individual or corporate defendant has had certain "minimum contacts" with the district in which that court resides.[4] If an accused infringer has had no contact whatsoever with, for example, the state of Florida, then suit cannot be filed there. The "minimum contacts" doctrine has constitutional origins in the due process clause. The rules are subtle and depend in part on the jurisdictional rules of the state where the court is located. If the accused infringer has an office in the district, or regularly transacts business in the district,

---

[3] For example, in April 1998 the Federal Circuit rendered an opinion in *Hughes Aircraft Co. v. U.S.*, a case filed in 1973. *See* 46 U.S.P.Q.2d 1285 (Fed. Cir. 1998).

[4] *See International Shoe Co. v. State of Washington*, 326 U.S. 310, 316, 66 S. Ct. 154, 158 (1945) (defendant must have "certain minimum contacts with [the forum] such that the maintenance of the suit does not offend 'traditional notions of fair play and substantial justice.' " (citation omitted)). The defendant's contacts with the forum must be such that "he should reasonably anticipate being haled into court there." *See World-Wide Volkswagen Corp. v. Woodson*, 444 U.S. 286, 297, 100 S. Ct. 559, 567 (1980). The emphasis is on deliberate or "purposeful" contacts rather than those that may occur by accident. *See Beverly Hills Fan Co. v. Royal Sovereign Corp.*, 21 F.3d 1558, 1565 (Fed. Cir. 1994).

or conducts infringing activity in the district, the "minimum contacts" test will likely be satisfied. It may even be sufficient that the infringer intended the accused products to enter the district via the "stream of commerce."[5]

If a court has in personam jurisdiction over the defendant, the next question is one of "venue." The rules of venue create further restrictions on where suit can be filed. In a patent case, venue is appropriate in the following districts:

- Where the defendant "resides," *or*
- Where the defendant has committed acts of infringement *and* has a regular and establishehed place of business.[6]

In 1988, the federal venue statutes were altered so that corporate defendants are held to "reside" in any district where the corporation is subject to in personam jurisdiction—in other words, wherever it has established "minimum contacts."[7] Since most patent cases are filed against corporations rather than against individuals or partnerships, the "minimum contacts" standard is generally the test of whether a suit can or cannot be filed in a particular judicial district.

Because a corporate defendant typically has "minimum contacts" with several states (possibly with all 50), patent owners may have a number of choices in deciding where to file suit. The choice is likely to be governed by factors such as geographical convenience, the experience of the court in dealing with patent litigation,[8] whether the court's docket permits a speedy trial and any perceived "home field" advantages. Within the limits set by the rules of in personam jurisdiction and venue, the location of the lawsuit is generally within the control of the plaintiff. However, if the defendant can show that another district would be more suitable (for the "convenience of parties and witnesses" and "in the interest of justice"[9]), the court in which the suit was filed has the power to transfer the case to another district, if it is a district in which the suit could have been filed in the first instance.

[5] *See North American Philips Corp. v. American Vending Sales, Inc.*, 35 F.3d 1576, 1580 (Fed. Cir. 1994); *Beverly Hills Fan*, 21 F.3d at 1565 ("The allegations are that defendants purposefully shipped the accused fan into Virginia through an established distribution channel. The cause of action for patent infringement is alleged to arise out of those activities. No more is usually required to establish specific jurisdiction.").

[6] 28 U.S.C. § 1400(b).

[7] *See* 28 U.S.C. § 1391(c); *VE Holding Corp. v. Johnson Gas Appliance Co.*, 917 F.2d 1574 (Fed. Cir. 1990).

[8] If suit is filed in, for example, the Northern District of California, there is a greater likelihood that the judge assigned to the case will have handled patent cases before, in comparison to locations where technology-driven businesses are less common.

[9] 28 U.S.C § 1404(a).

11.2 DECLARATORY JUDGMENT

Patent cases generally arise when a patent owner files suit against a party it accuses of infringement. However, it is also possible for the accused infringer to launch a preemptive strike by filing suit against a patentee. A suit of this kind is called an action for "declaratory judgment" because it asks the court to declare that the party filing suit is *not* liable to the patent owner, either because the patent is invalid, or not infringed, or for some other reason.[10] The potential infringer, in such a case, is nominally the plaintiff and the patent owner is the defendant.[11]

If it were not for declaratory judgment actions, parties accused of infringement would have to wait until the patent owner chose to litigate before the dispute could be resolved. In the meantime, the accused infringer would have to give in to the patent owner's demands, or proceed as before with the risk that investments would be lost, and accumulated damages assessed, when the patent owner finally did sue. A suit for declaratory judgment allows the potential infringer to bring matters to a head. It also gives the accused infringer more control over the forum in which the case will be heard.

Federal courts generally follow a "first to file" rule in deciding where a case will be tried.[12] Suppose that a patent owner in California accused a company in Illinois of infringement. For the sake of convenience, and possibly in the hopes of sympathy from a "home town" jury, the patent owner would likely prefer that any litigation take place in California, while the accused infringer, for the same reasons, would prefer Illinois. If the accused infringer sues for declaratory judgment in Illinois before the patent owner sues in California, the "first to file" rule generally means that the case will be heard in Illinois. The "first to file" rule is not absolute, however. An exception can be made if the interests of justice or expediency so require.[13]

On the other hand, a federal court can only try a case if there is a genuine dispute—a "case or controversy" in constitutional terms.[14] A potential infringer cannot file an action for declaratory judgment simply because there is a hypothetical possibility that a patent owner will allege infringement. The threat must be far more immediate and concrete. The party filing for declaratory judgment must have acted, or prepared to act, in a potentially infringing manner, *and* the patent owner must have made

---

[10] *See* 22 U.S.C. § 2201 (Declaratory Judgment Act).

[11] Even if the patent owner initiates the lawsuit, the accused infringer may choose to file a *counterclaim* for declaratory judgment.

[12] *See Genentech, Inc. v. Eli Lilly & Co .*, 998 F.2d 931, 937 (Fed. Cir. 1993).

[13] *See Serco Services Co. v. Kelley Co.*, 51 F.3d 1037, 1039 (Fed. Cir. 1995); *Genentech*, 998 F.2d at 937.

[14] *See Genentech*, 998 F.2d at 936.

an explicit accusation of infringement, or must at least have acted in such a way as to create a reasonable apprehension of litigation.[15]

A potential infringer might receive a letter from a patent owner advising the recipient (1) that the patent owner has an extensive patent portfolio and (2) that the recipient should discuss the terms of a license. This warning would likely be considered so general (not referring to a specific patent, a specific product or a specific intention to file suit) that it would not create a "reasonable apprehension" of imminent litigation.[16] In fact, the patent owner may deliberately refrain from a more concrete warning, specifically to prevent the potential infringer from filing suit.

11.3 BURDEN OF PROOF

The patent owner has the burden of proving infringement by a "preponderance of the evidence."[17] In other words, based on the evidence presented, it must be more likely than not that the patent is infringed. If the evidence on both sides is equally persuasive, the claim must fail.

If the accused infringer raises a defense of invalidity or unenforceability, the defendant bears the burden of proof with respect to that defense.[18] Moreover, the burden is one of "clear and convincing" evidence, a higher standard of proof than a mere preponderance of the evidence.[19] The evidence not only must favor the infringer's version of the facts, it must be sufficient to produce an "abiding conviction" that the facts are "highly probable."[20] The reason for this higher standard of proof is the "presumption of validity" discussed in Section 8.2. The heavier burden of proof for establishing invalidity, as compared to infringement, provides a tactical advantage to patent owners.

11.4 THE ROLE OF JUDGE AND JURY

Litigants in a patent case are entitled to trial by jury,[21] although this right can be waived, by consent of both parties, in favor of a bench trial

---

[15] *See Phillips Plastics Corp. v. Kato Hatsujou K.K.,* 57 F.3d 1051, 1052 (Fed. Cir. 1995); *Serco,* 51 F.3d at 1038.

[16] *See Phillips,* 57 F.3d at 1053–54 (ongoing license negotiations were not sufficient to create a reasonable apprehension of litigation).

[17] *Conroy v. Reebok Int'l, Ltd.,* 14 F.3d 1570, 1573 (Fed. Cir. 1994); *Wilson Sporting Goods Co. v. David Geoffrey & Assoc.,* 904 F.2d 677, 685 (Fed. Cir. 1990).

[18] 35 U.S.C. § 282; *Greenwood v. Hattori Seiko Co.,* 900 F.2d 238, 240–41 (Fed. Cir. 1990).

[19] *Greenwood,* 900 F.2d at 241; *Jamesbury Corp. v. Litton Indus. Prods., Inc.,* 756 F.2d 1556, 1559 (Fed. Cir. 1985).

[20] *Price v. Symsek,* 988 F.2d 1187, 1191 (Fed. Cir. 1993); *Buildex, Inc. v. Kason Indus., Inc.,* 849 F.2d 1461, 1463 (Fed. Cir. 1988).

[21] *See Markman v. Westview Instruments, Inc.,* 116 S. Ct. 1384, 1389 (1996) ("there is no dispute that infringement cases today must be tried to a jury, as their predecessors were more than two centuries ago").

in which all issues are left to the judge.[22] Even if the trial does involve a jury, the judge will still decide certain questions. Generally speaking, a judge decides "questions of law," whereas the jury decides "questions of fact."[23] In reality, most questions have a factual aspect and a legal aspect. For example, to decide if an accused product is "equivalent" to a claimed invention, one has to address questions of fact (how does the accused product differ from the claimed invention?) and questions of law (how much can the accused product differ from the claimed invention before the law no longer considers them "equivalent"?).

Because there is no practical way to separate every nuance of fact and law, certain issues have, somewhat arbitrarily, been deemed "questions of law" for the judge, and others "questions of fact" for the jury.[24] For example, anticipation is a question of fact for the jury,[25] but obviousness is a question of law for the judge.[26] Claim interpretation is a question of law,[27] but infringement is a question of fact.[28] Some questions of law, such as obviousness, depend in part on underlying issues of fact which can be submitted to the jury.[29]

In addition to "questions of law," the judge also rules on "equitable" claims and defenses. In the eighteenth century, there were two varieties of court—courts of law and courts of equity—and they differed somewhat in the kinds of claims that could be heard and the remedies that could be granted. Only courts of law provided a right to a jury trial. In the United States, courts of law and equity were merged long ago, so the distinction would be little more than an historical curiosity if not for the language of the Seventh Amendment of the Constitution. In lieu of setting forth the right to a jury trial in explicit terms, the Seventh Amendment

---

[22] *See* Rule 38 of the Federal Rules of Civil Procedure.

[23] *See Jurgens v. McKasy*, 927 F.2d 1552, 1557 (Fed. Cir. 1991) ("In a jury trial, there are two decisionmakers, the judge and the jury. In general, the judge decides issues of law and issues committed to his discretion, and the jury decides issues of fact that are material to the case and in genuine dispute.").

[24] The arbitrariness of the distinction is suggested by the frequent disagreements among the Federal Circuit judges as to whether an issue is really a question of law or a question of fact. *See, e.g., Markman*, 52 F.3d 967 (*en banc* panel split on whether claim interpretation is an issue of law decided by the judge alone); *Lough v. Brunswick Corp.*, 103 F.3d 1517 (Fed. Cir. 1997) (Federal Circuit split on whether "experimental use" in the context of § 102(b) is a question of fact or law).

[25] *Hoover Gp., Inc. v. Custom Metalcraft, Inc.*, 66 F.3d 299, 302 (Fed. Cir. 1995); *Glaverbel Societe Anonyme v. Northlake Marketing & Supply, Inc.*, 45 F.3d 1550, 1554 (Fed. Cir. 1995).

[26] *Para-Ordnance Mfg., Inc. v. SGS Imports Int'l, Inc.*, 73 F.3d 1085, 1088 (Fed. Cir. 1995); *Stiftung v. Renishaw PLC*, 945 F.2d 1173, 1182 (Fed. Cir. 1991).

[27] *Markman*, 116 S. Ct. at 1384.

[28] *Hilton Davis Chemical Co. v. Warner-Jenkinson Co.*, 62 F.3d 1512, 1520–21 (Fed. Cir. 1995) (*en banc*).

[29] *See Miles Labs., Inc. v. Shandon Inc.*, 997 F.2d 870, 877 (Fed. Cir. 1993); *Jurgens*, 927 F.2d at 1557.

provides that "the right of trial by jury shall be *preserved*" as it was under English common law. Accordingly, to this day courts are required to examine claims from an historical perspective and try to determine whether, applying eighteenth-century standards, the claim is "legal" or "equitable." If the latter, there is no right to a jury.

For purposes of patent litigation, it is enough to know that a claim seeking *money damages* is a legal claim with a right to a jury trial, but a claim to an *injunction* is an equitable claim. In the rare instance that a patentee chooses to forego damages and sue only for an injunction, neither party has a right to a jury trial.[30] Certain defenses are also "equitable" and reserved to the judge to decide. The most important of these are inequitable conduct[31] (discussed in Section 9.1), laches and estoppel[32] (discussed in Sections 11.8.3.3–11.8.3.4). However, the majority of the Federal Circuit recently held that infringement under the doctrine of equivalents (discussed in Section 10.6), often referred to as the "*equitable doctrine of equivalents*," is in fact a matter for decision by a jury.[33]

In spite of the latter development, there may be a trend toward assigning more decision-making responsibility to judges and less to juries. At least certain disapproving Federal Circuit judges perceive such a trend.[34] This shift, if there is one, may reflect a feeling that juries have been overmatched by the complex and difficult issues often presented in patent cases.

11.5 BIFURCATION

Patent cases are often tried in phases rather than all at once. A trial divided into two phases is "bifurcated," but division into three or more phases is also possible. The purpose of holding trial in stages is to focus the issues, avoid confusion and save unnecessary effort.

One common practice is to hold separate trials on liability and damages. If the infringer is not found liable, there is no need to proceed with the damages phase. Another option is to hold a preliminary bench trial on those issues that do not require fact finding by the jury. For example, if a patent has been challenged on grounds of inequitable conduct (an "equitable" defense reserved to the judge), that part of the case can be tried before any jury has been selected.

---

[30] *See In re Lockwood,* 50 F.3d 966, 977 (Fed. Cir. 1995).

[31] *See Kingsdown Medical Consultants, Ltd. v. Hollister, Inc.,* 863 F.2d 867, 876 (Fed. Cir. 1988) ("the ultimate question of whether inequitable conduct occurred is equitable in nature").

[32] *See A.C. Aukerman Co. v. R.L. Chaides Construction Co.,* 960 F.2d 1020, 1028 (Fed. Cir. 1992).

[33] *See Hilton-Davis,* 62 F.3d at 1521.

[34] See Judge Newman's dissent in *Lough,* 103 F.3d at 1519 ("In converting the factual question of experimental purpose into a matter of law, our court has cut another notch in the removal of patent issues from the trier of fact.").

When the Supreme Court held in *Markman v. Westview Instruments*[35] that claim interpretation is a matter within the province of the judge, rather than the jury, a question was raised as to how and when a judge should decide questions of claim interpretation, and how the judge should communicate his findings to the jury. Some courts have responded by scheduling a "*Markman* hearing" before the jury trial.[36] In connection with the hearing, the court receives evidence from both parties as to their proposed claim interpretations. The judge's findings can then be incorporated into the jury instructions.

11.6 PRELIMINARY INJUNCTIONS

Patent litigation often begins with a motion for a "preliminary injunction."[37] A preliminary injunction is a court order that prevents the accused infringer from making, using, selling, offering to sell or importing the accused product until the case has been decided. In effect, it forces the accused infringer to put its activities on hold. A motion for a preliminary injunction is made to the judge, and the decision to grant or deny the motion is generally based on the following factors:[38]

- The likelihood that the patent owner will ultimately prevail in the litigation—in other words, the likelihood that the patent will be held valid, enforceable, and infringed. This requires the judge to make a preliminary assessment of the evidence, including any defenses that may be raised by the accused infringer.
- Whether the patent owner would suffer "irreparable harm" if the injunction were denied. Irreparable harm is harm that cannot be cured by the eventual payment of money damages. If the only harm to the patentee is a temporary loss of royalty income pending trial, this loss is one that probably can be made up, with interest, when damages are ultimately awarded. However, the harm might be irreparable if, for example, the accused infringer would not have the funds to pay damages after trial, or if sales of infringing articles would create some form of intangible harm. For example, if the patent owner itself sold an article within the scope of the patent, the infringer's sales of an inferior product pending trial might injure the patent owner's reputation and market share in ways that would be difficult to translate into a payment of money. Note that if the patent owner fails to seek a preliminary injunction at the first opportunity, it may be difficult to convince the court that there is a threat of immediate harm.[39]

---

[35] 116 S. Ct. 1384 (1996).

[36] *See, e.g., Ethicon Endo-Surgery, Inc. v. U.S. Surgical Corp.*, 93 F.3d 1572, 1577 (Fed. Cir. 1996).

[37] *See* 35 U.S.C. § 283.

[38] *See Reebok Int'l, Ltd. v. J. Baker, Inc.*, 32 F.3d 1552, 1555 (Fed. Cir. 1994); *New England Braiding Co. v. A.W. Chesterton Co.*, 970 F.2d 878, 882 (Fed. Cir. 1992).

[39] *See, e.g., High Tech Medical Instrumentation , Inc. v. New Image Indus., Inc.*, 49 F.3d 1551, 1557 (Fed. Cir. 1995) ("Absent a good explanation, not offered or found here, 17 months is a substantial period of delay that militates against the issuance of a preliminary injunction by demonstrating that there is no apparent urgency to the request for injunctive relief.").

- The balance of hardships if the motion is granted or denied. In other words, would the harm to the patent owner if the injunction were denied outweigh the harm to the accused infringer if the injunction were granted? The harm to the accused infringer is often more tangible and immediate. If the accused product accounts for a substantial portion of the accused infringer's business, the loss of that business pending trial could result in diminished profits, employee layoffs or even bankruptcy. A court is unlikely to grant an injunction with such severe consequences unless it is very clear that the patent owner will prevail on the merits.

- The public interest. A court may hesitate to grant an injunction that would deny the public an important product—for example, a drug or medical device—even temporarily. On the other hand, the enforcement of valid patents ultimately benefits the public by encouraging innovation.

A court must weigh each of these factors and determine whether a preliminary injunction is appropriate. The stronger the patent owner's case, the lesser the showing of irreparable harm necessary to justify an injunction.[40]

11.7 SUMMARY JUDGMENT

Sometimes the merits of a case are so clear that it is unnecessary to conduct a full-blown jury trial. The mechanism for cutting short such a case is known as "summary judgment." Summary judgment is granted if a judge finds that there is no "genuine issue of material fact" for decision by a jury.[41] In other words, the evidence is so one-sided that the outcome of the case cannot be reasonably disputed, and no reasonable jury could reach a contrary decision.[42] Either party to a patent infringement suit may bring a motion for summary judgment, supported by evidence in its favor (usually in the form of documents and sworn testimony), or pointing out the absence of evidence supporting claims on which the other party bears

---

[40] *See New England Braiding,* 970 F.2d at 883 n.5.

[41] Rule 56(c) of the Federal Rules of Civil Procedure states that summary judgment "shall be rendered forthwith if the pleadings, depositions, answers to interrogatories, and admissions on file, together with the affidavits, if any, show that there is no genuine issue as to any material fact and that the moving party is entitled to a judgment as a matter of law." Summary judgment is not precluded by a genuine dispute as to an "immaterial fact"—that is, one that need not be decided to render a judgment. *See Jonsson v. Stanley Works,* 903 F.2d 812, 820 (Fed. Cir. 1990); *London v. Carson Pirie Scott & Co.,* 946 F.2d 1534, 1537 (Fed. Cir. 1991) ("There can be 'no genuine issue as to any material fact' where the . . . proof is deficient in meeting an essential part of the applicable legal standard, since such failure renders all other facts immaterial.").

[42] *See London,* 946 F.2d at 1538 (motion for summary judgment can be defeated only if " 'the evidence is such that a reasonable jury could return a verdict for the non-moving party.' " [quoting *Anderson v. Liberty Lobby, Inc.,* 477 U.S. 242, 248, 106 S. Ct. 2505, 2510 (1986)]).

the burden of proof.[43] The opposing party naturally submits its own evidence in an attempt to convince the judge that there is, at least, a "genuine issue of material fact" to be decided.

An entire matter may be decided by summary judgment, or the judge may determine that individual questions raise no genuine issue of fact, even if they do not resolve the entire case.[44] For example, a court might grant summary judgment (or "summary adjudication") finding that a particular invention pre-dates the patentee's invention, while leaving to the jury the genuinely disputed question of whether the prior invention anticipates the claims at issue. It is only on rare occasions that courts grant summary judgment that a patent is infringed.[45] Usually the accused infringer can at least raise a "genuine issue of fact" regarding alleged differences between the accused product and the claimed invention. More frequently, a patent is held *not* infringed on summary judgment,[46] often because infringement is precluded by the principle of prosecution history estoppel.[47] Sometimes courts grant summary judgment that patents are invalid or unenforceable.[48] Since liability can be found only if a patent is valid, enforceable *and* infringed, a negative judgment on one of these issues can dispose of the entire case.

11.8 REMEDIES

When a court, with or without a jury, finds a patent both valid and infringed, then it must decide what remedies to grant the patentee. A permanent injunction against further infringement is one remedy that is granted almost routinely.[49] This is simply a court order that describes in

---

[43] *See Johnston v. IVAC Corp.*, 885 F.2d 1574, 1577 (Fed. Cir. 1989); *Celotex Corp. v. Catrett*, 477 U.S. 317, 325, 106 S. Ct. 2548, 2553 (1986).

[44] See Rule 56(d) of the Federal Rules of Civil Procedure.

[45] *See, e.g., Quantum Corp. v. Mountain Computer Inc.*, 5 U.S.P.Q.2d 1103 (N.D. Cal. 1987).

[46] *See, e.g., Glaverbel Societe Anonyme v. Northlake Marketing & Supply, Inc.*, 45 F.3d 1550, 1562 (Fed. Cir. 1995); *London*, 946 F.2d at 1537; *Jonsson*, 903 F.2d at 821; *Townsend Eng'g Co. v. Hitec Co.*, 829 F.2d 1086 (Fed. Cir. 1987).

[47] See Section 10.6.8.

[48] *See, e.g., United States Gypsum Co. v. Nat'l Gypsum Co.*, 74 F.3d 1209 (Fed. Cir. 1996) (best mode); *Quantum Corp. v. Rodime, PLC*, 65 F.3d 1577 (Fed. Cir. 1995) (claims improperly broadened during reexamination); *Paragon Podiatry Lab., Inc. v. KLM Labs., Inc.*, 984 F.2d 1182 (Fed. Cir. 1993) (on-sale bar and inequitable conduct); *Constant v. Advanced Micro-Devices, Inc.*, 848 F.2d 1560 (anticipation and obviousness).

[49] Unless, of course, the patent has already expired. *See Richardson v. Suzuki Motor Co.*, 868 F.2d 1226, 1246–47 (Fed. Cir. 1989) ("Infringement having been established, it is contrary to the laws of property, of which the patent law partakes, to deny the patentee's right to exclude others from use of his property. . . . It is the general rule that an injunction will issue when infringement has been adjudged, absent a sound reason for denying it."). A rare exception might be granted if an injunction would deny the public a product essential to health or safety. *See Rite-Hite Corp. v. Kelley Co.*, 56 F.3d 1538, 1547–48 (Fed. Cir. 1995) (*en banc*).

specific terms the activities that the infringer must henceforth avoid.[50] If the infringer does not abide by the terms of the injunction, it can be enforced by contempt proceedings.[51]

11.8.1 Damages

The other remedy available to a patentee is an award of money damages to compensate for past infringement. While injunctions are a matter within the discretion of the judge, the calculation of damages is a question for the jury.[52] A patentee can elect to pursue damages in either of two forms. One is *lost profits* attributable to the infringement.[53] This form of recovery is appropriate if the infringer competed with the patentee in the marketplace, and it can be shown that sales made by the infringer were sales lost to the patentee.[54] The standard of proof is one of "reasonable probability."[55]

The calculation of lost profits is often complicated by disputes over collateral sales that the patentee might have lost together with sales of the patented item. Suppose, for example, that the patent covered a *component* of a larger item—perhaps an improved lens for a flashlight. The patentee would demand the profits that could have been made from the sale of *flashlights* if the infringer had not misappropriated the lens design. The infringer, on the other hand, might attempt to apportion the profits in some way so that only profits from the *lens* could be recovered. At the same time, the patentee might argue that lost flashlight sales also resulted in lost sales of accessories and spare parts—for example, spare bulbs, bat-

---

[50] The injunction should be more specific than simply prohibiting any further infringement. *See Additive Controls & Measurement Sys., Inc. v. Flowdata, Inc.*, 986 F.2d 476, 479–80 (Fed. Cir. 1993) (injunction must give fair warning of the specific conduct that is enjoined).

[51] *See Arbek Mfg., Inc. v. Moazzam*, 55 F.3d 1567, 1569–70 (Fed. Cir. 1995).

[52] *Festo Corp. v. Shoketsu Kinzoku Kogyo Kabushiki Co.*, 72 F.3d 857, 866 (Fed. Cir. 1995). The award can, however, be modified by the judge if it is "grossly excessive, clearly not supported by the evidence, or based on speculation or guesswork." *See Id.* at 867.

[53] The infringer cannot be compelled to turn over *its* profits in lieu of calculating the *patentee's* lost profits, except where the infringed patent is a design patent. *See* 35 U.S.C. § 289.

[54] *See Festo*, 72 F.3d at 867. Lost profits are most easily proven in a two-supplier market, but they can also be based on suppositions relating to market share. *See King Instruments Corp. v. Perego*, 65 F.3d 941, 953 (Fed. Cir. 1995). In the two-supplier situation (the two suppliers being the patentee and the infringer), proof of lost profits typically focuses on the following factors: (1) the demand for the patented product; (2) the absence of acceptable substitutes; (3) the capacity of the patentee to exploit the demand had there been no infringement (for example, did the patentee have the manufacturing capacity to make the sales that the infringer made?); and (4) the amount of profit the patentee would have made if the patentee, rather than the infringer, had made the sales. *See Standard Havens Prods., Inc. v. Gencor Indus., Inc.*, 953 F.2d 1360, 1373 (Fed. Cir. 1991).

[55] *See Standard Havens*, 953 F.2d at 1372.

teries and so forth. The infringer would likely attempt to exclude these from the calculation.

These disputes are resolved by the "entire market value rule." This rule has been articulated in different ways, but according to the most recent and authoritative holdings of the Federal Circuit, the entire market value rule allows recovery for profits from patented *and* unpatented items if together they are "components of a single assembly or parts of a complete machine," or if together they constitute "a single functioning unit."[56] Recovery cannot be had for unpatented items that "have essentially no functional relationship to the patented invention" but that "may have been sold with an infringing device only as a matter of convenience or business advantage."[57] Returning to the example, the entire flashlight would likely be held the appropriate base for calculating lost profits because the patented lens, together with the unpatented bulb and housing, form a "single functioning unit." On the other hand, if the flashlights were sold as part of a tool kit, the other tools would likely be excluded from the calculation of lost profits because their use and function are unrelated to the patented lens.[58]

Another issue recently addressed by the Federal Circuit is whether a patentee can recover profits lost on sales of an *unpatented* item that competes with sales of an *infringing* item. Suppose, for example, that the inventor of the improved flashlight lens decided, for whatever reason, to market only flashlights that are *not* covered by the patent. Meanwhile, the infringer marketed flashlights that *are* covered by the patent. Can the patentee recover the profits that it would have made on unpatented flashlights if not for the sales of the infringing ones? According to the Federal Circuit, those profits *can* be recovered, as long as it can be shown that the sales of the unpatented flashlights would have been made if not for the infringement.[59]

In many cases lost profits are difficult to calculate, or the patentee did

---

[56] *Rite-Hite Corp. v. Kelley Co.*, 56 F.3d 1538, 1550 (Fed. Cir. 1995) (*en banc*).

[57] *Rite-Hite*, 56 F.3d at 1550. Earlier cases had focused on whether *customer demand* for the entire item could be attributed to the patented component or feature. *See Rite-Hite*, 56 F.3d at 1549. While *Rite-Hite* refers to these cases, it is not certain what role this factor is meant to play in future applications of the "entire market value rule."

[58] The flashlight *batteries* might be a close call. They are a necessary part of a functioning flashlight but are often sold separately. The infringer might argue that when batteries are sold with a flashlight, it is done only as a matter of "convenience and business advantage." Alternatively, a distinction might be drawn between the original batteries, which are sold as a part of the flashlight, and replacement batteries, which the patentee could not have expected to sell. *See Kaufman Co. v. Lantech, Inc.*, 926 F.2d 1136, 1144 (Fed. Cir. 1991) (whether "accessories" should be included in the calculation of lost profits depends on whether there is a reasonable probability that the patentee would have made the sale if not for the infringement).

[59] *Rite-Hite*, 56 F.3d at 1548–49; *King Instruments*, 65 F.3d at 947.

not lose any profits through competition because the patentee did not sell a product of its own. In these situations, the patentee may choose to pursue a *reasonable royalty* as the measure of damages. This is, by statute, the minimum that a patentee can be awarded.[60] A "reasonable royalty" is the amount that the infringer would have paid the patentee if, instead of infringing the patent, it had negotiated for a license. This is generally assessed as a percentage of the sales price of the infringing goods, multiplied by total sales.

The best guide to calculating a reasonable royalty is evidence of an *established* royalty.[61] If, for example, the patentee has already licensed the patent to others at a standard of royalty of 3 percent, then 3 percent appears to be an amount that the market will bear, and that is adequate to satisfy the patentee. If there is no established royalty, then a reasonable royalty must be determined through a difficult mental exercise. One must imagine what would have occurred if, at the time the infringement began, the patentee and the infringer sat down together and negotiated the terms of a patent license. The amount that the patentee would have been willing to accept, and that the infringer would have been willing to pay, is the amount of a reasonable royalty.[62]

The courts have identified a number of factors that should be considered in the context of this "hypothetical negotiation." These are commonly known as "Georgia-Pacific" factors—a reference to one of the first opinions to set them down.[63] The Georgia-Pacific factors include the following:[64]

- Any evidence of an established royalty rate.
- Rates paid by the infringer for rights to similar patents.
- Whether the patentee had a policy of refusing licenses.
- Whether the patentee and the infringer were competitors.
- Whether sales of the patented item would generate (for the infringer or the patentee) additional sales of non-patented items, including such things as accessories and spare parts. These additional sales are known as "convoyed sales" or "derivative sales."

---

[60] 35 U.S.C. § 284 ("Upon finding for the claimant the court shall award the claimant damages adequate to compensate for the infringement, but in no event less than a reasonable royalty for the use made of the invention by the infringer, together with interest and costs as fixed by the court.").

[61] *Nickson Indus., Inc. v. Rol Mfg. Co.*, 847 F.2d 795, 798 (Fed. Cir. 1988) ("Where an established royalty exists, it will usually be the best measure of what is a 'reasonable' royalty.").

[62] *See Unisplay, S.A. v. American Electronic Sign Co.*, 69 F.3d 512, 517 (Fed. Cir. 1995); *Rite-Hite*, 56 F.3d at 1554.

[63] *Georgia-Pacific Corp. v. United States Plywood Corp.*, 318 F. Supp. 1116 (S.D.N.Y. 1970).

[64] *See Georgia-Pacific*, 318 F. Supp. at 1120.

- The time remaining before the patent expired.

- The established success and profitability of items within the scope of the patent.

- The advantages of the patented invention over available substitutes.

- The portion of both selling price and profits that could be attributed to the patented invention rather than to other product components or features.

The "hypothetical negotiation" exercise is difficult and imprecise, in part because it requires the jury, or the judge in a bench trial, to imagine the state of affairs as they existed when the infringement began, putting aside knowledge of subsequent events.[65] It also requires that the patentee and the infringer be pictured as a willing licensor and a willing licensee, respectively, when the reality may have been very different.

Even if the "hypothetical negotiation" could be imagined perfectly, basing a damages figure on the result would seem to make infringement a "no-lose" proposition.[66] The potential infringer who would otherwise pay for a license might decide to take its chances, knowing that, at worst, it would be forced to pay after litigation no more than would have been required for a license. In reality, however, things are not so easy for the would-be infringer. First, the courts recognize that the "hypothetical negotiation" is only a mental exercise. In the end, an infringer may be compelled to pay more than an actual licensee would have paid.[67] More importantly, if the infringement was "willful," damages can be increased as a punishment.

11.8.2 Willful Infringement

Although unintentional infringement is still infringement, the law recognizes a difference in culpability between the infringer who was unaware of its trespass, and the infringer who acted deliberately. A court can as

---

[65] *See Unisplay,* 69 F.3d at 518; *Hanson v. Alpine Ski Area, Inc.,* 718 F.2d 1075, 1079 (Fed. Cir. 1983) (" 'The key element in setting a reasonable royalty . . . is the necessity for return to the date when the infringement began.' "). However, in seeming contradiction to this rule, some cases have approved the use of later information to suggest what a reasonable royalty might have been. *See Fromson v. Western Litho Plate & Supply Co.,* 853 F.2d 1568, 1575 (Fed. Cir. 1988) (the law "permits and often requires a court to look to events and facts that occurred thereafter and that could not have been known to or predicted by the hypothesized negotiators").

[66] *See Fromson,* 853 F.2d at 1574–75; *Panduit Corp. v. Stahlin Bros. Fibre Works, Inc.,* 575 F.2d 1152, 1158–59 (6th Cir. 1978).

[67] *See King Instruments,* 65 F.3d at 951 n.6; *Fromson,* 853 F.2d at 1575 n.11 ("Courts have on occasion recognized the need to distinguish between royalties payable by infringers and non-infringers.").

much as triple the damages assessed against a "willful" infringer.[68] Willfulness is a question of fact, and the standard of proof is one of clear and convincing evidence.[69] If infringement is found to be willful, whether or not to increase the damages, and by how much, is a decision left to the discretion of the judge.[70] The test of willfulness is whether, under all of the circumstances, a reasonably prudent person would have continued the challenged activity with any confidence that the patent would, in the end, be held invalid or not infringed.[71] Willfulness depends on the state of mind of the infringer but is judged from the standpoint of objectively reasonable behavior. Until the infringer is *aware* of the patent, the infringement cannot be willful.[72]

Because willfulness is only an issue after a court has held a patent valid and infringed, any conviction that the infringer held to the contrary was obviously mistaken. The question is not whether the infringer's point of view was correct, but whether it was reasonable and maintained in good faith. Although willfulness is judged under the totality of the circumstances,[73] a dominant consideration is whether the infringer, when made aware of the possibility of a claim, sought out and relied on competent advice of counsel. There is no absolute requirement that an accused infringer seek legal advice, but it is normally expected as part of the accused infringer's duty of due care.[74] Accordingly, any potential infringer is well advised to seek competent legal advice at the first opportunity.

If the accused infringer failed to seek advice of counsel, this goes a long way toward proving willful infringement. On the other hand, an accused infringer who *does* seek advice of counsel is not guaranteed immunity.[75] In order for an accused infringer to reasonably rely on it, the advice of

---

[68] *See* 35 U.S.C. § 284 ("the court may increase the damages up to three times the amount found or assessed"). Although the statute does not specify the circumstances under which damages may be increased, the courts have held that " 'enhancement of damages must be premised on willful infringement or bad faith.' " *Beatrice Foods Co. v. New England Printing Lithography Co.*, 923 F.2d 1576, 1578 (Fed. Cir. 1991) (citation omitted).

[69] *Pall Corp. v. Micron Separations, Inc.*, 66 F.3d 1211, 1221 (Fed. Cir. 1995).

[70] *Graco, Inc. v. Binks Mfg. Co.*, 60 F.3d 785, 792 (Fed. Cir. 1995).

[71] *See Minnesota Mining & Mfg. Co. v. Johnson & Johnson Orthopaedics, Inc.*, 976 F.2d 1559, 1580 (Fed. Cir. 1992); *State Indus., Inc. v. Mor-Flo Indus., Inc.*, 883 F.2d 1573, 1581 (Fed. Cir. 1989).

[72] *Gustafson, Inc. v. Intersystems Industrial Prods., Inc.*, 897 F.2d 508, 511 (Fed. Cir. 1990) ("a party cannot be found to have 'willfully' infringed a patent of which the party had no knowledge"). The issue of willful infringement often begins with the moment that the patentee notifies the infringer of its claims, but infringement can be willful even where the infringer discovers the patent entirely on its own. *See Jepson Inc. v. Makita USA Inc.*, 32 U.S.P.Q.2d 1107, 1111 (C.D. Cal. 1994).

[73] *Ortho Pharmaceutical Corp. v. Smith*, 959 F.2d 936, 944 (Fed. Cir. 1992).

[74] *Minnesota Mining & Mfg.*, 976 F.2d at 1580; *Ortho*, 959 F.2d at 944.

[75] *Minnesota Mining & Mfg.*, 976 F.2d at 1580.

counsel must be competent. In other words, it must come from an attorney who is qualified to render an opinion, it must show that the advice is based on a thorough investigation, and it must explain its conclusions in reasonable detail.[76] Needless to say, the opinion also must be favorable to the accused infringer's position. An opinion of counsel supporting the view that the patent is valid and infringed only makes willfulness more apparent if the advice was ignored.

Normally, communications between attorney and client are privileged. However, if an accused infringer chooses to rely on an opinion of counsel to refute allegations of willful infringement, that privilege must be waived. This can create a dilemma for an accused infringer. If it decides to maintain the privilege by not disclosing the opinion (as it has every right to do), the court may infer that no advice of counsel was received, or that if it was received it was unfavorable.[77] On the other hand, if the accused infringer chooses to rely on the opinion, then it must disclose *all* communications from counsel related to the same subject matter, which may mean disclosing some information that the accused infringer would rather keep under wraps. The accused infringer cannot disclose only so much of the advice as favors its position, while maintaining in confidence the rest. It is all or nothing.[78]

In addition to advice of counsel, or the lack of it, a court may consider as evidence of willfulness whether the infringer deliberately set out to copy the patentee's invention.[79] On the other hand, an attempt to "design around" the claims of the patent (in other words, to make any changes necessary to avoid the scope of the claims) may be viewed as evidence of good faith.[80] Some courts have suggested that the conduct of the infringer

---

[76] See *Graco*, 60 F.3d at 793–94; *BIC Leisure Prods., Inc. v. Windsurfing Int'l, Inc.*, 1 F.3d 1214, 1223 (Fed. Cir. 1993); *Minnesota Mining & Mfg.*, 976 F.2d at 1580; *Ortho*, 959 F.2d at 944; *Read Corp. v. Portec, Inc.*, 970 F.2d 816, 829 (Fed. Cir. 1992); *Underwater Devices Inc. v. Morrison-Knudsen Co.*, 717 F.2d 1380, 1390 (Fed. Cir. 1983). An opinion obtained from an outside counsel is generally afforded more weight than one obtained from a presumably less objective in-house counsel. See *Underwater Devices*, 717 F.2d at 1390. Similarly, written opinions are generally considered more favorably than oral opinions, since it can be difficult to reconstruct the latter. See *Minnesota Mining & Mfg.*, 976 F.2d at 1580. It does not, however, matter that the advice ultimately proved incorrect. If it had been correct, the issue of willfulness would never have arisen. See *Ortho*, 959 F.2d at 944.

[77] See *L.A. Gear, Inc. v. Thom McAn Shoe Co.*, 988 F.2d 1117, 1126 (Fed. Cir. 1993); *Fromson*, 853 F.2d at 1572–73.

[78] See *McCormick-Morgan Inc. v. Teledyne Indus. Inc.*, 21 U.S.P.Q.2d 1412, 1416 (N.D. Cal. 1991) ("The law is clear: [an accused infringer] cannot waive the attorney-client privilege as to certain communications regarding infringement, validity, and unenforceability, but not others.").

[79] *Read*, 970 F.2d at 827.

[80] See *Rolls-Royce Ltd. v. GTE Valeron Corp.*, 800 F.2d 1101, 1109–10 (Fed. Cir. 1986).

during litigation, and the closeness of the questions decided against it, also may be weighed in the balance.[81]

Another potential remedy against a willful infringer is an award of reasonable attorneys' fees. The general rule in the United States is that each litigant must bear its own legal costs, regardless of the outcome of the case, but 35 U.S.C. § 285 provides for an award of attorneys' fees in an "exceptional case." Willful infringement may be found to create such an "exceptional case,"[82] though it is still a matter for the judge's discretion.[83] On occasion, attorneys' fees are awarded to an accused infringer who prevails in the litigation, generally when the patentee committed inequitable conduct in prosecuting the patent or the claim of infringement was frivolous.[84] However, it is by no means proper to award attorneys' fees to the prevailing party as a matter of routine.[85]

11.8.3 Limitations

Recovery of damages for patent infringement can be limited under certain circumstances. The most important limiting factors are the statute of limitations, failure to properly mark products or give notice of infringement, laches and equitable estoppel.

11.8.3.1 Statute of Limitations

35 U.S.C. § 286 provides that no damages may be recovered for infringement that occurred more than six years prior to the filing of a claim. This "statute of limitations" is equivalent to those found in many other areas of the law, and the purpose is the usual one of encouraging the prompt disposition of potential claims. Note that § 286 does not prevent the filing of a suit, unless the only relief that could be granted is damages for infringement more than six years ago. If, for example, the defendant

---

[81] *Read*, 970 F.2d at 827.

[82] *L.A. Gear*, 988 F.2d at 1128; *Avia Gp. Int'l, Inc. v. L.A. Gear California, Inc.*, 853 F.2d 1557, 1567 (Fed. Cir. 1988). Even if the infringement was not willful, "vexatious conduct" by the infringer in the course of the litigation may be held sufficient to make an "exceptional case" and justify an award of attorneys' fees. *See Beckman Instruments, Inc. v. LKB Produkter AB*, 892 F.2d 1547, 1551–52 (Fed. Cir. 1989).

[83] *Delta-X Corp. v. Baker Hughes Production Tools, Inc.*, 984 F.2d 410, 414 (Fed. Cir. 1993); *Avia*, 853 F.2d at 1567.

[84] *See Haynes Int'l, Inc. v. Jessop Steel Co.*, 8 F.3d 1573, 1579 (Fed. Cir. 1993) (a "frivolous" lawsuit justifying an award of attorneys' fees is one which "the patentee knew or, on reasonable investigation, should have known, was baseless"); *Cambridge Prods., Ltd. v. Penn Nutrients, Inc.*, 962 F.2d 1048, 1050–51 (Fed. Cir. 1992); *Stevenson v. Sears Roebuck & Co.*, 713 F.2d 705, 713 (Fed. Cir. 1983) ("There must be some finding of unfairness, bad faith, or inequitable conduct on the part of the unsuccessful patentee.").

[85] *See Revlon, Inc. v. Carson Prods. Co.*, 803 F.2d 676, 679 (Fed. Cir. 1986).

had infringed continuously for the past ten years, the patentee could still sue to recover damages for the most recent six years of infringement and could obtain an injunction against future infringement.

11.8.3.2 Notice and Marking

Many manufactured articles bear a notice referring to a specific patent or patents. For example, a close look at the base of a Texas Instruments pocket calculator may reveal a list of patent numbers molded into the plastic in barely legible type. These are the result of 35 U.S.C. § 287, which states that such a list provides "notice to the public" that the article is patented. It may not be *actual notice* to a particular individual who has never seen the article, but the law considers it "constructive" notice to anyone.[86] If it is not practical to list patent numbers on the article itself, they can be listed on packaging.[87]

If a patent owner or licensee makes, sells, offers to sell or imports into the United States articles covered by the patent but not marked in this fashion, no damages for infringement can be recovered until (1) such marking begins, or (2) the infringer receives from the patent owner *actual notice* of the infringement.[88] Imagine the following scenario: A patent issues on January 1, 1995. Between January 1, 1995 and January 1, 1996, the patent owner sells goods in the United States that are covered by the patent but not properly marked. An infringer also sells goods during that period, but the patent owner fails to provide actual notice of the infringement. On January 1, 1996, the patent owner begins to mark its goods as contemplated by § 287. If the patent owner files suit in 1999, damages can be recovered only on infringing sales that occurred after January 1, 1996. This limitation of damages provides an incentive to patent owners to mark their goods and provide at least that much notice to the public.

The marking of goods must be "substantially consistent and continuous."[89] If a large shipment of unmarked goods is sold, this re-sets the damages clock, so to speak. If only a few unmarked goods slip through, this may be overlooked. Note that the obligation to mark applies to goods made or sold by the patent owner *or* licensee (express or implied).[90] Patent owners therefore have to make sure that licensees are properly marking their goods, or the patent owner's ability to recover damages for infringement will be impaired. Section 287 does not apply to patents with just method claims, for the simple reason that a method cannot be

---

[86] *See American Medical Sys., Inc. v Medical Eng'g Corp.*, 6 F.3d 1523, 1538 (Fed. Cir. 1993).

[87] 35 U.S.C. § 287(a).

[88] *See* 35 U.S.C. § 287(a); *American Medical,* 6 F.3d at 1537.

[89] *American Medical,* 6 F.3d at 1537.

[90] *Amstead Indus. Inc. v. Buckeye Steel Castings Co.*, 24 F.3d 178, 185 (Fed. Cir. 1994).

marked.[91] If a patent includes both method and apparatus claims, and the method is related to an apparatus that can be marked, such marking will likely be required, at least if both method and apparatus claims are infringed.[92] If neither the patent owner nor the patent owner's licensees have sold any products covered by the patent, no marking or other notice is required to begin the accumulation of damages for infringement.

If products have not been properly marked, the patentee can provide *actual notice* to the infringer. The notice can come in the form of a warning letter from the patentee or without ceremony in the form of a suit for infringement.[93] Once such notice has been provided, damages with respect to that infringer can begin to accrue. The notice must come from the patent owner; it is not sufficient that the accused infringer discovered the infringement on its own.[94] Moreover, the notice must identify the patent, and it must specifically charge the recipient with infringement of that patent. In *Amstead Indus. Inc. v. Buckeye Steel Castings Co.*,[95] the infringer (Buckeye) received a form letter from the patent owner mentioning the patent and warning it not to infringe. The same letter had been sent to other companies throughout the industry. The court found that this was not "actual notice" of infringement to Buckeye because it did not specifically charge Buckeye with infringement, nor did it identify any infringing device.[96]

11.8.3.3 Laches

The equitable principle of "laches" may also bar recovery of damages accrued before suit was filed. As explained by the Federal Circuit in *A.C. Aukerman Co. v. R. L. Chaides Construction Co.*,[97] laches may bar the recovery of pre-filing damages if (1) the patentee unreasonably and inexcusably delayed in filing suit, and (2) the accused infringer was materially harmed by the delay.[98] If the patentee delayed filing suit for more than six years, measured from the time it first knew or should have known of the alleged

---

[91] *American Medical,* 6 F.3d at 1538; *see also Hanson v. Alpine Valley Ski Area, Inc.,* 718 F.2d 1075, 1083 (Fed. Cir. 1983).

[92] *See American Medical,* 6 F.3d at 1538–39.

[93] *See American Medical,* 6 F.3d at 1537.

[94] *See American Medical,* 6 F.3d at 1537 n.18.

[95] 24 F.3d 178, 185–87 (Fed. Cir. 1994).

[96] *Amstead,* 24 F.3d at 187.

[97] 960 F.2d 1020 (Fed. Cir 1992) (*en banc*).

[98] *Aukerman,* 960 F.2d at 1032; *see also Gasser Chair Co. v. Infanti Chair Mfg. Corp.,* 60 F.3d 770, 773 (Fed. Cir. 1995); *Meyers v. Asics Corp.,* 974 F.2d 1304, 1307 (Fed. Cir. 1993). However, even if these facts are demonstrated, enforcement of the laches defense is still left to the judge's discretion and sense of fairness. *See Gasser,* 60 F.3d at 773. If the infringer itself has behaved unfairly (perhaps by deliberately copying the patentee's invention), the court may decline to exercise its equitable powers. *See Id.*

infringement, laches is *presumed*, though that presumption can be overcome with the introduction of contrary evidence.[99]

The harm to the accused infringer can be either "economic" or "evidentiary."[100] Economic harm means the loss of investments or the incurring of additional damages that could have been avoided if suit had been filed earlier. For example, during the period of delay, the accused infringer might have made unrecoverable investments in a factory to manufacture the accused product. A patentee cannot delay unreasonably while such investments are made, nor can it "lie silently in wait watching damages escalate."[101] Evidentiary prejudice refers to the loss of evidence that the accused infringer might have used in its defense had the case been brought sooner. Such prejudice can arise where, for example, important documents have been lost, memories have faded or witnesses have died.[102]

Laches is an equitable defense that depends on the exercise of the judge's discretion, in view of all the circumstances.[103] Those circumstances include the length of the delay and any excuses or justifications offered by the patentee. Excuses for delay that may be acceptable include the demands of other litigation, negotiations with the accused infringer and disputes over ownership of the patent.[104] Fairness may sometimes require that the patentee notify the accused infringer of the reason for its delay.[105]

The effect of a successful laches defense is to bar recovery of damages incurred *before* the lawsuit was filed.[106] The patentee can still recover damages for subsequent infringement, as well as an injunction against future infringement.

11.8.3.4 Equitable Estoppel

"Equitable estoppel" is an equitable defense similar to laches, but it depends on a somewhat different set of circumstances. In order for this defense to apply, the patentee must somehow have *communicated* to the potential infringer the idea that the patentee would not press a claim.[107] This "communication" can be in the form of words, conduct or even

---

[99] *Aukerman*, 960 F.2d at 1028, 1037–39.

[100] *Aukerman*, 960 F.2d at 1033.

[101] *Aukerman*, 960 F.2d at 1033. However, the court must find that the potential infringer would have acted differently if the infringer had made its claim more promptly. In other words, the losses must have been *caused* by the delay. *See Gasser*, 60 F.3d at 775.

[102] *Aukerman*, 960 F.2d at 1033.

[103] *Aukerman*, 960 F.2d at 1032.

[104] *Aukerman*, 960 F.2d at 1033.

[105] *See Aukerman*, 960 F.2d at 1033; *Vaupel Textilmaschinen KG v. Meccanica Euro Italia S.P.A.*, 944 F.2d 870, 877 (Fed. Cir. 1991) (for the "other litigation" excuse to apply, the patentee must inform the accused infringer of the other litigation and of its intention to enforce the patent when the other litigation is concluded).

[106] *Aukerman*, 960 F.2d at 1041.

[107] *A.C. Aukerman Co. v. R.L. Chaides Construction Co.*, 960 F.2d 1020, 1042 (Fed. Cir. 1992).

silence if, under the circumstances, one would expect the patentee to voice any objections to the potential infringer's activities.[108] In addition, the potential infringer must have *relied* on that communication and suffered material harm as a result of that reliance.[109] Equitable estoppel is most easily applied where, for example, the patentee told the potential infringer that it would not interfere with its activities, the potential infringer relied on that communication and invested in a new factory, and the patentee then reversed itself and filed suit.[110] The more difficult cases are those where the patentee did nothing, and the potential infringer interpreted that inaction as tacit permission.

As in applying the laches defense, the court must weigh all of the circumstances and determine what fairness dictates.[111] If the defense of equitable estoppel is held to apply, it bars *any* relief to the patentee.[112] In this respect, the consequences are more severe than laches, which prevents only the recovery of past damages.

11.9 THE INTERNATIONAL TRADE COMMISSION

If allegedly infringing products are being *imported* into the United States, a patent owner can request an investigation by the International Trade Commission (ITC). In many ways, an ITC investigation is similar to a suit for patent infringement in a District Court, but there are important differences.

First, the matter will be handled by an Administrative Law Judge (ALJ) rather than a conventional judge or jury. The decision of the ALJ is reviewed by the ITC Commissioners and, if an exclusion of infringing goods is ordered, by the President of the United States.[113] Second, the patent owner must demonstrate that importation of infringing articles threatens a "domestic industry" in those articles—in other words, there must be significant business activity in the United States, either underway or imminent, that will be injured by the illicit competition of infringing

---

[108] *Aukerman*, 960 F.2d at 1041–42. If the "communication" is in the form of inaction, then there must have been some contact or relationship with the patentee that would allow the inaction to be reasonably interpreted as a sign of abandonment. *Id.* at 1042. For example, the patentee might have threatened immediate enforcement of its patents and then failed to follow through, which could reasonably be interpreted as a change of heart. *See Meyers v. Asics Corp.*, 974 F.2d 1304, 1309 (Fed. Cir. 1993). Ironically, the patentee who insists most emphatically that it will enforce its patent rights is the patentee most likely to be found to have abandoned those rights by its subsequent inaction.

[109] *Aukerman*, 960 F.2d at 1042–43.

[110] Note that, unlike the laches defense, equitable estoppel does not require any element of delay. *Aukerman*, 960 F.2d at 1041–42.

[111] *Aukerman*, 960 F.2d at 1043.

[112] *Aukerman*, 960 F.2d at 1041.

[113] *See* 19 U.S.C. § 1337(c), (j).

goods.[114] Third, the ITC can award no money damages for past infringement. It can only order that the importation of infringing goods be stopped.[115] Finally, while an ITC investigation involves much of the same effort as a suit in a District Court, the schedule is generally more compressed. An ITC investigation, from start to finish, is generally completed in little more than a year.

11.10 JUDGMENTS OF INVALIDITY

When a court has held a patent invalid, and all avenues of appeal have been exhausted, the patent cannot in the future be asserted against any potential infringer.[116] In a sense, a patent owner has only one chance to defend the validity of the patent. On the other hand, an unsuccessful attempt by one accused infringer to challenge the validity of a patent generally does not preclude another accused infringer from raising similar arguments.

---

[114] *See* 19 U.S.C. § 1337(a)(2)-(3).
[115] *See* 19 U.S.C. § 1337(d).
[116] Assuming that the patent owner had a "full and fair opportunity" to defend the patent. *See Blonder-Tongue Labs., Inc. v. University of Illinois Foundation,* 402 U.S. 313, 328, 91 S. Ct. 1434, 1442 (1971).

CHAPTER 12

Special Topics

This final chapter covers a number of specialized topics outside of the mainstream of patent law, but still worthy of discussion. These include design patents, plant patents, foreign patents and the complex problem of extending patent protection to computer software.

12.1 DESIGN PATENTS

Throughout this book, the term "patent" generally refers to a *utility patent.* A utility patent is a patent on a device, method or composition of matter having a practical use.[1] Most of the inventions one would commonly think of, from mousetraps, to pharmaceuticals, to communications satellites, are things properly the subject of a utility patent. However, the Patent Office also issues *design patents.* A design patent is a curious hybrid similar in some respects to an ordinary utility patent, but applied to the kinds of artistic (or at any rate decorative) expression that are also the subject of copyright or trademark protection.[2] Whereas utility patents exist to promote the "useful arts," design patents exist to promote the "decorative arts."[3]

Design patents are granted to new, original and ornamental designs, as they are embodied in a manufactured object.[4] The "design" can be a

---

[1] "Utility" is defined rather broadly, however, and can be applied to inventions such as toys that have minimal practical value. See Section 8.4.

[2] See Sections 2.1–2.2.

[3] *Avia Group Int'l, Inc. v. L.A. Gear California, Inc.,* 853 F.2d 1557, 1563 (Fed. Cir. 1988).

[4] 35 U.S.C. § 171.

surface ornament, such as a pattern on a cream pitcher, or it can derive from the shape and configuration of the object itself. For example, if one conceived of a sleek new shape for a telephone, that shape could be the subject of a design patent. Copies of three design patents can be found at Appendix B. They depict a chandelier, a fishing lure and a Rolls Royce automobile, respectively.

A design patent cannot be awarded to an entirely abstract design, not associated with any particular utilitarian object. One could not, for example, obtain a design patent on a painting of sunflowers.[5] One could, however, obtain a design patent on a vase that bears the same painting as a decoration. Although a design patent must claim an article of manufacture, the design cannot be dictated by functional considerations.[6] If the shape of a new tennis racket were dictated by a scheme to enlarge the "sweet spot," that shape should not be the subject of a design patent. Instead, the shape should be protected by a utility patent, assuming that it meets the criteria of patentability. One factor to consider in judging whether a design is functional or ornamental is whether the same functions could be accomplished by designs of significantly different appearance.[7]

Although neither the Patent Office nor the courts may be well suited to judge artistic merit, a design is required to be "ornamental" before it can be granted a design patent. The design need not be a fine example of artistic expression, but it must, in some way, appeal to the "aesthetic sense." On occasion, design patents have been denied because the depicted article failed to meet this criterion.[8] On the other hand, design patents can be granted to numerous objects that would not ordinarily be thought of as having an "ornamental" aspect—for example, a hip prosthesis.[9] Apparently, a physician selecting a hip prosthesis might be moved to select the one that appeals to the eye.

---

[5] *See* M.P.E.P. § 1504.01A.

[6] *See L.A. Gear, Inc. v. Thom McAn Shoe Co.*, 988 F.2d 1117, 1123 (Fed. Cir. 1993); *Avia*, 853 F.2d at 1563.

[7] *See L.A. Gear*, 988 F.2d at 1123 ("When there are several ways to achieve the function of an article of manufacture, the design on the article is more likely to serve a primarily ornamental purpose."); *Avia*, 853 F.2d at 1563. Note that even if every element of the design has a function, the overall configuration may be a matter of patentable aesthetic expression. *See L.A. Gear*, 988 F.2d at 1123; *Avia*, 853 F.2d at 1563.

[8] *See, e.g., Blisscraft of Hollywood v. United Plastics Co.*, 294 F.2d 694, 696 (2d Cir. 1961) (holding a design patent on a pitcher invalid because the pitcher was not sufficiently ornamental in design: "Plaintiff's pitcher has no particularly aesthetic appeal in line, form, color, or otherwise. . . . The reaction which the pitcher inspires is simply that of the usual, useful and not unattractive piece of kitchenware."). In the more recent cases, a design is not likely to be criticized on the grounds that it fails to appeal to the eye. Instead, the debate is likely to center on whether the form is dictated by aesthetic aspirations (however successful) or by functional necessity.

[9] *See In re Webb*, 916 F.2d 1553 (Fed. Cir. 1990).

Since design patents are meant to protect a visually appealing design, objects that are hidden from view may be denied a design patent.[10] A vacuum cleaner bag, for example, has been denied a design patent on that ground.[11] Nevertheless, a design may be found sufficiently "ornamental" to warrant a design patent if its appearance is a "matter of concern" during some significant portion of its life cycle.[12] The hip prosthesis, for example, is not visible in use, but it is visible when displayed at a trade show or in advertising.

Where a utility patent generally has many pages describing the invention in words, a design patent usually includes little description apart from the drawings. This is appropriate since the purpose of the patent is to protect a visual design. Where a utility patent can have many claims, a design patent can have only one,[13] typically in the form "The ornamental design for the [object] as shown."[14] The bracketed portion would name the kind of object depicted—for example, chandelier, fishing lure or automobile.

A design patent carries no requirement of "utility," but the design must be new and non-obvious.[15] Obviousness is inherently difficult to judge in aesthetic matters,[16] and the prior art available for the Patent Office to consult (primarily earlier design patents and utility patents) may barely scratch the surface. Nevertheless, a design patent, like a utility patent, carries a presumption of validity.

The term of a design patent is fourteen years from the date of issue.[17] An object can infringe a design patent if it presents substantially the same appearance to an ordinary observer,[18] and if the accused product includes

[10] *See Webb*, 916 F.2d at 1557.

[11] *See Ex Parte Fesco*, 147 U.S.P.Q. 74 (Pat. Off. Bd. App. 1965).

[12] *See Keystone Retaining Wall Sys., Inc. v. Westrock, Inc.*, 997 F.2d 1444, 1451 (Fed. Cir. 1993); *Webb*, 916 F.2d at 1557–58.

[13] *See* 37 C.F.R. § 1.153.

[14] *See* M.P.E.P. § 1503.03.

[15] 35 U.S.C. §§ 171, 103; *L.A. Gear*, 988 F.2d at 1124; *Avia*, 853 F.2d at 1563.

[16] As in the case of a utility patent, the factors to consider include the scope and content of the prior art, the differences between the prior art and the claimed subject matter, the level of ordinary skill in the art, and secondary considerations such as commercial success or copying. *Avia*, 853 F.2d at 1564. See Section 8.9.6. In the case of a design patent, obviousness is to be judged from the perspective of a designer of ordinary capabilities. *Litton Sys., Inc. v. Whirlpool Corp.*, 728 F.2d 1423, 1443 (Fed. Cir. 1984).

[17] 35 U.S.C. § 173.

[18] " '[I]f, in the eye of an ordinary observer, giving such attention as a purchaser usually gives, two designs are substantially the same, if the resemblance is such as to deceive such an observer, inducing him to purchase one supposing it to be the other, the first one patented is infringed by the other.' " *Avia*, 853 F.2d at 1565 (citation omitted). *See also Keystone*, 997 F.2d at 1450; *Oakley, Inc. v. Int'l Tropic-Cal, Inc.*, 923 F.2d 167, 169 (Fed. Cir. 1991). Note the similarity of this test to the test of infringement for a trademark, discussed at Section 2.2. The proper comparison, however, is between the accused product and the

the aspects of the claimed design that distinguished it from the prior art.[19] It is not an infringement to copy only the functional aspects of a patented design.[20]

The patentee can recover the "entire profit" of an infringer who has sold an article covered by a design patent.[21]

12.2 PLANT PATENTS

A new plant variety can be the subject of a utility patent,[22] but only if the variety is "non-obvious,"[23] and only if the patent disclosure satisfies the usual requirements, such as the "enablement" and "written description" requirements.[24] These requirements are often problematic in the case of a plant variety. For example, if the difference between a newly discovered rose and a known variety is a subtle difference in color and perfume, it is difficult to describe these differences in words and equally difficult to decide if the differences are "non-obvious." Congress addressed these difficulties by providing a special form of patent for plant varieties, thereby putting agriculture on a more even footing with industry when it comes to encouraging, and rewarding, innovation.

A plant patent can be granted to one who "invents or discovers and asexually reproduces any distinct and new variety of plant, including cultivated spores, mutants, hybrids, and newly-found seedlings, other than a tuber propagated plant or a plant found in an uncultivated state."[25] Asexual reproduction refers to reproduction by grafting, budding and similar procedures that reproduce a genetically identical plant from a portion of the first plant or its progeny.[26] The "invention" is complete only when

design depicted in the patent, not between the accused product and the patentee's own commercial embodiment, which may include features not depicted in the patent. *See Sun Hill Indus., Inc. v. Easter Unlimited, Inc.*, 48 F.3d 1193, 1196 (Fed. Cir. 1995).

[19] *See Sun Hill*, 48 F.3d at 1197 ("The patentee must prove both substantial similarity and appropriation of the 'point of novelty.' "); *Litton*, 728 F.2d at 1444.

[20] *See Lee v. Dayton-Hudson Corp.*, 838 F.2d 1186, 1189 (Fed. Cir. 1988).

[21] 35 U.S.C. § 289.

[22] *See Diamond v. Chakrabarty*, 447 U.S. 303, 100 S. Ct. 2204 (1980).

[23] See Section 8.9.6.

[24] See Sections 8.6.8 and 8.8.

[25] 35 U.S.C. § 161. According to the Manual of Patent Examining Procedure, tubers (such as potatoes) are excluded because "this group alone, among asexually reproduced plants, is propagated by the same part of the plant that is sold as food." M.P.E.P. § 1601. The term "plant" is used in its popular sense rather than a strict scientific sense, so species such as bacteria are also excluded. *Id.*

[26] See M.P.E.P. § 1601. The Plant Variety Protection Act, 7 U.S.C. § 2321 *et seq.*, provides similar legal protection for sexually-reproduced plant varieties (e.g., plants grown from seed), but not as a part of the patent system. The Plant Variety Protection Act is administered by the Department of Agriculture.

the new variety has been discovered, its distinguishing characteristics have been identified and it has been asexually reproduced. If the asexually reproduced plant has the distinctive characteristics of its parent, this demonstrates that the characteristics likely represent a genetic rather than an environmental variation.

A patent cannot be granted for the discovery of a new plant in the wild—that is, in an "uncultivated state." However, patents can be granted for varieties that arise from unplanned sports or mutations of cultivated crops. *Imazio Nursery, Inc. v. Dania Greenhouses*,[27] for example, discusses a patented variety of heather discovered as a seedling in a cultivated field. This variety, dubbed "Erica Sunset," blooms during the Christmas season, much earlier than the ordinary heather from which it arose.

Plant patents have only one claim, which typically refers to the plant variety "shown and described" in the specification, usually with a brief recital of the characteristics that distinguish the new variety.[28] In contrast to a utility patent, a description found in a plant patent need only be "as complete as is reasonably possible."[29] Because of their function in identifying the patented variety, illustrations are an important part of a plant patent, and they must be "artistically and competently executed."[30]

A plant variety is patentable if it is "distinct and new"[31]—a threshold of novelty less demanding than "non-obviousness." The patent confers the right to exclude others from asexually reproducing the claimed plant or from using or selling such a plant.[32] It is not an infringement of a plant patent to grow the claimed plant from seed. It is also not an infringement to develop independently a variety that is indistinguishable from the patented variety. An infringement occurs only if the accused variety is an *offspring* of the original, which means that an element of proving infringement is evidence that the accused infringer had access to the original plant or its asexually reproduced progeny.[33] This is in contrast to the usual rule (applied to utility patents) that independent development is not a defense to infringement.

---

[27] 69 F.3d 1560 (Fed. Cir. 1995).

[28] *See* 35 U.S.C. § 162 ("The claim in the specification shall be in formal terms to the plant shown and described.").

[29] 35 U.S.C. § 162.

[30] M.P.E.P. § 1606. Either drawings or color photographs are acceptable. *Id.* Examples of plant patents have been omitted from the Appendix due to the difficulty of reproducing the illustrations.

[31] 35 U.S.C. § 161.

[32] 35 U.S.C. § 163.

[33] *See Imazio Nursery,* 69 F.3d at 1569–70.

12.3 FOREIGN PATENTS

An inventor who wishes to protect an invention in a foreign country must apply for a patent in that country.[34] Foreign patent systems generally convey rights similar to those obtainable in the United States, but there are important differences.

Other countries award a patent to the *first person to file a patent application*, whereas the United States awards a patent to the *first to invent*. The first-to-file system provides a far simpler way to resolve issues of priority, which in the United States must be resolved by complex inquiries into conception, reduction-to-practice and diligence.[35] It is often proposed that the United States adopt the first-to-file rule in order to make its practice consistent with that of the rest of the world. However, there is something to be said for rewarding the person who is first to invent, rather than the person who wins the "race to the Patent Office."

Many other countries allow a degree of public participation in the process of patent examination. In Japan, for example, applications are "laid open"—that is, made public—eighteen months after a patent application is filed. At this time, members of the public, most likely competitors of the applicant, may submit prior art that bears upon the patentability of the claimed invention. If the Patent Office still determines that the patent should issue, the public is notified again and anyone who opposes issuance of the patent is allowed to file an opposition. This system ensures a more rigorous examination than typically occurs in the United States, where prosecution is conducted in secret and the government hears only from the applicant.

An applicant for a United States patent can take the benefit of an earlier filing date in most foreign countries, if the foreign application was filed no more than twelve months before the United States filing date.[36] This earlier effective filing date does not remove any "statutory bar" problems raised by 35 U.S.C. § 102(b).[37] The foreign filing date can, however, be used to establish an earlier constructive reduction to practice,[38] possibly

---

[34] Many countries, including the United States, are parties to a Patent Cooperation Treaty which provides for a standardized patent application acceptable for filing in any of the participating countries. However, the patent laws of the participating countries differ, so an invention that is patentable in one country may be denied a patent in another.

[35] See Sections 8.9.2–8.9.3.

[36] *See* 35 U.S.C. § 119.

[37] "[B]ut no patent shall be granted on any application for patent for an invention which had been patented or described in a printed publication in any country more than one year before the date of the actual filing of the application in this country, or which had been in public use or on sale in this country more than one year prior to such filing." 35 U.S.C. § 119(a). The § 102(b) "statutory bar" provisions are discussed in Section 8.10.

[38] *See In re Mulder*, 716 F.2d 1542, 1544–45 (Fed. Cir. 1983). Constructive reduction to practice is discussed in Section 8.9.2.

avoiding certain prior art references or improving the applicant's position in an interference contest.[39] On the other hand, an inventor who files an application in a foreign country should wait no longer than twelve months before filing in the United States. Otherwise, the foreign patent, if it issues before the United States application is on file, may constitute invalidating prior art under 35 U.S.C. § 102(d).[40]

12.4 PATENTING COMPUTER PROGRAMS

In recent years, one of the thorniest questions in patent law has been whether, and under what circumstances, a computer program can be patented. Because the issue is increasingly important as the number of software patents grows, and because the precedent is difficult to sort out, we will digress on this topic at some length.

At first blush, there may seem no reason to doubt that a computer program constitutes patentable subject matter. A program is, literally, a "process"—one of the categories of patentable subject matter set out in 35 U.S.C. § 101. A programmed computer might also be claimed as a "machine." Moreover, computer programs are undoubtedly *technological* in nature. Even though the process of writing a computer program involves a degree of personal "expression," the purpose of the program is to control the operation of a physical device. Finally, from a constitutional perspective, there is no reason to suppose that progress in the art of computer programming is less dependent on patent protection than progress in the arts of circuit design, pharmaceuticals or any other field in which patents are granted routinely. Why then have software patents met with resistance?

The source of the difficulty lies in two long-standing doctrines. The first is the unpatentability of "mathematical algorithms." A "mathematical algorithm" is a series of precisely defined steps for performing a mathematical operation. The following is an example of a mathematical algorithm that begins with two quantities a and b:

1. Raise a to the power 2, and call the result x.
2. Raise b to the power 2, and call the result y.
3. Add x and y, and call the result z.
4. Take the square root of z, and call the result c.

As we have seen, a patent cannot be granted on a "principle of nature" such as a mathematical formula. The truths of mathematics are consid-

---

[39] See Section 5.4.
[40] See Section 8.11.

ered beyond the possibility of ownership, even by the first person to discover those truths. Accordingly, Pythagoras could not have patented his famous theorem. When the mathematical truth expresses a relationship, as in the case of the Pythagorean theorem, the relationship also suggests a *process* by which one set of numbers can be converted, by mathematics, to another. As the reader may already have recognized, the algorithm set forth above is simply a sequence of steps, based on the relationship expressed in the Pythagorean theorem, by which one could derive the length (*c*) of the hypotenuse of a right triangle, given the lengths of the two sides (*a* and *b*).

If the formula itself cannot be patented, it seems to follow that an algorithm based on the formula cannot be patented either. If it were otherwise, only the patentee could *use* the formula, and the effect would be the same as if the patentee owned the formula itself.[41] Hence, courts have categorized "mathematical algorithms" as unpatentable subject matter, akin to "principles of nature" and "abstract ideas."

Computers carry out their myriad functions by performing, at tremendously high speeds, a number of very fundamental mathematical and logical operations. These operations are controlled by a computer program, which dictates the sequence of steps that the computer is to perform. If expressed in slightly different terms, the algorithm set forth above could be made a computer program that would cause a computer to calculate, in an instant, the length of hypotenuse *c*. If a programmer attempted to patent such a program, the question would arise whether the program was a practical advancement in the technological art of computer programming or nothing more than an unpatentable "mathematical algorithm."

The other source of doubt as the patentability of computer programs is the so-called mental steps doctrine, which holds that a process is unpatentable if an essential step of the process requires human thought. In the past, this theory has been relied upon to deny the patentability of processes that called for human judgment, calculation or perception. The rationale for the doctrine appears to be that human thought processes are too abstract, too remote from the technological "useful arts" or too difficult to capture in terms of a patent disclosure, to be suitable for patent protection. One court simply pronounced it "self-evident that thought is not patentable," perhaps inferring that exclusive rights to a mental process would impinge too greatly on human freedoms.[42] The doctrine is now

---

[41] If various algorithms could be devised that would achieve the same mathematical result, one could argue that patenting one of those algorithms would not monopolize the underlying abstract principle. On the other hand, one could argue that algorithms associated with any mathematical relationship are themselves "abstract ideas" or "fundamental truths," in which case they would also not be available for patenting.

[42] *In re Abrams*, 89 U.S.P.Q. 266, 269 (C.C.P.A. 1951).

discredited, or at least displaced by other debates, but the notion that a computer program is a mechanical analogue of human thought processes seems to account for some of the early hostility toward the patenting of computer software.

12.4.1 The Supreme Court Trilogy

Any discussion of the patentability of computer software must include a trilogy of Supreme Court cases decided in the 1970s and early 1980s: *Gottschalk v. Benson*, 409 U.S. 64, 93 S. Ct. 253 (1972), *Parker v. Flook*, 437 U.S. 584, 98 S. Ct. 2522 (1978) and *Diamond v. Diehr*, 450 U.S. 175, 101 S. Ct. 1048 (1981).

12.4.1.1 Gottschalk v. Benson

The *Benson* case involved an attempt to patent a process for converting binary-coded decimal (BCD) numbers into pure binary numbers.[43] The method did not rely on a new kind of computer. It could be performed with any computer, then existing or yet to be invented. The Supreme Court held the claims unpatentable, on the ground that the claimed method embodied an abstract idea, or a mathematical truth, rather than the application of an idea to a specific technological end.

Regarding "process" claims in general, the court observed that "[t]ransformation and reduction of an article 'to a different state or thing' is the clue to the patentability of a process claim that does not include particular machines."[44] If this statement is taken at face value, it would appear that no computer program would be patentable as such, since programs involve the manipulation of information, not the physical transformation of an article to "a different state or thing." However, the court denied that it intended to bar the patentability of computer programs altogether. Instead, it focused on the preemptive effect of allowing an inventor to patent a method that is "not limited to any particular art or technology, to any particular apparatus or machinery, or to any particular end use":[45]

It is conceded that one may not patent an idea. But in practical effect that would be the result if the formula for converting BCD numerals to pure binary numerals

---

[43] Binary numbers are expressed in base two, rather than in the base ten of the decimal system. The only numerals needed to represent binary numbers are 1 and 0. The number 13, for example, is expressed in binary as 1101. In binary-coded decimal notation, each base ten *digit* is independently represented by a binary number. In that notation, 13 would be expressed as 0001 0011—the binary equivalent of 1, followed by the binary equivalent of 3. Binary numbers are important because of their use in computing.

[44] *Benson*, 409 U.S. at 70, 93 S. Ct. at 256.

[45] *Benson*, 409 U.S. at 64, 93 S. Ct. at 254.

were patented in this case. The mathematical formula involved here has no sub-stantial practical application except in connection with a digital computer, which means that if [a patent were granted], the patent would wholly preempt the math-ematical formula and in practical effect would be a patent on the algorithm itself.[46]

Although the reasoning of *Benson* has been debated by scholars, it seems to be as follows: (1) the conversion of BCD numerals to pure binary is an abstract idea, or a mathematical principle; (2) if Benson were allowed to patent his algorithm, the public, as a practical matter, would be denied all use of that principle, even in applications that had not yet been in-vented; (3) no process claim that denies the public all use of a mathe-matical principle can be considered within the realm of patentable subject matter under 35 U.S.C. § 101. *Benson* left open the question of whether one could patent a computer program embodying a mathematical algo-rithm if the use were limited to a particular technological application. This issue was presented in *Flook*.

12.4.1.2 Parker v. Flook

The claim at issue in *Flook* involved a method of updating an "alarm limit." An "alarm limit" is a number that is used to indicate an abnormal, or possibly dangerous, condition arising during the catalytic conversion of hydrocarbons. If temperature, pressure or some other operating con-dition exceeds its respective "alarm limit," the process is not going as planned. However, an "alarm limit" should not always be fixed; during certain stages of operation, the "alarm limit" needs to be adjusted or "updated." Flook's contribution was to devise an algorithm for updating an "alarm limit."

As in *Benson*, the court held that the "mathematical algorithm" was unpatentable subject matter. Even though the algorithm was to be used only in connection with a catalytic conversion process, and even though a certain amount of specific "post-solution activity" followed the calcula-tion (namely, the adjustment of the "alarm limit"), the court still found that patenting the process would be tantamount to patenting an abstract idea or phenomenon of nature. As a part of its analysis, the court adopted an odd mixture of the patentable subject matter standard of 35 U.S.C. § 101 and the standard of novelty under 35 U.S.C. § 102. The court found that if the algorithm were treated *as though it were already known*, the claim as a whole would describe no patentable invention.[47]

---

[46] *Benson*, 409 U.S. at 71–72, 93 S. Ct. at 257.

[47] *Flook*, 437 U.S. at 594, 98 S. Ct. at 2527–28. The court apparently reasoned as follows: For a method to be a patentable "invention," some part of that method must be outside of the public domain. Although a principle of mathematics may not be "already known," it is in the public domain just as if it were. Hence, if the algorithm part of a method is in the public domain as a principle of mathematics, and the rest is in the public domain

In some respects *Flook* is a troubling decision, because it seems to blur the distinction between principles of nature, which in the abstract are not patentable, and specific, technological applications of those principles, which seemingly should be patentable. Perhaps if the claim had been more specific as to how the "alarm limit" was to be used in the catalytic conversion process, the court would have regarded the claim as less of an abstraction.

12.4.1.3 Diamond v. Diehr

The Supreme Court revisited these issues in the *Diehr* case. While the facts in *Diehr* are curiously similar to those in *Flook*, the result was very different. Diehr's invention involved a process for curing rubber inside a molding press. In order to determine the proper time to open the press and remove the finished article, Diehr's method called for constant measurement of the temperature inside the press. This data was fed to a computer, which used the well-known Arrhenius equation to periodically recalculate the time necessary for the rubber to cure. When the calculated optimum and the actual curing time were the same, the computer would open the press automatically. This time, the court found that the use of the algorithm did not take the claims outside of the scope of patentable subject matter.

The *Diehr* case was decided not long after *Chakrabarty*, and it reflects a similarly expansive interpretation of the Patent Act. The majority viewed the invention not as a mathematical algorithm per se, but as a method of curing rubber that happened to make use of a mathematical algorithm. Viewed in this light, Diehr's method was an industrial process for "transforming . . . an article . . . into a different state or thing"—the kind of process that has always been considered patentable.[48] The process was not made unpatentable simply because various steps of the process involved the use of an equation and a programmed computer.

As in *Benson*, the court referred to the issue of preemption, finding that Diehr did not seek a monopoly on the Arrhenius equation itself, but only on the use of that equation with other steps in a process for curing rubber. Although *Flook* had seemingly dismissed "field of use" limitations as the key to patentability, the *Diehr* court distinguished *Flook* as a case in which the claimed method did nothing more than calculate a "number," with hardly a mention of the physical process steps associated with that calculation. The implication is that if the claims in *Flook* had been drafted with additional references to the catalytic conversion process itself, the claims

---

because it was already known, there is nothing about the method that can be the basis of a patent. However, it could be argued that even if the algorithm and the remainder of the claim, individually, are in the public domain, the *combination* of the two, or the *application* of the algorithm to the known process steps, might be novel and not abstract.

[48] *Diehr*, 450 U.S. at 184, 101 S. Ct. at 1055.

might have been patentable *as a catalytic conversion process*, even if the only novel aspect of the process had been the use of the mathematical algorithm.[49]

Diehr seems to mark a significant change in the Supreme Court's attitude toward the patentability of computer software. However, since *Diehr* did not overrule *Flook*, the lower courts, and the Federal Circuit in particular, have been left with the difficult task of reconciling and applying the rules set out in *Benson*, *Flook* and *Diehr*.

12.4.2 The Federal Circuit Decisions

The application of patent law to computer software has provoked as much dissension, and as many seemingly contradictory opinions, in the Federal Circuit Court of Appeals as in the Supreme Court. However, one can piece together from the case law at least some guidelines for determining whether a claim to a computer program, or a process involving a computer program, will be held patentable subject matter.

One approach adopted by the Federal Circuit is known as the *Freeman-Walter-Abele* test, after a trio of cases that played a part in its evolution. The Court has characterized the test as the following:

It is first determined whether a mathematical algorithm is recited directly or indirectly in the claim. If so, it is next determined whether the claimed invention as a whole is no more than the algorithm itself; that is, whether the claim is directed to a mathematical algorithm that is not applied to or limited by physical elements or process steps. Such claims are nonstatutory. However, when the mathematical algorithm is applied in one or more steps of an otherwise statutory process claim, or one or more elements of an otherwise statutory apparatus claim, the requirements of section 101 are met.[50]

Thus, the Federal Circuit has distinguished between patent claims drawn to mathematical algorithms in the abstract, and claims that call for

---

[49] *Flook* had suggested that a method would be unpatentable if the only novel aspect of the method were the use of a mathematical algorithm: "[Flook's] process is unpatentable under § 101, not because it contains an algorithm as one component, but because once that component is assumed to be within the prior art, the application, considered as a whole, contains no patentable invention." The *Diehr* court did not retract this statement, but it stressed that claims must be viewed as a whole, and that even known elements in the combination should not be ignored when addressing patentability under § 101. The *Diehr* opinion also holds it "commonplace that the application of a law of nature or mathematical formula to *a known structure or process* may be patentable," a statement that seems to contradict the *Flook* approach. 450 U.S. at 187, 101 S. Ct. at 1057. Since the *Diehr* court declined to contradict the comment in *Flook*, it is unfortunate that it did not provide a clearer statement of how it should be interpreted.

[50] *Arrhythmia Research Technology, Inc. v. Corazonix Corp.*, 958 F.2d 1053, 1058 (Fed. Cir. 1992).

application of an algorithm to a *physical* process, or claims that call for a specific *machine* to perform the algorithm. For example, the Federal Circuit has rejected claims to a method of conducting an auction, where the mathematical algorithm was neither tied to specific computer hardware nor used to accomplish any physical transformation.[51] It has similarly denied a patent to an algorithm for constructing a "bubble hierarchy" to define the space around an object. This algorithm could be used to keep industrial robots from colliding with fixed objects, but, significantly, the challenged claims did not refer to this specific use.[52] On the other hand, the Federal Circuit held patentable an apparatus claim reciting various *physical* components, one of which used an "auto-correlation" algorithm to recognize patterns in signals (e.g., for voice recognition).[53]

The approach taken by the Federal Circuit raises two significant, but difficult, questions: (1) Does the inclusion in the claimed method of steps for *gathering data* to be processed by the algorithm and/or *displaying a result* provide sufficient connection with the physical world to make the algorithm more than an "abstract idea?" and (2) Can questions of patentability be avoided by the simple expedient of describing the invention as a *physical machine* (i.e., computer) for performing the mathematical algorithm?

The first question has no clear answer, as can be seen by comparing *In re Grams*[54] with *Arrhythmia Research Technology, Inc. v. Corazonix Corp.*[55] The former case concerned a method for diagnosing an abnormal condition in a patient, which depended on gathering data on a variety of patient "parameters," and processing this data by a mathematical algorithm to identify the possible cause of any unusual findings. The only physical process step involved data gathering. The court held that this did not bring the claim within the scope of patentable subject matter. Since a mathematical algorithm can be used only by plugging data into the equation, a patent claim that merely added to the algorithm a step for gathering data would be, in effect, the same as a patent on the algorithm itself.[56] The court declined to hold that a mathematical algorithm combined with data-gathering steps would always be unpatentable, but it noted that in this case there was little specific disclosure relating to the data-gathering steps, leading to the impression that "applicants are, in essence, claiming the

---

[51] *In re Schrader*, 22 F.3d 290 (Fed. Cir. 1994).

[52] *In re Warmerdam*, 33 F.3d 1354 (Fed. Cir. 1994).

[53] *In re Iwahashi*, 888 F.2d 1370 (Fed. Cir. 1989).

[54] 888 F.2d 835 (Fed. Cir. 1989).

[55] 958 F.2d 1053 (Fed. Cir. 1992).

[56] " 'If the steps of gathering and substituting values were alone sufficient, every mathematical equation, formula, or algorithm having any practical use would be per se subject to patenting as a 'process' under § 101.' " *Grams*, 888 F.2d at 839 (citation omitted).

mathematical algorithm, which they cannot do under *Gottschalk v. Benson.*"[57]

The patentee in *Arrhythmia* claimed a method of analyzing electrocardiographic signals in order to detect dangerous heart conditions. The method involved a mathematical algorithm to be performed by a computer. As in *Grams,* the method consisted essentially of gathering data from a patient and using an algorithm to detect an abnormality. However, this time the court held the method to be patentable. According to the court, the signals analyzed by the process were "not abstractions" because they were "related to the patient's heart function," and "the resultant output is not an abstract number, but is a signal related to the patient's heart activity."[58] In addition, the processing of the data involved "physical process steps that transform one physical, electrical signal to another."[59] Thus, the claimed method was not an algorithm in the abstract, but the specific application of an algorithm to a process for analyzing electrocardiographic signals.

Grams and *Arrhythmia* are difficult to reconcile. Although the data analyzed in *Arrhythmia* represented the functioning of an actual human heart, the data analyzed in *Grams* represented the condition of an actual human patient. While in *Arrhythmia* the data processing involved the transformation of "one physical, electrical signal into another," the same might be said of the data processing in *Grams.* In fact, computerized data processing always involves some manipulation of "physical, electrical signals."[60] Comparing *Grams* with *Arrhythmia,* the most one can conclude with any confidence is that if a claim is limited a specific application, and if it includes disclosure of physical process steps or manipulation of "physical signals," it is more likely to be found patentable subject matter.

The question of whether one can avoid the patentability issue merely by claiming a physical apparatus (i.e., computer) to perform the algorithm is also a troubling one. In *In re Warmerdam,* the court rejected the "bubble hierarchy" *method* claims, but as to the *apparatus* claim the court merely stated that "[c]laim 5 is for a machine, and is clearly patentable subject matter."[61] Yet the claim required nothing more than "A machine having

---

[57] *Grams,* 888 F.2d at 840.

[58] *Arrhythmia,* 958 F.2d at 1059.

[59] *Arrhythmia,* 958 F.2d at 1059.

[60] The courts have seemed more willing to accept as patentable algorithms that analyze a "signal," as opposed to algorithms that derive a result based on discrete values. *Arrhythmia* is one example, as is *In re Taner,* 681 F.2d 787 (C.C.P.A. 1982), where the "signal" analyzed ("converted," in the court's terminology) by the algorithm was a seismic energy wave generated to explore geologic strata. However, it is difficult to see why processing a stream of data in the form of a "signal" should be treated differently in terms of patentability than processing discrete data values, where both are obtained by measuring physical properties or conditions.

[61] *Warmerdam,* 33 F.3d at 1360.

a memory which contains data representing a bubble hierarchy generated by the method of any of [unpatentable!] Claims 1 through 4."

In *In re Alappat,*[62] the Federal Circuit considered whether the Patent Office had properly rejected Alappat's claims to an improved rasterizer for an oscilloscope display, which used a software algorithm to make jagged lines appear smoother. The claims called for an apparatus comprising a combination of "means" to perform the necessary functions of calculation and display.[63] The majority of the court held the claims patentable, stressing the disclosure of specific memory and logic circuits to perform the functions recited in the claims: "This is not a disembodied mathematical concept which may be characterized as an 'abstract idea,' but rather a specific machine to produce a useful, concrete, and tangible result."[64] Moreover, because the claim to the "machine" required specific hardware, it would not "wholly pre-empt" the use of the formula.

Two of the dissenting judges in *Alappat* complained that the "apparatus" on which the majority relied was nothing more than conventional computer hardware, and the only thing that Alappat had invented (or discovered) was a mathematical operation. In the dissenters' view, Alappat's choice to describe the invention not as mathematics per se, but as conventional hardware to perform the mathematics, should not have determined the question of whether the "invention" was patentable subject matter.

Alappat suggests that virtually any software invention can be patented, as long as it is claimed in terms of a *machine* to perform the necessary functions, and the corresponding circuitry is disclosed in the specification. This is so even if the circuitry is nothing more than what one would find in any run-of-the mill computer. In the majority's view, "[new] programming creates a new machine, because a general-purpose computer in effect becomes a special purpose computer once it is programmed to perform particular functions pursuant to instructions from program software."[65] On the other hand, some judges may persist in the view that such claim drafting choices are matters of form rather than substance, and the question of patentability runs deeper than superficial questions of claim drafting. Even *Alappat* suggests that an apparatus claim can be only a "guise."[66]

The subject of software patentability continues to be a controversial one, so it would be foolish to conclude that the current state of the law is necessarily the last word on the subject. The Supreme Court, or Congress,

---

[62] 33 F.3d 1526 (Fed. Cir. 1994).
[63] See the discussion of "means-plus-function" claims at Section 7.7.4.
[64] *Alappat,* 33 F.3d at 1544.
[65] *Alappat,* 33 F.3d at 1545.
[66] *Alappat,* 33 F.3d at 1541.

may have more to contribute to the debate. However, for now the Patent Office has adopted the liberal view reflected in *Alappat.* Its recently published guidelines require a patent examiner to presume that a programmed computer is a statutory "machine," a computer-readable memory used to store a computer program is a statutory "manufacture" and a series of steps to be performed by a computer (i.e., a program) is a statutory "process."[67] Although these are only presumptions, they represent a dramatic change in attitude toward the acceptance of computer programs as suitable material for patent protection. As a result, software developers are more than ever looking to patents as a means to protect their creations, and in the coming years it is likely that software patents will account for an increased percentage of cases litigated.

[67] M.P.E.P. § 2106.

Note on Sources

In any area of the law, there is no substitute for the original sources. In the specific case of patent law, the primary source is Title 35 of the United States Code. BNA Books publishes a convenient one-volume reference, entitled **Patent Trademark and Copyright Laws** (Jeffrey M. Samuels, ed.), which combines Title 35 with other statutes relating to copyrights and trademarks. Rules and regulations specifically relating to patent applications and prosecution can be found in Title 37 of the Code of Federal Regulations, published by the Office of the Federal Register, National Archives and Records, and the Manual of Patent Examining Procedure (or MPEP), published by the Department of Commerce.

Judicial opinions cited in this book can be found in any good law library. Supreme Court decisions are found in the **United States Reports** (abbreviated in case citations as U.S.) or the **Supreme Court Reporter** (S. Ct.), published by West Publishing Co. Published decisions of the Federal Circuit Court of Appeals are found in West's **Federal Reporter** (F.2d or F.3d). District Court opinions are found in West's **Federal Supplement** (F. Supp.), or BNA's **United States Patent Quarterly** (U.S.P.Q. or U.S.P.Q.2d).

Several multi-volume treatises provide very detailed surveys of United States patent law, including its historical development. The one the author turns to most frequently is Professor Donald S. Chisum's **Chisum on Patents**, published by Matthew Bender. Ernest Bainbridge Lipscomb's **Lipscomb's Walker on Patents**, published by Clark Boardman Callaghan, is also a valuable resource. Robert L. Harmon's **Patents and the Federal Circuit**, published by BNA Books, is a work that concentrates on the development of the law in the Federal Circuit Court of Appeals. Any of these works would be a useful supplement to this book when greater detail is required.

Sample Utility Patents

US005502918A

United States Patent [19]

Oviatt

[11] **Patent Number:** **5,502,918**

[45] **Date of Patent:** **Apr. 2, 1996**

[54] **MOUSETRAP FOR CATCHING MICE LIVE**

[76] Inventor: **Bill Oviatt**, 1375 Highway 71 North, Springdale, Ark. 72764

[21] Appl. No.: **347,890**

[22] Filed: **Dec. 1, 1994**

[51] **Int. Cl.^{6}** **A01M 23/02**

[52] **U.S. Cl.** **43/61**; 43/60; 43/66

[58] **Field of Search** 43/66, 67, 61, 43/60, 58, 75

[56] **References Cited**

U.S. PATENT DOCUMENTS

944,926 12/1909 Turnbo 43/66

1,226,641	5/1917	Cushing	43/60
4,768,305	9/1988	Sackett	43/61

Primary Examiner—Kurt Rowan
Attorney, Agent, or Firm—Rick Martin

[57] **ABSTRACT**

A "Y" shaped mousetrap lures a mouse into an open end of the "Y" by means of smelly bait located at a closed end of the bottom of the "Y". The "Y" is pivotally supported horizontally by a stand. As the mouse walks past the pivot point, a ping pong ball rolls from the opposite short "Y" tube member and down to the entrance of the open ended tube member. The mouse is trapped alive and can be drowned by immersing the mousetrap.

8 Claims, 3 Drawing Sheets

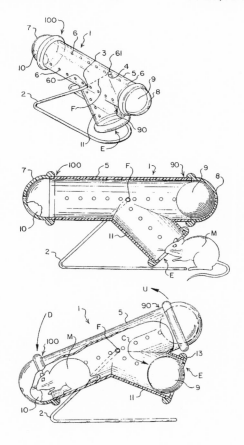

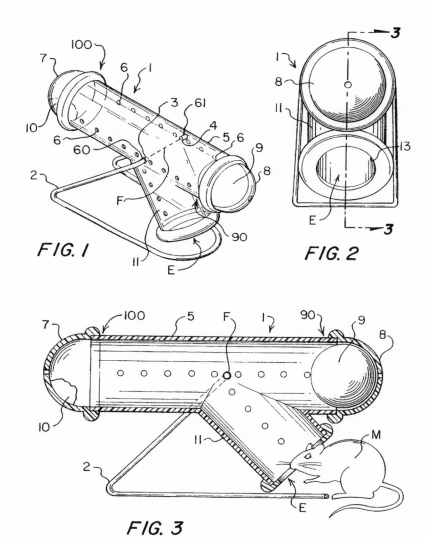

FIG. 1

FIG. 2

FIG. 3

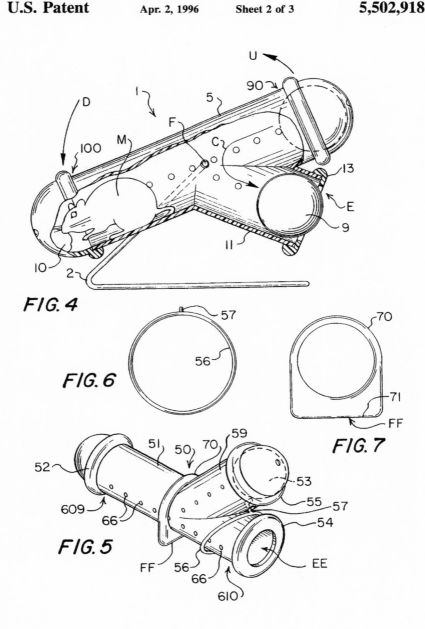

FIG. 4

FIG. 6

FIG. 7

FIG. 5

194

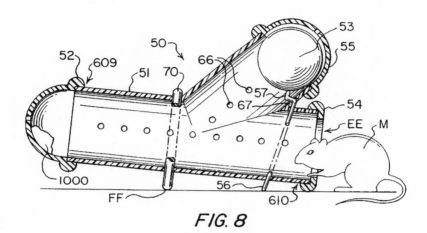

FIG. 8

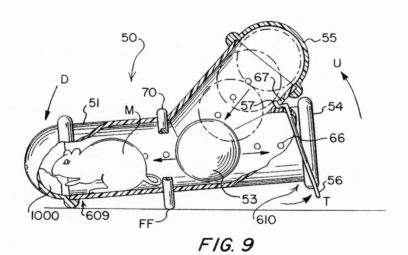

FIG. 9

1

MOUSETRAP FOR CATCHING MICE LIVE

FIELD OF INVENTION

The present invention relates to a better mousetrap.

BACKGROUND OF THE INVENTION

Mice can be a nuisance and/or a health menace. Traditional mousetraps are comprised of either a mechanical or chemical killing means. When a mouse is killed in a household, many health problems can arise. These health problems include the release of body fluids containing viruses inside the household. Parasites including worms or lice can be released. Decomposition bacteria will cause odors and cause injury to pets or children who ingest them.

The present invention eliminates these hazards by catching the mouse alive. A simple, cylindrical, teeter-totter contains bait at a closed end of the cylinder. The mouse enters the open end of the cylinder and walks toward the bait. As the mouse passes a fulcrum the cylinder tilts the bait end of the cylinder downward. The mouse becomes trapped by a downward rolling ping pong ball. The trap containing the trapped mouse can be brought outside where the entire trap can be thrown in a bucket to drown the mouse.

SUMMARY OF THE INVENTION

The main object of the present invention is to trap a mouse alive.

Another object of the present invention is to provide an inexpensive trap.

Yet another object of the present invention is to allow the trap to be easily dropped into a bucket of water to drown the mouse.

Still yet another object of the present invention is to reuse the trap.

Other objects of this invention will appear from the following description and appended claims, reference being had to the accompanying drawings forming a part of this specification wherein like reference characters designate corresponding parts in the several views.

BRIEF DESCRIPTION OF THE DRAWINGS

FIG. 1 is a top perspective view of the preferred embodiment.

FIG. 2 is a front plan view of the preferred embodiment shown in FIG. 1.

FIG. 3 is a longitudinal sectional view taken along line 3—3 of FIG. 2.

FIG. 4 is a side plan view with a partial cut-away showing the mouse of FIG. 3 trapped.

FIG. 5 is a top perspective view of an alternate embodiment.

FIG. 6 is a front plan view of the retaining ring of FIG. 5.

FIG. 7 is a front plan view of the pivot stand of FIG. 5.

FIG. 8 is a longitudinal partial sectional view of the embodiment of FIG. 5 in the process of trapping a mouse.

FIG. 9 is a partial cut-away of the embodiment shown in FIG. 8 having caught the mouse.

Before explaining the disclosed embodiment of the present invention in detail, it is to be understood that the invention is not limited in its application to the details of the particular arrangement shown, since the invention is capable

2

of other embodiments. Also, the terminology used herein is for the purpose of description and not of limitation.

DESCRIPTION OF THE PREFERRED EMBODIMENT

Referring first to FIG. 1 the trap 1 is comprised of a support stand 2 preferably made of wire. Support stand 2 has wire ends 3, 4 which form a fulcrum for the main tube 5. Main tube 5 preferably is a plastic cylinder having holes 6, 60, 61. Holes 60, 61 removably attach to the wire ends 3, 4 thereby permitting the main tube 5 to teeter-totter around the fulcrum F. Holes 6 also provide an entrance for water when the trap 1 is immersed to kill a mouse.

A pair of removable end caps 7, 8 seal the ends of main tube 5. Before the end caps 7, 8 are secured to main tube 5, the bait 10 and the ping pong ball 9 are inserted as shown at bait end 100 and ball end 90.

An entrance tube 11 forms a "Y" with the main tube 5. Entrance tube 11 depends downward from main tube 5 and points away from the bait end 100.

FIG. 2 shows a mouse eye view of the trap 1. The lure of the bait 10 emanates from entrance E. In FIG. 3 the mouse M is entering entrance E of entrance tube 11. The main tube 5 is in the loaded position which is horizontal. Thus, the ping pong ball 9 rests at ball end 90.

Referring next to FIG. 4 the mouse M has had it. He's eating the bait 10. But as he walked past the fulcrum F his weight caused the main tube 5 to pivot around fulcrum F so that the bait end 100 fell down in direction D and the ball end 90 rose up in direction U. The ping pong ball 9 urged by gravity rolled in path C to close the entrance E. A rim 13 prevents the ping pong ball 9 from rolling past the entrance E.

When finished eating mouse M will turn around and walk past fulcrum F. Main tube 5 will teeter back to a horizontal position. However, ping pong ball 9 will prevent the egress of mouse M out of entrance E. All mouse M can do is travel back and forth in main tube 5 and entrance tube 11, thereby causing the trap 1 to teeter-totter around fulcrum F. Trap 1 can then be immersed in water to drown mouse M or opened at end caps 7, 8 to release mouse M. Of course, in an alternate use one could kill mouse M with poison bait and trap him in the same manner.

Referring next to FIGS. 5, 6, 7a trap 50 is shown. FIG. 5 shows the trap 50 in the horizontal loaded position. In this alternate embodiment a main tube 51 teeter-totters around fulcrum FF. Preferably a plastic ring 70 has a flat base 71 which acts as fulcrum FF. The entrance EE is at the entrance end 610 of the main tube 51. A removable cap 52 seals the bait end 609 of the main tube 51. Holes 66 can allow water to enter main tube 51 during immersion.

The trapping mechanism is comprised of a retaining tube 59 forming a "Y" with the main tube 51. Retaining tube 59 rises obliquely from main tube 51 away from the bait end 609 of the main tube 51. The ping pong ball 53 is held up in the load position by retaining prong 57 of swivel ring 56.

Referring last to FIGS. 8, 9 mouse M is first entering in FIG. 8 entrance EE. The swivel ring 56 is resting on the ground in the cocked position. The retaining prong 57 is pivotally supported in hole 67. Retaining prong 57 is holding up the ping pong ball 53.

When the mouse M passes the fulcrum FF he becomes trapped. The main tube 51 teeters so that the bait end 609 falls in direction D, and the entrance end 610 rises in direction U. The swivel ring 56 pivots in direction T because the prong 57 is urged downward by ping pong ball 53. Hole 67 acts as a fulcrum. The ping pong ball 53 is restrained from exiting entrance EE by rim 54. End caps 52, 55 prevent the mouse's egress.

Although the present invention has been described with reference to preferred embodiments, numerous modifications and variations can be made and still the result will come within the scope of the invention. No limitation with respect to the specific embodiments disclosed herein is intended or should be inferred.

I claim:

1. A mousetrap comprising:

a main tube having a central fulcrum means, a bait end, and a ball end;

a base stand having a means to support the main tube at the fulcrum;

said bait end further comprising mouse bait and a main tube closure;

said ball end further comprising a ball and a main tube closure;

an entrance tube depending down from the main tube at the central fulcrum means, and angled toward the ball end;

said entrance tube having a mouse entrance adjacent a supporting surface for the base stand; and

said main tube having a horizontal load position wherein said ball rests at the ball end, wherein a mouse enters the mouse entrance, walks toward the bait up the entrance tube, and passes the fulcrum means, thereby causing the main tube to teeter down at the bait end, and cause the ball to roll down the main tube then down the entrance tube, functioning to block an egress of the mouse out the mouse entrance.

2. The mousetrap of claim 1 wherein said central fulcrum means further comprise holes in the main tube.

3. The mousetrap of claim 2 wherein said means to support further comprises a pair of prong ends fittingly engaged in the holes in the main tube.

4. The mousetrap of claim 1 wherein the ball further comprises a ping pong ball.

5. The mousetrap of claim 3 wherein said central fulcrum means further comprises a support stand depending from the main tube.

6. A mousetrap comprising:

a main tube having a closed bait end, a mouse entrance end, and a central fulcrum means supporting the main tube on a support surface;

a ball tube angularly rising from the main tube;

said ball tube further comprising a closure, a ball, and a ball support means, functioning to hold the ball against the closure when the main tube is teetered in a cocked position;

a bait in the bait end, functioning to lure a mouse into the mouse entrance, past the central fulcrum means, thereby causing the main tube to teeter downward at the bait end, and causing the ball support means to release the ball to roll into the main tube and thereby block an egress of the mouse out the mouse entrance.

7. The mousetrap of claim 5 wherein said ball support means further comprises a swivel ring suspended from a hole in the ball tube by a prong, wherein said prong swings away from the ball, thereby releasing it when the main tube is teetered downward at the bait end.

8. A mousetrap comprising:

a "Y" shaped tube pivotally supported at a center point by a stand;

said "Y" shaped tube having a straight tube closed at both ends, and having bait at one end, and a ball at an opposing ball end, said ball end being adjacent to an open tube member;

said open tube member depending from the straight tube so as to form a mouse entrance when the straight tube is suspended horizontally, whereby a mouse attracted by a bait at the bait end passes the center point and causes the straight tube to teeter with the bait end down, thereby causing the ball to travel to the open tube member, thus trapping the mouse.

* * * * *

United States Patent [19]

Fisher

[11] Patent Number: 4,662,101

[45] Date of Patent: May 5, 1987

[54] **RAT OR MOUSE TRAP**

[76] Inventor: **Harry L. Fisher,** 9336 S. 208th St., Kent, Wash. 98031

[21] Appl. No.: **880,285**

[22] Filed: **Jun. 30, 1986**

[51] Int. Cl.⁴ A01M 23/04
[52] U.S. Cl. 43/69
[58] Field of Search 43/69

[56] **References Cited**

U.S. PATENT DOCUMENTS

121,608	12/1871	Francisco	43/69
290,580	12/1883	Harwell	43/69
1,208,206	12/1916	Poynter	43/69
1,525,349	2/1925	Yamasaki	43/69

FOREIGN PATENT DOCUMENTS

81327 8/1934 Sweden 43/69

Primary Examiner—Gene P. Crosby
Attorney, Agent, or Firm—Bruce A. Kaser

[57] **ABSTRACT**

A mousetrap (**10**) is made of a pivoting platform (**12**) suspended over a pitfall (**14**). The platform (**12**) is balanced in a manner such that it normally assumes a horizontal position, thus giving a mouse an appearance of a stable bridge over the pitfall. When the mouse (**42**) steps onto the platform (**12**) for the purpose of obtaining bait placed thereon, however, the platform (**12**) spins and dumps the mouse into the pitfall thereby trapping it.

1 Claim, 5 Drawing Figures

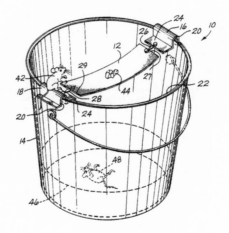

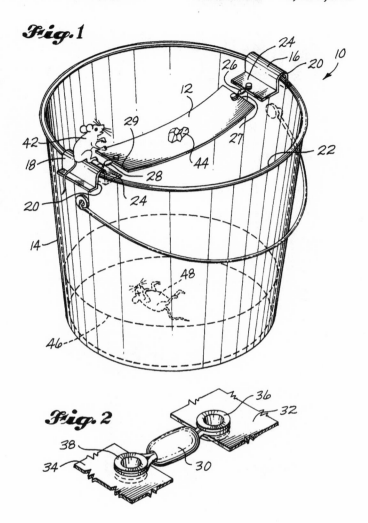

Fig.1

Fig.2

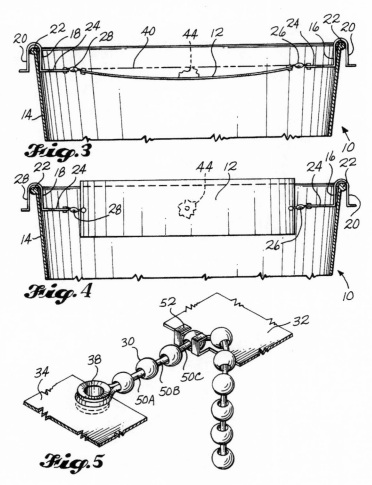

Fig.3

Fig.4

Fig.5

1

RAT OR MOUSE TRAP

TECHNICAL FIELD

This invention relates to animal traps, and in particular, traps for rats, mice and/or similar vermin.

BACKGROUND ART

The damage caused by rats and mice to agricultural products is well known. Every year these pests cause incalculable damage to crops, whether they be in the field or stored, and other foodstuffs of a similar nature. Further, the problems associated with rat or mice infestation of domestic household environments are well known.

Man has continuously engaged in war with these pests and has engaged in various attempts at eradicating and/or controlling them. The present invention provides yet another attempt which has certain advantages over previous ones. As will become apparent, the present invention is, quite literally, the better mousetrap.

DISCLOSURE OF THE INVENTION

The present invention provides a trap for rats, mice and similar vermin. This invention employs a pit or pitfall into which these pests fall and are trapped. Once there, they may be either killed or maintained in a live condition.

A platform is suitably supported over the pitfall in a manner such that the platform can freely turn or pivot about a center line axis. The platform is balanced in a manner such that it normally assumes a horizontal position thereby giving a vermin an appearance of providing a secure supporting surface over the pitfall. The vermin can access the platform from the edge of the pitfall, and when the vermin moves onto the platform, the vermin's weight causes the platform to become unbalanced and turn, thus causing the vermin to fall into the pitfall. Of course, the vermin would be enticed onto the platform by a suitable bait placed on the platform but out of reach from the edge of the pitfall's opening.

Preferably, the pitfall is made of a bucket or another suitable container of like nature. The platform is supported over the bucket's opening by a pair of supporting members hooked to the bucket's rim. One supporting member is positioned directly across the bucket's opening from the other.

The platform comprises a generally rectangular sheet of material which spans the distance between the supporting members, with each end of the platform being pivotally connected to the end's respective adjacent supporting member. These connections are symmetrical, that is, the mid-point of each end of the rectangular platform is pivotally connected to a supporting member. This makes a pair of pivot points which define the center line axis, such axis extending generally horizontally across the bucket or pitfall's opening and about which the platform is free to turn.

The rectangular platform is curved sufficiently that its center of gravity is offset from the center line axis. Since the platform can freely turn, this causes the platform to normally assume the above-mentioned horizontal position. After the weight of a mouse or rat on the platform unbalances it, causing it to turn, the platform naturally turns back to the horizontal position after the mouse or rat falls off.

Each supporting member may have an inwardly projecting ledge from the rim or edge of the bucket or

2

pitfall which provides vermin-access onto the platform. Swivel members are provided for making the pivotal connection between each ledge and the ends of the platform.

An advantage to the present invention is that it is effective in controlling vermin without using poison. Poison, of course, has been known to be one of the most effective methods of controlling vermin. However, it is undesirable to use poison in situations where the poison may get mixed into foodstuffs that are eventually to be consumed by humans. This invention is ideally suited for use in these kinds of situations.

Another advantage to the present invention is that it may be used as a live trap, or otherwise, if so desired. The bottom of the bucket may be filled with a few inches of water into which a mouse or rat will fall after being dumped by the platform. Eventually, the mouse or rat drowns. However, by leaving the bucket empty, they may be trapped alive.

BRIEF DESCRIPTION OF THE DRAWINGS

In the drawings, like reference numerals and letters refer to like parts throughout the various views, and wherein:

FIG. 1 is a pictorial view of a preferred embodiment of the invention, and shows a curved rectangular platform pivotally supported over the opening of a bucket;

FIG. 2 is an enlarged fragmentary pictorial view showing a swivel member which connects the platform shown in FIG. 1 to a supporting member connected to the rim of the bucket;

FIG. 3 is a side elevational view of the platform shown in FIG. 1;

FIG. 4 is a view like FIG. 3 but shows the platform in a pivoting or turned condition; and

FIG. 5 is a view like FIG. 2 but shows an alternative embodiment for connecting the rectangular platform in FIGS. 1, 3 and 4 to a supporting member on the bucket's rim.

BEST MODE FOR CARRYING OUT THE INVENTION

Referring now to the drawings, and first to FIG. 1, therein is shown at 10 a preferred embodiment of the invention. The invention includes a rectangular platform 12 which is suspended over the upwardly directed opening of a bucket 14. The platform 12 is attached to the bucket 14 by a pair of supporting members 16, 18. Each supporting member has a hook portion 20 that is attached to the bucket's rim 22. Further, each member 16, 18 has an inwardly projecting ledge portion 24 that provides vermin-access from the edge of the bucket 22 onto the platform 12.

The platform 12 is pivotally connected at each of its ends 27, 29 to respective adjacent supporting members 16, 18 as shown at 26, 28. These connections are better illustrated in FIG. 2 which shows a swivel member 30 interconnecting a first member 32 and a second member 34. The swivel member 30 is connected to the two members 32, 34 by rivets 36, 38, or other suitable means, and permits the first member 32 to pivot relative to the second member 34.

Referring back to FIG. 3, each swivel member 26, 28 connects the approximate center point of the platform's ends 27, 29 to the supporting members 16, 18. The swivel members 26, 28 thus define two points through which a horizontal center line axis 40 passes. The plat-

3

form **12** is free to turn about this axis **40** and is curved slightly so that its center of gravity is offset from the axis. This offset causes the platform **12** to be normally balanced in the horizontal position shown in FIGS. **1** and **3**.

Referring again to FIG. **1**, therein is shown a mouse **42** poised on the rim **22** of the bucket **14**. A suitable bait **44** is positioned on the center of the platform **12** and attracts the mouse **42**. It should be understood that a suitable ramp or similar structure would be provided to permit the mouse **42** to access the bucket's rim **22**. This is not shown in the drawings, however. The bait **44** would, of course, be positioned on the center of the platform **12** so that its weight would not unbalance the platform.

The horizontal position of the platform **12** gives the mouse **42** the appearance that the platform provides a bridge across the opening of the bucket **14**. However, when the mouse **14** steps onto the platform **12**, in its desire to obtain the bait **44**, the mouse's weight unbalances the platform, causing it to turn as shown in FIG. **4**, and thus dumps the mouse **42** into the bucket **14**. The offset center of gravity of the platform **12** then causes the platform to return to the horizontal position after the mouse falls therefrom.

It should be appreciated that the above-described curved platform **12** could be replaced by a straight platform having a suitable counterweight attached thereto. This would not be a preferred embodiment, however.

The bottom of the bucket **14** may be filled with a few inches of water as indicated by the dashed lines **46**. The mouse **42** may be able to swim in the water for a certain period of time but will eventually become tired and drown as shown at **48**.

FIG. **5** shows an alternative embodiment of the swivel member **30** shown in FIG. **2**. This embodiment may be used if it is desired to adapt the platform **12** to a bucket or other container having a different diameter. In this embodiment, the swivel member **30** comprises a plurality of swivel links as indicated at **50***a*, **50***b*, and **50***c*. The length of this alternative swivel member **30** is therefore adjustable by catching and releasing the links

4

50*a*, **50***b*, **50***c* from a link-catch **52** which is suitably connected to member **32**.

The above description is presented for exemplary purposes only. This description is not meant to limit patent protection insofar as it is understood that certain departures may be taken from the above-described embodiments without departing from the overall spirit and scope of the invention. With regard to patent protection, the invention is to be limited not by the above description but only by the subjoined patent claims, in accordance with the well-established legal doctrines of patent claim interpretation.

What is claimed is:

1. A trap for mice, rats or vermin of a similar nature, and for use in connection with a pitfall having an upwardly directed opening, comprising:

a generally rectangular platform having a top surface and a bottom surface, and having a thin cross section;

a pair of platform supporting members, each of which is connected to the edge of said pitfall's opening, wherein one of said supporting members is positioned across said opening from the other, and wherein said platform substantially spans the distance between said supporting members, with a first end of said rectangular platform being pivotally connected to one of said members, and with a second end of said platform being pivotally connected to the other of said members, wherein such connections generally define a pair of points through which a center line axis extends across said pitfall's opening, said center line axis being an axis of symmetry for said platform and said platform being freely pivotably about said center line axis, and wherein

said platform's cross section is curved so that said top surface is concave and said bottom surface is convex, to cause said platform's center of gravity to be slightly offset from said center line axis, and to cause said platform to normally pivot into a position where said center of gravity is positioned below said center line axis, so that said platform is balanced in a manner that said platform's top surface provides said vermin with an appearance of a bridge across said pitfall.

* * * * *

50

55

60

65

United States Patent [19]

Fodor

[11] **Patent Number:** **4,819,368**

[45] **Date of Patent:** **Apr. 11, 1989**

[54] **DISPOSABLE MOUSETRAP**

[76] Inventor: **John Fodor,** 13 Village Park Cir., Morgantown, W. Va. 26505

[21] Appl. No.: **552,153**

[22] Filed: **Nov. 14, 1983**

[51] Int. Cl.[4] A01M 23/18; A01M 23/02
[52] U.S. Cl. **43/61**
[58] Field of Search 43/61, 60, 62, 67, 70

[56] **References Cited**

U.S. PATENT DOCUMENTS

2,573,228	10/1951	Slauth	43/61
2,598,007	5/1952	McCormick	43/61
3,729,852	5/1973	Holmes	43/61
3,823,504	7/1974	Dosch	43/61
4,142,320	3/1979	Marcolina	43/61
4,231,180	11/1980	Bare	43/61
4,232,472	11/1980	Muelling	43/61
4,238,902	12/1980	Holl et al.	43/61

Primary Examiner—Kurt Rowan
Attorney, Agent, or Firm—Mason, Fenwick & Lawrence

[57] **ABSTRACT**

A disposable rodent trap is formed of an aluminum beverage can comprising an internal chamber, a bottom end wall with an opposite end wall including an entry opening therein of sufficient size to permit a rodent to pass into the internal chamber. A door member in the form of a can end is positioned externally of said end wall and movable into a closed position covering and blocking the entry opening by a rubber band. A latch means normally holds the door open by engagement with an edge surface of the entry opening but is movable by rodent contact inside the chamber to unlatched position to permit the rubber band to move the door member to its closed postion to trap the rodent in said internal chamber.

15 Claims, 2 Drawing Sheets

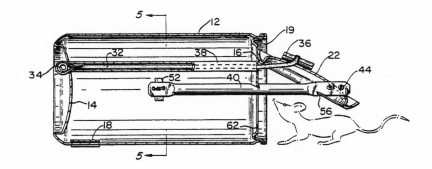

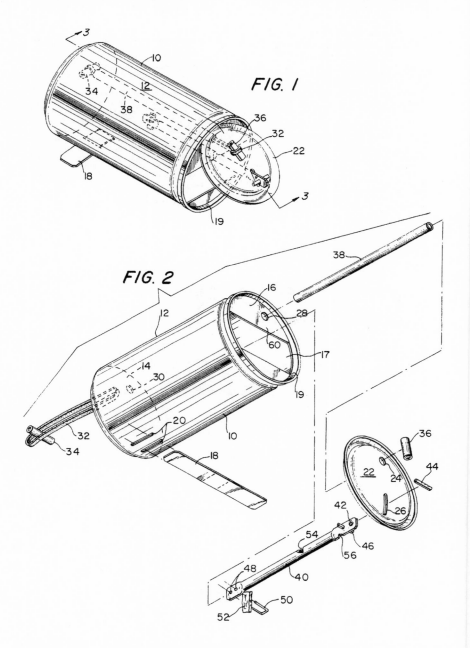

FIG. 1

FIG. 2

204

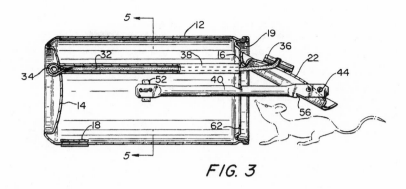

FIG. 3

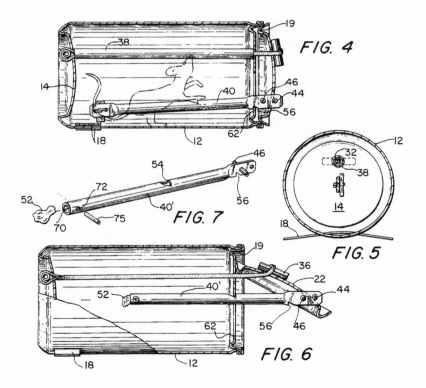

FIG. 4

FIG. 7

FIG. 5

FIG. 6

1

DISPOSABLE MOUSETRAP

BACKGROUND OF THE INVENTION

The present invention is in the field of animal trapping devices and is more specifically directed to a unique disposable rodent trap of particular value for capturing mice.

Numerous devices have evolved over the years for either capturing or killing mice. Many of the known devices have suffered from a number of shortcomings such as failing to operate properly and being overly expensive to fabricate. The most relevant prior known U.S. Patents comprise U.S. Pat. Nos. 100,986; 924,237; 1,261,189; 1,326,662; 1,372,663; 1,415,093; 1,861,478; 2,087,646; 2,434,031; 2,437,020; 2,573,228; 2,608,018; 3,426,470; 3,729,852; 3,733,735; 3,992,802. The present invention overcomes the shortcomings of the foregoing patents in providing a fool-proof functionally operational device that is quick and effective for capturing mice or other rodents and which is economical to fabricate and assemble due to the use of well-known widely available materials many of which are presently thrown away as scrap. It is consequently possible to simply dispose of the subject invention following the capture of a mouse or other rodent.

Therefore, it is the primary object of the present invention to provide a new and improved rodent trap which is functionally more effective than prior known rodent traps and is also economical to fabricate and assemble.

SUMMARY OF THE INVENTION

Achievement of the foregoing objects is enabled by the preferred embodiment of the invention in a remarkably effective manner. More specifically, the preferred embodiment of the invention comprises a container in the form of an aluminum beverage can of the type normally used for beer, soft drinks or the like. Such cans comprise a cylindrical wall member having a bottom end wall and a dispensing end wall with the dispensing end wall of the can used in the present invention including an elongated transverse entry opening of sufficient size to permit the passage of a rodent into the interior of the can.

A movable door is positioned adjacent the dispensing end wall of the can and is connected to an elongated latch member comprising an elongated tubular rod which extends into the interior of the can. Also, a rubber band extends from the bottom wall of the can through the length of the can outwardly through an opening provided in the dispensing end wall and is connected to the movable door member so as to urge the movable door member toward a closed position in which it overlies the entry opening and completely blocks same. The latch member includes a transverse surface engagable with a catch surface adjacent the edge of the entry opening so as to hold the door member in an open position against the urging of the elastic rubber band member. A tubular metal sheath encloses the rubber band member across the span between the dispensing end wall and the bottom end wall of the can so as to prevent any captured rodent from gnawing through the rubber band to permit the door to then open.

The inner end of the tubular latch member is provided with means for retaining bait on the inner end of the latch member for the purpose of attracting mice or

2

other rodents so as to cause them to enter the interior of the can. When such a mouse has entered the can, he will attempt to eat the bait and will dislodge the tubular latch member from engagement with the catch surface so that the elastic rubber band member immediately snaps the door closed and the rodent is consequently entrapped within the confines of the can. Additionally, the latch member is also provided with a lock latch surface which engages a second catch surface along the inside edge of the entry opening upon closure of the door member so as to lock the door member in closed position. Thus, the operation of the elongated elastic rubber band member and the lock surface provides a dual locking function to preclude escape of a captured rodent. In one embodiment of the invention the latch tube receives the bait member in an open-ended recess adjacent the end of the latch member with a transverse bore opening being provided on opposite sides of the opening so as to permit impalement of the bait by a retaining pin extended therethrough. In a second embodiment the bait is retained on the end of the latch member by a wire clip or the like extending through openings provided in a flattened end of the latch member.

BRIEF DESCRIPTION OF THE DRAWING

FIG. 1 is a perspective view of the preferred embodiment of the invention illustrating the door member in open position;

FIG. 2 is an exploded perspective view of the embodiment of FIG. 1;

FIG. 3 is a sectional view taken along lines 3—3 of FIG. 1 and illustrating the door in an opened condition;

FIG. 4 is a sectional view similar to FIG. 3 but illustrating the door in the closed position for imprisoning a rodent;

FIG. 5 is a sectional view taken along lines 5—5 of FIG. 3;

FIG. 6 is a side elevation view of a second embodiment with portions removed for the sake of illustration; and

FIG. 7 is a perspective view of a second embodiment of tubular latch means employed in the invention.

DESCRIPTION OF THE PREFERRED EMBODIMENTS

The preferred embodiment of the invention as illustrated in FIGS. 1 etc. comprises a disposable rodent trap including a container 10 in the form of a disposable aluminum beverage container having a cylindrical body wall 12, a bottom end wall 14 and a dispensing end wall 16. It should be observed that the bottom end wall 14 is normally the "bottom" wall when the beverage can is used for its original purpose whereas the dispensing end wall 16 is the end from which the beverage contained within the container is dispensed. Dispensing end wall 16 includes an opening 17 of sufficient size to permit the passage of a rodent therethrough so as to enter the interior of the container can 10 and also includes a peripheral flange 19. A stabilizer tab 18 extends through slots 20 provided in the cylindrical body wall 12 as best shown in FIG. 2. Stabilizer tab 18 prevents the can from rolling on a supporting surface in an obvious manner.

A floating door 22 comprising an end wall from a similar can is positioned adjacent and in contact with the dispensing end wall 16. Floating door 22 is provided with an upper circular opening 24 and a lower slot 26.

The upper circular opening 24 is in general alignment with an opening 28 in the dispensing end wall 16. The bottom end wall 14 is provided with an opening 30 in alignment with the opening 28 of the dispensing end wall. Biasing means in the form of an elastic rubber band member 32 extends through the openings 28 and 30 with the end of the biasing elastic rubber band member 32 adjacent the bottom wall 14 being anchored by a tubular anchor lug 34 while the opposite end of the rubber band member which extends through openings 28 and 24 is anchored by a similar lug 36. The lug members 34 and 36 can for example be formed of rolled pieces of aluminum scrap or the like. Thus it will be seen that the tension in rubber band 32 tends to move the floating door member 22 toward a closed position. A protective sheath 38 formed of metal in the form of aluminum or the like extends between the bottom wall 14 and the dispensing end wall 16 to fully enclose the rubber band 32 to prevent any rodent on the interior of the can from gnawing or eating through the band so as to cause its failure.

An elongated tubular latch member 40 is provided internally of the container can 10 and includes a flat outer end 42 which extends through the slot 26 and is held in position by an outer keeper pin 44 and an inner keeper pin 46 which are respectively on opposite sides of the floating door member 22. The inner end of the elongated tubular latch member 40 is provided with a pair of openings 48 through which a bait retention loop or wire or the like 50 extends so as to permit the attachment of bait 52 to the end of the latch member. Latch member 40 includes a first transverse latch surface 54 and a second transverse oppositely facing lock surface 56.

When the floating door 22 is in its open position the latch surface 54 is engaged with an upper external catch surface 60 extending along entry opening 17 in the dispensing end wall 16. Thus, the latch member retains the floating door in its open position. A mouse or other rodent can enter the opening 17 and upon attempting to eat the bait 52 will effect dislodging of the latch surface 54 from the catch surface 60 to immediately result in a rapid and quick movement of the door member 22 from the open position of FIG. 3 to the closed position of FIG. 4. The rodent on the interior of the container will consequently be imprisoned. Moreover, movement of the floating door 22 to the closed position immediately results in the lock surface 56 becoming engaged with a lower catch inside surface 62 as shown in FIG. 4. Thus, the floating door member 22 will be held in closed position by operation of the lock surface 56 as well as the elastic urgings of the rubber band 32.

FIG. 6 illustrates a slightly simplified embodiment in which the protective sheath 38 is dispensed with and the bare rubber band extends between the bottom wall 14 and the dispensing wall 16. The advantage of this embodiment is that it is slightly easier to manufacture. Additionally, the embodiment of FIG. 6 is illustrated with a second embodiment latch member 40′ which is basically identical to the first latch member with the exception of the manner in which the bait 52 is connected to the inner end of the latch member. More specifically, the inner end of the latch member 40′ includes an open end chamber or cavity 70 through which diametric openings 72 extend with the chamber or cavity 70 being of sufficient size to receive the bait 52. A retention pin 75 extends through the opening 72 and the bait 52 to retain the bait 52 in the end of the

latch member in the manner shown in FIG. 6. Otherwise, the second embodiment operates in exactly the same manner as the first embodiment.

It should be understood that, while preferred embodiments of the invention are illustrated herein, numerous modifications of the disclosed embodiments will undoubtedly occur to those of skill in the art. For example, practice of the invention is not limited to the use of beverage cans and other type cans or containers of larger sizes could be employed. In fact, it would even be possible to practice the present invention by the use of such large containers as oil drums or the like for use in capturing larger animals. Consequently, the use of the term "rodent" as discussed herein and as set forth in the claims should be broadly interpreted to include other types of animals. For these reasons, the spirit and scope of the invention should be broadly interpreted.

I claim:

1. A disposable rodent trap comprising a container defining an internal chamber, an end wall having an entry opening therein of sufficient size to permit a rodent to pass therethrough so as to enter said internal chamber, a door member provided externally of said end wall and movable from an open position toward said end wall into a closed position covering and blocking said entry opening, biasing means comprising a rubber band for urging said door member toward its closed position, latch means having a portion inside said chamber and extending between said door member and a catch surface on, and forming part of, said end wall comprising an edge surface adjacent said entry opening for normally holding said door member in its open position but being movable by rodent contact inside said chamber out of contact with said catch surface to permit said biasing means to move said door member to its closed position to entrap the rodent in said internal chamber and wherein said container is a disposable beverage can having a cylindrical body wall, a bottom end wall and a dispensing end wall with said entry opening being provided in said dispensing end wall which comprises a wall from which beverage would normally be dispensed during usage of said beverage container for its original purpose.

2. The invention of claim 1 wherein said latch member comprises an elongated tube connected at one end to said door member and having a transverse latch surface medially of its length for engaging said catch surface adjacent one edge of said entry opening and further including a lock latch surface extending transversely of said tubular member at a location near the door member for engaging an inner edge surface of said entry opening for latching said door member in said closed position.

3. A rodent trap as recited in claim 2 additionally including a tubular sheath extending between said bottom end wall and said opening in said dispensing end wall for enclosing said rubber band portion inside said internal chamber for preventing any rodent in said chamber from chewing on said rubber band.

4. A disposable rodent trap as recited in claim 3 wherein said door member comprises a can end from a similar can which has one end engaged with said dispensing end wall, said dispensing end wall including a peripheral flange surface which retains said door member in position.

5. A rodent trap as recited in claim 4 wherein said latch member includes means on its end opposite its end connected to said door member for retaining rodent attracting means thereon.

5

6. A rodent trap as recited in claim 5 additionally including transversely extending means connected to said body wall and engagable with a supporting surface for said rodent trap for maintaining said rodent trap in fixed position on said supporting surface.

7. A rodent trap as recited in claim 6 wherein said bottom end wall is provided with an aperture through which one end of said rubber band extends to provide an external loop of said rubber band and wherein said rubber band is connected to said wall by an elongated anchor lug passed through said loop.

8. A rodent trap as recited in claim 7 wherein said door member is provided with an opening through which a loop of said rubber band extends and further includes an anchor lug extending through said loop for retaining said loop externally of said door member.

9. A rodent trap as recited in claim 8 wherein said door member includes a slot through which one end of said latch member extends and said latch member includes keeper pins extending transversely through said latch member on opposite sides of said door member so as to retain said latch member in said slot.

10. A rodent trap as recited in claim 4 wherein said latch member has an open-ended bait receiving cavity on its end opposite its connection to said door member.

11. A disposable rodent trap comprising a container defining an internal chamber, an end wall having an entry opening therein of sufficient size to permit a rodent to pass therethrough so as to enter said internal chamber, a door member provided externally of said end wall and movable from an open position toward said end wall into a closed position covering and blocking said entry opening, biasing means for urging said door member toward its closed position, latch means having a portion inside said chamber and extending between said door member and a catch surface on, and forming part of, said end wall for normally holding said door member in its open position but being movable by rodent contact inside said chamber out of contact with said catch surface to permit said biasing means to move

6

said door member to its closed position to entrap the rodent in said internal chamber and wherein said container is a disposable beverage can having a cylindrical body wall, a bottom end wall and a dispensing end wall with said entry opening being provided in said dispensing end wall which comprises a wall from which beverage would normally be dispensed during usage of said beverage container for its original purpose and wherein said biasing means comprises an elastic band having one end secured to said bottom end wall, said second end wall includes a small opening spaced from said entry opening and the opposite end of said elastic band extends through said small opening and is secured to said door member by retainer pin means.

12. The invention of claim 11 wherein said latch member comprises an elongated metal tube connected at one end to said door member and having a transverse latch surface medially of its length for engaging said catch surface and further including a lock latch surface extending transversely of said tubular member at a location near the door member for engaging an inner edge surface of said entry opening for latching said door member in said closed position.

13. A rodent trap as recited in claim 12 additionally including a tubular sheath extending between said bottom end wall and said opening in said dispensing end wall for enclosing said elastic band portion inside said internal chamber for preventing any rodent in said chamber from chewing on said rubber band.

14. A disposable rodent trap as recited in claim 13 wherein said door member comprises a can end from a similar can which has one end engaged with said dispensing end wall, said dispensing end wall including a peripheral flange surface which retains said door member in position.

15. A rodent trap as recited in claim 14 wherein said latch member includes attachment means on its end opposite its end connected to said door member for retaining rodent attracting means thereon.

* * * * *

45

50

55

60

65

Sample Design Patents

United States Patent [19]

Gill et al.

[11] **Patent Number:** **Des. 372,955**

[45] **Date of Patent:** ****Aug. 20, 1996**

[54] **SURFACE FISHING LURE**

[76] Inventors: **Everett R. Gill**, 403 Rapides Station Rd., Alexandria, La. 71303; **Jerry Jenson**, 814 10th St., Eldora, Iowa 50627

[**] Term: **14 Years**

[21] Appl. No.: **37,697**

[22] Filed: **Apr. 19, 1995**

[52] **U.S. Cl.** **D22/128**; D22/133

[58] **Field of Search** D22/126, 128, D22/131, 129, 133; 43/42.06, 42.35, 42.36, 42.05, 42.17, 42.16, 42.09, 42.28, 42.48, 42.45, 42.44

[56] **References Cited**

U.S. PATENT DOCUMENTS

D. 210,205	2/1968	Cordell, Jr.	D22/133
D. 218,932	10/1970	Perrin et al. .	
D. 223,490	4/1972	McClellan .	
D. 226,082	1/1973	Foster .	
D. 232,936	9/1974	Storm .	
D. 234,139	1/1975	McLaughlin	D22/133
D. 247,976	5/1978	Storm .	
D. 251,915	5/1979	Davis .	
D. 260,923	9/1981	Cope .	
1,131,909	3/1915	Clarkson et al.	43/42.06
1,608,375	11/1926	Dewey .	
1,878,015	9/1932	Steffensen .	
2,236,353	3/1941	Minser	43/42.05
2,245,061	6/1941	Wisniewski .	
2,542,447	2/1951	Adam et al. .	
2,714,779	8/1955	Heiner	43/42.23
2,734,301	2/1956	Fuqua	D22/128 X
2,854,780	10/1958	Dege	D22/133 X
2,878,611	3/1959	Netherton et al.	D22/133 X
3,094,804	6/1963	Walton et al.	43/42.23
3,205,608	9/1965	Dickinson	43/42.23
3,248,820	5/1966	Lamar	43/42.29
3,757,454	9/1973	Shurley	43/42.16
3,879,881	4/1975	Vick	43/41

4,144,665	3/1979	Dake	43/42.35
4,215,507	8/1980	Russell	
4,471,556	9/1984	Dworski	43/42.23
4,492,054	1/1985	Barnhart	43/42.23
4,642,933	2/1987	Brown	43/42.36
4,697,378	10/1987	Tunstall	43/42.09
4,700,504	10/1987	Mattison	43/42.33
4,733,491	3/1988	Wilson	43/42.45
4,739,576	4/1988	Davis	43/42.47
4,807,387	2/1989	Dougherty, Jr.	43/42.09
4,807,388	2/1989	Cribb	43/42.22
4,819,365	4/1989	Landuydt	43/42.47
4,873,781	10/1989	Bates	
4,873,782	10/1989	Gudermuth, Jr.	43/42.15
4,944,112	7/1990	Garmany	43/42.09
5,276,992	1/1994	Kato	43/42.06
5,379,543	1/1995	Avent	43/43.05 X

OTHER PUBLICATIONS

Seward and Petros. "New Lures What's Hot And How to Use 'Em!," *Fishing Facts*, 77–85, May 1990.

Bass Pro Shops "Johnny Moore's Outdoor World" 1991 Catalog; pp. 126, 127, 164–181, 183–185, 187–195, 197, 199, 200, 202, 204.

Primary Examiner—Doris V. Coles
Attorney, Agent, or Firm—Arnold White & Durkee

[57] **CLAIM**

The ornamental design for a surface fishing lure, as shown and described.

DESCRIPTION

FIG. 1 is a front, top and right side perspective view, showing our new design;

FIG. 2 is a top plan view thereof;

FIG. 3 is a front elevational view thereof;

FIG. 4 is a right side elevational view thereof;

FIG. 5 is a bottom plan view thereof;

FIG. 6 is a left side elevational view thereof; and,

FIG. 7 is a rear elevational view thereof.

1 Claim, 2 Drawing Sheets

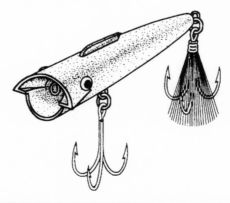

Fig. 1

Fig. 2

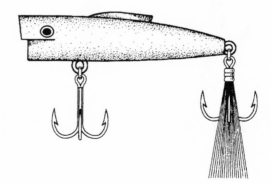

Fig. 3   Fig. 4

Fig. 5

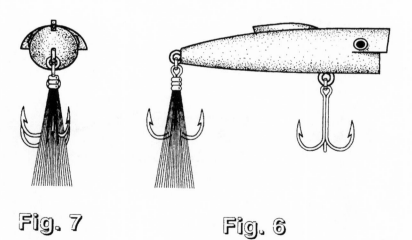

Fig. 7

Fig. 6

CERTIFICATE OF CORRECTION

PATENT NO. : D 372,955

DATED : August 20, 1996

INVENTOR(S) : Everett R. Gill and Jerry Jenson

It is certified that error appears in the above-identified patent and that said Letters Patent is hereby corrected as shown below:

Title page, please insert the following item:

"[73] Assignee: Sports Design & Development, Inc., Alexandria, LA."

Signed and Sealed this

Nineteenth Day of August, 1997

Attest:

BRUCE LEHMAN

Attesting Officer Commissioner of Patents and Trademarks

United States Patent [19]

Axe

[11] Patent Number:	**Des. 372,441**
[45] Date of Patent:	**∗∗Aug. 6, 1996**

[54] **MOTOR VEHICLE**

[75] Inventor: **Royden Axe**, Warwick, England

[73] Assignee: **Rolls-Royce Motor Cars Limited**, Crewe, England

[∗∗] Term: **14 Years**

[21] Appl. No.: **29,270**

[22] Filed: **Sep. 1, 1994**

[30] **Foreign Application Priority Data**

Mar. 1, 1994 [GB] United Kingdom 2037417
[52] **U.S. Cl.** **D12/92**
[58] **Field of Search** D12/82, 86; 296/185

[56] **References Cited**

U.S. PATENT DOCUMENTS

D. 236,706	9/1975	Pininfarina	D12/92
D. 327,238	6/1992	Honda et al.	D12/92
D. 353,351	12/1994	Heffernan	D12/92

OTHER PUBLICATIONS

Motor Trend (Jan. 1993) pp. 104–106, Bentley Continental.
Motor Trend (Sep. 1993) p. 88, Audi Cabriolet.

Primary Examiner—Brian N. Vinson
Attorney, Agent, or Firm—Cushman Darby & Cushman, L.L.P.

[57] **CLAIM**

The ornamental design for a motor vehicle, as shown and described.

DESCRIPTION

FIG. 1 is a front elevational view of a motor vehicle showing my new design;
FIG. 2 is a rear elevational view thereof;
FIG. 3 is a right side elevational view thereof;
FIG. 4 is a left side elevational view thereof;
FIG. 5 is a top plan view thereof; and,
FIG. 6 is a bottom plan view thereof.

1 Claim, 5 Drawing Sheets

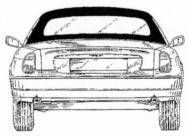

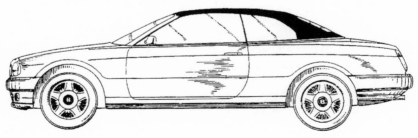

214

Fig.3

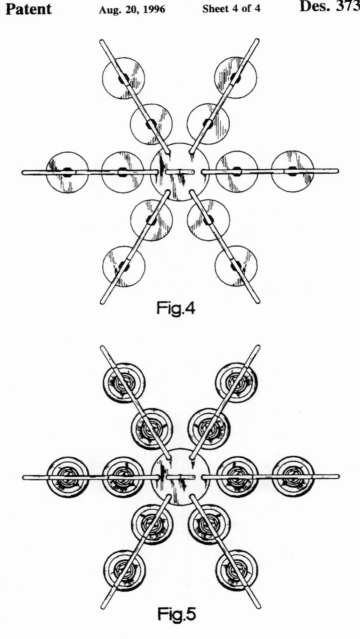

Fig.4

Fig.5

Index

About the Author

ALAN L. DURHAM is a Professor of Law at the University of Alabama, teaching courses in intellectual property and computer law. Professor Durham formerly practiced law in California's Silicon Valley with the Palo Alto offices of Brown & Bain and Morrison & Foerster LLP. During that time he specialized in high-technology intellectual property litigation, with a particular emphasis on patent matters.